ROGUE RIVER JOURNAL

Rogue River Journal

A WINTER ALONE

JOHN DANIEL

SHOEMAKER & HOARD
WASHINGTON, D.C.

Portions of this book first appeared, in different form, in *Audubon*, *Orion*, *Portland*, *Resurgence*, and *Writing Nature* magazines.

Library of Congress Cataloging-in-Publication Data is available.
ISBN 1-59376-051-5

Text design by Gopa & Ted2, Inc.
Printed in the United States of America

 Shoemaker & Hoard
A Division of Avalon Publishing Group, Inc.
Distributed by Publishers Group West

10 9 8 7 6 5 4 3 2 1

For Marilyn

Here

I wished to dive into some deep stream of thoughtful
and devoted life, which meandered through retired
and fertile meadows far from towns. I wished . . .
to lurk in crystalline thought like the trout under
verdurous banks, where stray mankind should only
see my bubble come to the surface. I wished to live,
ah! as far away as a man can think.

—H. D. THOREAU, *Journal* (1851)

Are men no better than sheep or cattle, that they must live
always in view of one another in order to feel a sense of safety?

—EDWARD ABBEY, *Desert Solitaire*

November 19, 2000

I'm here, and my right hand has nothing to reach for but a whiskey glass.

Time and again as I steered the truck south from home, down Knight Road and 126 and Territorial Road to Curtin, then on down I-5 to Roseburg, where I bought final supplies, during that hour-and-a-half and the next two hours too, the curvy, climbing, southwesterly way into the Klamath Mountains on progressively bumpier and narrower backwoods roads that at times skirt sheer drop-offs of several hundred feet—all the way here to Dutch Henry Homestead my hand kept reaching for the radio button that wasn't there. I wanted news. NPR, network, talk show, *something*. It's the week before Thanksgiving of the year 2000. We've voted, but we haven't elected a president. Like everyone else I've kept myself wired to the recounts, the tussles in court, the urgent posturings of the spinners and pundits, and of course the latest from or about the two principals themselves, each acting loose and cheery and confident and not at all queasy, as if the summit were a mere step away and it certainly wouldn't be *him* falling off the mountain instead.

I needed my fix, my loyal right hand went to fetch it, and came back empty each time. "Oh yeah . . ." I kept saying aloud. The radio button wasn't there because I had removed the stereo unit's face and left it at home, rendering the radio and tape player inoperable. The removable-face feature is meant to discourage theft. Today is the first time in five years I've used it, as I head off for the winter to a place where no one breaks into cars. No one human, anyway. Maybe a bear, but he'll have to be an oddball insomniac bear, and it won't be news he's after but the candy wrappers on the floor. I've defaced the radio to foil the only criminal and the only human I expect to be around for the next five months. A proven petty thief, a junkie with a serious habit. I'm going off news, my thwarted right hand kept reminding me. *Oh yeah . . .*

I've been working up to this venture for months. For years, actually. In August I started driving down here for a day or two at a time to get a fall garden going, cool-weather greens and root vegetables. Nestled in the Rogue River Canyon, with a considerable maritime influence from the Pacific Ocean only thirty air miles away, this is a place where you can take a garden through the winter—I hope. The man then in residence, a bearded poet from Washington State with the auspicious name Joe Green, kept the infant garden watered for me. In October I focused on firewood. With the help of the Brothers, two ministers of a certain Oregon faith who own the place in absentia and run it as a hermitage and poor farm for indigent writers, I rustled up five-odd cords of madrone, oak, and Douglas fir. Most of it has yet to be split, but that's the fun part.

Meanwhile, at home, I was collecting three hundred dollars from the ATM every day—all it would give me—and dispensing it to lucky businesses all across the greater vicinity of Eugene, Oregon. Cases of canned foods from Costco and Ray's Food Place. Granola and oats and rice and cheese in bulk from Oasis, the natural foods store. An expedition-grade first aid kit and most excellent fishing knife from REI. A used 12-gauge shotgun and supply of shells from Second Amendment Arms. Books from here, there, and everywhere. Notebooks and pads and mechanical pencils and leads and erasers and other writing sundries from Office Depot, manual typewriter ribbons and other rare items from local stationers. A modest supply of whiskey—too modest, I have a nagging feeling—obtained at the usual larcenous prices from the state liquor stores. A jillion purchases based on a lot of fretful guessing. How much toilet paper? (I mean, who keeps track?) How many D-cells, C-cells, Double As and Triple As, my only sources of electrical light? Enough vitamin supplements? Garbage sacks? Sweet potatoes? Fishing line? Paper clips? Socks? Matches? Excedrin?

I turned our garage into a depot for this freight, ferrying it down here one Toyota pickup load at a time. Once most of the supplies were laid in, my wife made a trip with me to help me get settled. She made sure I had things I might not have thought of and am glad to have—a sewing kit, a pastry knife and pastry cloth, a teapot, a set of red flannel sheets, pewter candlesticks and several dozen candles. She arrayed my hundreds of food cans—beef stew to Mandarin orange segments, sauerkraut to French cut string beans, albacore tuna to pickled okra—on storage shelves in the screened entry porch, where they make a formidable wall of Warholian art. Better than art—it can be eaten. This is an experiment in solitude, not in survival. Together we inventoried the kitchen implements and storage vessels and cleaning supplies already here, drawing up final lists of what was lacking.

When I first spoke of doing this, shortly after spending April through October here in 1994, Marilyn didn't count it as one of the best ideas I'd ever had. To her credit, though, she warmed to it. She appreciates solitude herself and understands my appetite for it. Nor is this the first eccentric thing I've done. She knew she was taking a risk when she married a poet and writer of literary nonfiction, but so far the money and glamour have made it worthwhile.

Still, four or five months apart is a long time. There came a point in August or September, while I was starting garden sprouts in seed trays and making lists and worrying out loud about getting the taxes paid come March, when we realized that I was really going to do this, and we stopped short. We felt it then, in a way we hadn't before. And so we had several weeks to say what we needed to say and do what we needed to do. Early this afternoon we hugged for a long time by the idling truck. She waved, I tooted the horn and drove off.

My original idea was to have no communication whatsoever with the world and to withdraw as completely as I could from human time. I didn't want to know the time of day or day of the week or what month it was. I wanted to live by the rhythms of light and dark, moon and weather, the tides of my own being. If I tallied time at all I wanted to do it as Robinson Crusoe had, cutting notches on a post. But this was a bit too extreme for Marilyn, who wanted periodic assurance that I was alive, if that was the case, and a way to reach me if an emergency should come along. So we compromised. There is a radio telephone in this cabin. It works only when turned on. I will turn it on every Wednesday night at ten o'clock and will call home to tell our answering machine a bit of news from the Rogue River Canyon, thus demonstrating that I am alive and indulging my wish not to engage in two-way conversation. At appointed times on two other evenings each week I will turn the phone on so that Marilyn, or one of a select group of friends, can reach me if necessary.

Getting out of here, if necessary, could be tricky, or at least exhausting. I almost didn't get in. The road tops out with a steep section at thirty-eight hundred feet on a north-facing ridge, informally known as the pass, half a mile higher than here at the homestead. A skiff of snow was on the pass a week ago when I made my final preparatory trip. This time there was seven or eight inches. My two-wheel-drive truck was loaded so groaningly full I thought I had a chance, but halfway up the steep stretch the wheels started to spin, the truck fishtailed, and my expedition came to a halt semi-crosswise in the road. The right rear wheel was about three feet from the brink of a slope that a logging crew must have used ropes to clear-cut.

My fear, as I stepped out in my high-top sneakers (not high enough), was not that I might be facing an eight-mile hike in the dark to the cabin or a longer-than-desirable night folded into the cab of my truck. My fear was this: *If I can't get myself out of this, someone else or several someone elses will have to know about it, and I will be acutely embarrassed.* Threaten a man with misery, even destruction, but please, please don't embarrass him. Don't let the world and especially his friends see him for the nincompoop he sometimes is.

Splayed out in the snow, fumbling with numbed fingers as dirty slush water dripped down my sleeves, I got the chains on by the light of my headlamp. I started the truck, eased out the clutch, and immediately threw one chain, the rear of the truck shifting a little closer to the brink. More slush water and some loud language as I unwrapped the chain from the axle and reinstalled it on the tire. This time it stayed on, both wheels slipped but gripped a little more than they slipped, and ever so delicately I cajoled my truck up the hill, pressing myself against the steering wheel to help it along. When we made the woods on top of the ridge I let out a holler. From that point on it was easy ups and downs along the ridgetop, the chains jingling like Christmas, then steadily down, out of the snow, into the Rogue River Canyon and my new home.

The truck is unloaded, the propane refrigerator stuffed full, the cabin warming to a fire in the Fisher woodstove, a dram of Scotch at my side. I've called Marilyn, as we agreed I would, to let her know I've made it. If all goes well, we won't speak again until early spring. In a few weeks, if it's a normal winter, the pass I just crept over will be buried under several feet of snow, much more than my truck can handle. Excellent. I'm here.

I'm elated, so elated I feel guilty. Tomorrow, a Monday, my wife will go to work as usual—she's a program manager for the Oregon Department of Environmental Quality—and she'll go to work as usual right through the winter, as I live the simple life in my spartan but comfortable cabin in the wilderness, with no phone to answer, no traffic to fight, no groceries to buy or bills to pay, no damnable election or anything else of the human world to grab me by the collar and boil my blood. A garden to eat from, a river to fish, backcountry to hike, wild animals where wild animals belong, a vast silence to soothe me, and no human light at night except the occasional satellite slipping inconspicuously among the stars. Yes, I feel guilty. But more elated than guilty.

Though I keep to myself more than anybody I know, I've never spent more than a week or two in the near-total isolation I'll experience here. I don't know what to expect, but I'm very much drawn to the prospect. I'm curious to find out what can be learned by stripping off, for a time, all human company and a good deal of human culture. I did bring books, of course—many books, because I couldn't conceive of not bringing books. On music I went back and forth. I was powerfully tempted to bring a Sony Discman and a tray of tunes, but in the end I decided against it. Too much like company. Same with the cat, which Marilyn and some of my friends urged me to bring. I love the cat, who is seventeen and almost as odd as I am, but I'll probably never do this again. I might as well keep the experiment as pure as I can. Besides, how would it look, bringing the cat and leaving my wife at home?

I will be working here, in my manner of work, and though my way of life will be simple the work will not. It never is. For several years I've been flailing and failing at the writing of a certain book, or rather an uncertain book, about growing up in the 1950s and '60s. I know there's a story to be told but I can't seem to discover its shape. It won't emerge from its background, just as red berries hide among green leaves from my partly color-blind eyes. In this spell of time, sealed off from distraction, I'm hoping I can find that story.

In my teens and twenties, I took it for granted when I thought about it at all that when I hit fifty I'd be worried about becoming an old man— would already *be* an old man. Well, I am kind of worried. The reflection in the window when I sit down to my desk at night is bespectacled and markedly white about the head. I'm not thrilled to see that guy. But on the other hand, he's generally quiet and doesn't claim much of my time. I've been thinking lately—as lately as three hours ago, during my chain-up adventure on the slippery hill—that maybe I've been seeing the problem upside down. Maybe it's not that I'm getting old, but that I never grew up.

I find myself keyed like a retriever on point to that time of my life in the late 1960s and early '70s when I came of age, or didn't, or did in some ways and didn't in others. Those years, and two of them in particular, stand in my memory like a job I began and for some reason abandoned, left like the framing of a house with a subfloor and part of a roof, the rooms roughed in, the studs and joists going gray through the years of sun and weather. I look back now and then to see if anyone's improved the place, and no one has. No one's going to, unless it's me.

And to do that, to imagine how it was that I became a man and how it was that I didn't, I know—I've known all along as I've tried to find this book—that I'll have to summon the memory of a certain extraordinary man who's been dead a quarter-century now, a strong and fragile and complicated man who himself was drawn to solitude, a man I admired and loved fiercely, hated at times, grew up with and left behind and never really knew. Stacked in the next room are several boxfuls of his letters to me and mine to him, his correspondence with others, speeches of his, newspaper clippings about him, interviews I've recorded with family members and some of his friends, miscellaneous other documents, some photographs, and a few mementos to bring him near. He's already near, of course. He's in that reflection in the window, and closer than that. In a way he's right where he always was. I need to understand where *I* am. I'm here to discover the story I belong to. I don't know where it begins.

November

I yet lack discernment to distinguish the whole lesson
of to-day; but it is not lost,—it will come to me at last.
My desire is to know *what* I have lived, that I may know
how to live henceforth.

—H. D. THOREAU, 1837
(ONE OF THE EARLIEST ENTRIES IN HIS *Journal*)

Life comes at you, my friend. You can't dodge it.

—FRANZ DANIEL, 1961

November 20

Morning, the first day, and the neighbors have called. A motley band of bucks loiters beneath the apple trees as I watch from the deck with my coffee. They came out of the woods from the west, sauntered up the drive with the mannered insouciance of teenagers displaying themselves at the mall. There's an antlerless little one born this year, a spikehorn, two forked-horns, and one four-point heavyweight who now and again lightly clacks antlers with one of the others to remind him of the natural order. Now they graze and loiter in edgy repose. Each of the five heads dips in its time for a mouthful of grass or old apple then suddenly lifts, the large ears shifting, the keen black nose also alert as the teeth chew—then down for another bite. One prances a few steps, another backs up, the little one starts and stops and quick-steps continually in response to his elders. They are five and one, a field of tense readiness. I sneak out of the cabin, slowly, with my camera. They chew, watch me, chew. I'm twenty-five feet away. Then, CHOOO!—a buck snort from one of them, like nothing so much as a sharp sneeze, and the five are running, bouncing, veering away into the meadow.

The meadow is the heart of this property, a ninety-four acre homestead on the north side of the canyon the Rogue River has worn to keep its course as the Klamath Mountains, over the last several million years, have risen around it. The canyon is a little over half a mile deep, its forested slopes steeply V-shaped, and it does a piece of fancy dancing in the stretch I now overlook. Flowing due north for a two-mile stretch, straight toward the homestead, the river deflects briefly to the east off a resistant rock mass, which it then wraps in a tight horseshoe bend—called Horseshoe Bend—and leaves behind, running off to the west of northwest toward its rendezvous with the Pacific. You don't see the river from the homestead—it's eight hundred vertical feet below, and some tall timber intervenes—but you look out on the spacious sculpturing it and its tributaries have accomplished, and the muted murmur of its rapids is always present when you remember to hear it.

Meadows of this size, about ten acres, are few and far between in the continuous forest of the Rogue Canyon, which is public land maintained as wilderness by the U.S. Bureau of Land Management. Private inholdings such as this homestead are rare also—a sparse scatter up and down the canyon, miles apart. The canyon is one of those places where progress has worked backwards. Almost empty of inhabitants now, from the 1850s well into the twentieth century it was sporadically busy with gold mining—small operations mainly, a long and loose community of sourdoughs sluicing the bars and tributary mouths, then larger outfits that ate into the riverbanks with hydraulic cannons when the easy gold had played out, and still later, during the Depression and the next few decades, a few sourdoughs again, scratching around for a subsistence living from what was left.

One of the early miners was a tall, bowlegged German named Henry Rosenbrook, who came to the Rogue in the 1860s. As Kay Atwood tells the story in *Illahe*, her invaluable account of settlement in the Rogue River Canyon, Rosenbrook found little gold but acquired a prominent and curiously dual reputation in local legendry. It seems commonly agreed that in separate incidents he murdered two of his mining partners—the first with a rifle butt during a business dispute, the other with an ax over an Indian woman. Dutch Henry, as Rosenbrook was known, though he wasn't Dutch, was tried and acquitted of both crimes, despite the fact that eyewitnesses testified against him in the first trial. After the second acquittal, perhaps as a gesture of contempt, Dutch Henry filed a new gold claim at Black Bar, which had been named for William Black, his second victim. Eventually he moved from the river to the meadow I'm now gazing upon. He built a cabin, planted fruit trees, ran a herd of Texas longhorns so ornery they'd gore anyone who came near who wasn't himself, packed in supplies by mule train for the miners on the river—making a better living than they did—and lived out his years uneventfully. At least one downriver mother had the habit of invoking the gangly murderer's name to control her kids—*If you don't behave I'll send you up to Dutch Henry!*—but it seems he also became a beloved figure to many in the sparse canyon community. People worried he'd die of pneumonia because he wore nothing heavier than a wool shirt. "He'd give you anything," one miner recalled. "He'd always say, 'You want some ah-pples? Some cha-a-a-a-ries?'"

Dutch Henry died in 1920, leaving his name on the homestead and also his bones. He was cared for in his last years by an Austrian immigrant, Bill Graiff, who took over the homestead and eventually proved it up—acquired outright ownership. Graiff, his great-great-granddaughter Jennifer Hall reports, had left his wife and family in the Washington coal country after a dispute over chickens or hunting dogs, one or the other. (Either way, one appreciates a man with clear priorities.) Here in the Rogue country he was a loner, like Dutch Henry and most of the miners, but he brought with him a tasteful Tyrolean domestic style. Culling doors, windows, and other makings from the river after a flood, Graiff built not a shack but a fine small house, complete with papered walls, two electric lights powered by a Pelton wheel in a tiny stream, and a rock-and-clay cellar he kept chuck full of home-stilled applejack, wine from his own grapes, and hundreds of pounds of bear meat put up in jars. Few guests would partake of the bear meat, but the same is not said of the drinkables.

Graiff vowed he'd live a hundred years but fell a few short. His heirs sold the homestead in 1968 to a Portland surgeon and his wife, the Doctor and Mother Margery, founders and progenitors of the Oregon faith, who had been packing in to the Horseshoe Bend of the Rogue since the 1940s for the hunting and steelhead fishing. The pair built a cabin on the place, Graiff's house having deteriorated, and later a second cabin down the drive to house a caretaker. The Brothers, sons of Mother Margery and the Doctor and present shepherds of the place, had the ingenious idea of awarding annual use of the homestead to a deserving writer with a preference for bears over humans as neighbors. The Brothers get their caretaker, and the writer gets up to a full year of backcountry solitude to seek out the paystreaks of his or her own kind of gold.

I had the residency in 1994. I fell in love with the place, as all residents do, and to stay in contact with it I've worked with the Brothers as a kind of lay facilitator, helping them manage the residency program. In '94 I watched fawns mature from wobbly-legged infants into spotless young deer. I saw Bill Graiff's walnut trees green up in the misty, dripping spring and go intensely yellow in the chilly light of fall. I encountered a cougar, the only one I've seen in the wild, and had peaceful relations with several black bears. I lay on a rock and watched, so close I could have touched them, chinook salmon three feet long cooling themselves where Kelsey Creek flows into the Rogue. I left on the first of November with a pang, wishing I could round out a full year at the place, wishing also for a long stay unbroken by trips in and out for groceries and the demands of the world.

And so, six years later, here I am, once again occupying the Route 66 Distinguished Chair in Creative Writing at Dutch Henry Homestead. Fall has always been my season. I get stirred up, shaken out of my summer sleep, when night and morning come with a bite and the days are suffused with a rich slant light, the light of lastnesses, and the wind strips bright leaves from the trees. This for me is the true season of renewal, when Nature shows her essential self. I like the withering bracken as well as I like the uncurling fronds of spring. Poets know the excellence of fall, or the good ones do, and so do mushrooms. As bears are denning up and crickets going quiet, the fungi push up bodily, heaving aside needle duff and even the trampled soil of the trails. Nothing can stop them—turn around and you spot a new one. Grouse explode from the grass at forest edges, quail run twittering zigzags across the drive, and in the river, the cool and green and clear-flowing river, steelhead and coho salmon press upstream, lit with their old and urgent desire.

The garden likes fall too. I've got fountaining broccoli plants, thickets of brazen Red Giant mustard, various green and purple cabbages lifting their leaves like glad hands, small stately spires of Romaine lettuce, two rows of sassy arugula, Hi-Ball onions scattered hither and thither, Winterbor and Winter Red kale, Purple Cape cauliflower, Flash collards, and many kohlrabi, those purple-clad baseballs of crisp peppery sweetness. This horde has burgeoned over the last three months under diaphanous white sheets of crop cover, which have admitted water and sun while pretty well excluding bugs and birds. The broccoli and cabbage have pressed the covers up taut, straining their edges against the staples that pin them to the ground. As I pull staples and lift sheets, I can actually hear a soft uncrinkling of burdened biomass.

Those are the greens, the flourishing greens. My root vegetables, on the other hand, have suffered casualties. Every carrot in the garden has been neatly clipped of its top. The thumb-sized carrots themselves are intact, but thumb-sized is all they will ever be. These are carrots, understand, in which I've invested myself. I started them from seed at home, fried the first batch in too much sun, rotted the second in too much shade, got it right with the third and transplanted the sprouts into this cushy, laboriously tilled and fertilized soil, where they took and began to thrive, only to become salad for—I suspect—digger squirrels, the lousy dirt rats who did in Joe Green's bean crop last summer and pillaged my own turnips and rutabagas earlier this fall. Or it might have been a deadbeat grouse I've seen skulking around, sneaking in where the covers were loose. The evidence is inconclusive. We will study the matter, and we will respond.

But all in all the garden's a rip-roaring success. It's the first fall garden I've tried. I'm putting off the unpacking of boxes and other chores of settling in to admire it, to snap a few photos and entertain the agreeable question of what to eat first.

Since my mid-twenties, almost everywhere I've lived I've put at least a few tomato plants into the ground, maybe some beans and cucumbers, and I've never turned the first spadeful of earth without thinking of my father. Except possibly in Denver, our one year in a mile-high city, he always grew a garden. In South and North Carolina, at all four of our houses in the Maryland suburbs of Washington, D.C., at our cabin on the Blue Ridge of northern Virginia. I know from letters that he gardened before my brother and I were born—in Philadelphia, at a shanty he built in Tennessee, even, I think, in the French Quarter of New Orleans in the early 1940s when he was trying to get into the military and join the war. He grew up in rural southwestern Missouri, where the family had a milk cow, a flock of Rhode Island Reds, a couple of hogs, and always a vegetable garden. My father returned to Missouri at various times in his life to lick his wounds, both physical and psychic, until his mother died in 1954. His gardens, I think, were a way of bringing Missouri with him, of grounding himself, literally, in a career that shifted dizzyingly from place to American place over the course of thirty-nine years and consumed all the passionate energy he had, and a bit more.

My father had an ease about him when he worked the ground. I picture him best in the little plot he had toward the end of the 1950s when we lived in Bannockburn, an early suburban development out MacArthur Boulevard from D.C. A nameless creek ran through a grassy and wooded bottomland, a commons between two sections of the suburb. My brother and I played baseball there with our friends, and out in far left-center, near the creek, my father had his tomato patch. When he wasn't traveling he'd come down after work on summer evenings in baggy trousers and undershirt, maybe sober, maybe half-lit in his beery, cheery phase. He'd hoe weeds, stake up his tomato vines, maybe plant something new, maybe spray his crops with some no doubt highly toxic pesticide, using an old-fashioned pump sprayer with the tank up front. He'd still be there sometimes when our game broke up at dusk, puttering, fireflies blinking around him, a lit Chesterfield hanging from the side of his mouth. "My tomatoes are lookin' awful good, Johnny," he might say, and I'd stop to pretend to admire them. I didn't care much about gardening but I cared about him, and I liked to please him.

And I cared about baseball. I'd tell him if I'd gotten a hit—most of the players were my brother's friends, bigger and stronger than me, so getting a hit meant something—and he'd say, "Attaboy, my friend." My father and I had some of our best times together watching ball games in the basement recreation room of our Bannockburn house, which stayed cool on the muggiest afternoons. Our team was the hapless Washington Senators (who would later play better as the Minnesota Twins), but even a bad team has moments. We rejoiced when our slugger, Roy Sievers, smacked another home run. We heaped praise on the curve ball of Camilo Pascual, the Cuban who once won seventeen games for the cellar-bound Senators. We noted our respect for the fortitude of catcher Clint Courtney—Old Scrapiron, as he was known, a man composed, according to my father, solely of bruises, knitted bones, and sheer grit.

I had the simplistically heroic view of the game that most kids have.

My father showed me its subtleties. "There's no percentage in *that* god-damn swing," I remember him grousing once when Jim Lemon, an outfielder who too often lived up to his name, had struck out yet again, trying to clobber a high fastball with no one on base and the Senators down four to nothing. "The bum," said my father. "We need baserun-ners, not heroes." Until then I had considered swinging for the fences an absolute good, the thing every batter should do when he comes to the plate. It had never occurred to me that he should sometimes try to draw a walk or hit a mere single or even get hit by a pitch. My dogma bled a drop of doubt.

My father put great stock in the sacrifice bunt, explaining when it was and wasn't the right move. He preached on the solemn duty of a runner sliding into second to do everything in his power, even gash the shortstop with his spikes, to break up the double play. He'd once seen Ty Cobb, he told me many times, sitting on the dugout steps, a fat Georgia grin on his face, conspicuously sharpening his spikes with a file before he came up to bat. And especially, my father shed light on the tense territorial warfare of the pitcher-batter confrontation. "Look at him dig in," he'd say of Moose Skowron or Vic Power. "Camilo's got to brush him back, Johnny. He's got to lay him in the dirt right now." And sometimes Camilo did exactly that.

My father would drink beer as we watched, Schlitz or National Bohemian, sipping straight from the cans he punched open between innings with a church key. The beer made him buoyantly amiable, his face relaxed in a steady loose smile, as if there were nothing in the world incapable of delighting him. He could maintain himself for hours in that state, and I liked him best that way. Everyone did. It was his story-telling state, his state of exulting with Beethoven. His spirit was huge and lively. Sober he was much more reserved, less delightable, and when he got drunker—when Bob Bradley came over to watch the game with a pitcher of martinis, or when my father on his own turned to bour-bon—his beery happiness sagged into intervals of brooding, his ciga-rette burning unnoticed between the yellowed first two fingers of his right hand, growing a long arc of ash that sometimes fell to the floor before he remembered to flick it into the ashtray.

November 21

I've got baseball on my mind, I suppose, because the World Series ended not long ago, ended the way it too often did when I was a kid. The New York Yankees, now as then the most boringly great team in baseball, won it again. Some things never change. For months I've been watching and listening to my team, the San Francisco Giants, as they put together a great second half of the season and then belly-flopped in the playoffs. On my trips here to provision the place, I brought a radio so I could listen to Giants night games, which came in lucidly clear from four hundred miles south. Now, my third night here, after a dinner of pork chops and Kyuna Mizuna mustard greens—can't say it, but I grew it—I drift around the cabin and outside for the stars and back in again, unable to settle on what to do. I'm realizing how used I am to something playing—a game, music, the news—something in the air. Without it I feel vaguely dull. I guess I've addicted myself to that stimulation, engaging enough to entertain me while demanding next to nothing. Something to liven my mood—or, if it was a Giants game and the Giants lost, to turn it sour.

Some things never change. My father, a boxing fan and an impromptu boxer himself, had a characteristic way of expressing his hurt when the wrong team won. It was put on, but genuine too. "*Ooh*," he'd say, part grunt part exclamation, as if he'd been punched in the midsection. "*Ooh, ooh*," with quick shakes of his head. "That hurts, Johnny. That hurts."

He'd had long experience of the wrong team winning because he'd devoted his life to coaching the underdog. He left Missouri in the early 1920s for Centre College in Kentucky, the University of Wisconsin, and then Union Theological Seminary in New York City—tending chickens on a railcar to get there—to study for the Presbyterian ministry, but even as an undergraduate he had been hearing a different call. The Daniel family was not well-heeled while my father was growing up and, for a time, after his father died, was quite poor. While working in the Frisco railroad shops in Springfield, though, to earn money to continue his education, my father got to know men who enjoyed no middle-class advantages at all, decent men who led lives of grinding drudgery. The shop workers went out on strike in 1922. My father, then eighteen, saw U.S. Marshals rounding up the strikers—men he knew— like so many cattle, beating them with guns and nightsticks, corralling them in the dry goods store, hauling them away. Nothing changed in the shops except that new bodies took up the same brutal jobs, but in my father a passion was waking.

At Wisconsin he encountered the manifesto of the Industrial Workers of the World, which had been first enunciated, he liked to say, by the legendary Utah miner and agitator Big Bill Haywood, pounding a table with a two-by-four in a Chicago union hall. The manifesto states:

> The working class and the employing class have nothing in common. There can be no peace so long as hunger and want are found among millions of working people, and the few, who make up the employing class, have all the good things of life. Between these two classes a struggle must go on.

It rang true, and when my father got to Union, so did the talks and writings of activist clergymen such as Walter Rauschenbusch, Harvey Ward, and Reinhold Niebuhr, who were preaching the Social Gospel, reinterpreting Christianity's prophetic ethical tradition as a call for social justice and the economic betterment of the poor. "We were going to right the wrongs of the world. We believed Jesus was leading us," my father would write forty-five years later, and he and his cohorts had a distinct, class-based attitude about their Christ. My father kept and sometimes recited an unattributed stanza of poetry from that time:

> Thanks to St. Matthew
>   Who had been
> At mass meetings in Palestine,
>   We know whose side was spoken for
> When Comrade Jesus had the floor.

Student preaching, working with boys clubs on the lower east side of Manhattan, making trips to poor mill towns in the Carolinas and the coal country of Harlan County, Kentucky, my father saw the human misery underlying the blithe prosperity of the late '20s and the crushing violence visited on workers who tried to improve their lot. And he saw something else—he saw "in the heart of mankind an indomitable desire for decency. In ugly, desolate mill villages where no man dared to raise his voice, there burned a fierce, unquenchable flame dedicated to justice." Henry Sloane Coffin, the seminary president, saw my father's own unquenchable flame and gift for oratory and urged him toward the pulpit, but my father was inclined more and more toward "applied" religion. He organized the Morningside Heights chapter of the American Socialist Party, led mass demonstrations to prevent eviction of the poor from apartments they couldn't afford, and began a chronic habit of sampling prison hospitality. (When he and other Union students were jailed for picketing Bloomingdale's, reporters asked President Coffin if he was embarrassed for his institution. "Christians have been thrown in jail for two thousand years," Coffin replied. "Haven't you heard of Paul and Silas?" "Sir," responded one reporter, "do you have their last names?")

In 1930 my father left Union without writing his dissertation and took up a job for $2.50 a week as a Socialist Party organizer in Philadelphia, where he worked and caroused with other activists who lived in a semi-communal three-story home on North 5th Street, a residence known—to its neighbors; its residents were vehemently anti-Communist—as Soviet House. "Franz had the voice for oratory," his Socialist comrade Alice Cook recalled to me a year before she died. "I remember once heading for a rally and hearing his unamplified voice from four or five blocks away." He had a knack, she and others have told me, for enunciating labor movement ideals in a down-to-earth style livened with anecdote. An intellectual with rural roots, he could rouse audiences of blue-collar, poorly educated workers that more purely intellectual speakers couldn't touch. He would sit for hours with those workers, too, drinking with them, drawing them out with stories, jokes, and what Alice Cook called "his encouraging little chuckle."

My father worked with several trade unions in his Party capacity, and in 1932 he was hired by Sidney Hillman to organize for the Amalgamated Clothing Workers of America, a rising powerhouse of a union. Garment and textile workers were the poorest-paid and most abused of all industrial laborers; it was the needle trades that gave birth to the term "sweatshop." My father was a lieutenant in the Amalgamated's successful campaign to organize shirt factories in the anthracite region of western Pennsylvania, where manufacturers had relocated to avoid union strength in urban areas. The employees, who were almost entirely daughters and wives of coal miners, became known as the "Baby Strikers"—two-thirds of them were under sixteen. My father went on to spend most of the thirties and forties as a leader in the Amalgamated's far less successful organizing drives in the Southeast, where the labor movement was up against not only the mill bosses and the sheriff's office, but also a culture of resentment toward Yankee meddling, preachers who demanded that workers choose between God and the union, and frequently enough the Ku Klux Klan.

My mother also organized for the Amalgamated. She met my father at a house party on the Maine coast in 1930 and married him in 1934, my father in a suit reeking of whiskey—his bottle had come uncorked in his suitcase. Elizabeth Day Hawes, the rebel daughter of a New England Unitarian minister, was four years younger than Franz Daniel and a graduate of Vassar College, where she had become a passionate leftist. They must have cut quite a figure. My father, over six feet tall, bigframed and dark-haired, had a broadly handsome Germanic face, a commanding baritone voice, and an unfailing magnetism. He could not enter a room unnoticed, according to friends, and the same was true of the young Zilla Hawes, with her dark curly hair, her exuberant spirit, and her virile intensity that many men found intimidating. Through the thirties, before and after their wedding, they lived rootless and frequently separate lives, shifting around the South on various organizing drives. They spent time together when they could at Highlander Folk School near Monteagle, Tennessee, where my mother taught and my father built a shanty—"Zilla's Doll House," he called it—where they could hole up.

There's a story from that time I liked as a kid, though I didn't know all its details then, because it was about my parents adventuring together. The Amalgamated sent them to Rockwood, Tennessee, to invigorate a strike at a hosiery plant that wasn't going well. The workers there, as in most clothing and textile mills in the South, put in crushing twelve-hour shifts, endured job speed-ups and miserable conditions, and often didn't make enough in a week to avoid falling still further behind at the company store. The hosiery company was intimidating the strikers, firing them, hiring scabs to take their places. When my parents arrived at the plant, my father handed his watch and wallet to my mother and told her to wait while he went to rally the picketers.

He came back with a rag tied around his bloodied head. "Let's get the hell to Knoxville," he said. "The son-of-a-bitch sheriff's got a warrant on me." My father, a labor movement star on the rise, was sometimes greeted with an arrest warrant before he'd had a chance to break any laws.

They jumped into his Ford coupe, my mother driving, and as she turned onto the highway a car roared up behind them. The sheriff was driving. Three deputies leaned out the windows, each with a sawed-off shotgun.

My father said, "You'd better pull over, Zil."

My mother said, "Like hell!" She hit the gas and took the curves of the mountain highway at seventy, as she remembered it decades later, tires squealing, the two of them lurching side to side with the force of the turns. The sheriff stayed on their tail. As the Ford slowed on a long grade, one of the deputies fired a shot at the rear tires. A blowout might have sent the car off the road and down the mountainside. My mother pulled over.

The sheriff pronounced my father—as my mother liked to remember it—a goddamned Red Russian Bolshevik Jew and took him into custody, where he would remain until the union lawyer bailed him out. My mother, on the other hand, the sheriff let off without so much as a speeding ticket. "Ma'am," he told her, turning courtly, "you are the best woman driver I have ever seen in Roane County."

My mother, by the end of the thirties, would convince my father that they should have children and would quit her labor career. My father would work on, organizing and troubleshooting for the Amalgamated, the Textile Workers Organizing Committee, the United Auto Workers, and the Marine & Shipbuilding Workers, then serving in the forties as a regional director in the Carolinas for the Congress of Industrial Organizations, a national association of unions founded during the New Deal as the labor movement caught fire. He rose to the position of field assistant to Walter Reuther, the president of the CIO, and in 1955, when the CIO merged with the older American Federation of Labor, he became assistant director of organization for the national AFL-CIO.

That was his job when we lived in Bannockburn. He spent at least half his time on the road, working with various unions. When he was home, he worked at the AFL-CIO's shiny new headquarters on 16th Street in downtown Washington. He left the house in the morning dressed in suit and tie and fedora hat, just like other men in Bannockburn, who mainly were government workers, academics, and other professionals. He smelled of aftershave and made small talk with the neighbors, but he had a past I couldn't imagine in the neighbors. He had scars on his hands and arms from fights with cops and security guards, strikebreakers and company goons. He'd been hit with blackjacks and brass knuckles, slashed with a beer opener. He'd been many times in jail. He'd even been shot point blank in the chest with a pistol and survived it—shrugged off the slug like Superman in the ten-cent comics I liked to read.

I was proud of my father, and in awe of him, but I was at times uncomfortable that he did something and was someone so out of the ordinary. It felt a little odd to hear myself say, when asked what my father did for a living, that he was a labor organizer. The questioner's reaction sometimes told me that not everyone viewed the American labor movement as we did in our house, where "Joe Hill" or "Solidarity Forever" was as likely to be playing on the hi-fi as Beethoven or Duke Ellington. The climate of the Cold War was settling in then, and unions, to some, were nothing but cells of Red subversion. That sort of embarrassment was salutary, though, in the long run. It helped me focus my sense of self. I was more troubled by a different kind.

My father was in his garden one evening when we were playing ball.

I saw him watching us from left field, then a few minutes later he walked over and stood behind first base, declaring runners out or safe with loud calls and exaggerated motions of his arms. His smile was loose, too loose. His voice slurred a little when he shouted approval of someone's base hit to center.

It was a big game, eight or maybe a full nine on each team. It was beginning to get dark, the fireflies sparking. Someone on the other team left to go home, and my father, at his own suggestion or someone's invitation, took over first base. By now it was feeling like a bad dream. I came up to bat with two outs. My father crouched in theatrical readiness, borrowed glove forward, cigarette dangling from his lips. I swung too hard and hit a soft grounder. The second baseman bobbled it, kept it in front of him, scooped it up and threw in plenty of time. As I ran it out my father was there to take the throw, his glove hand reaching, his smile boundless, and the ball passed several inches beneath his glove and hit him squarely in his ample gut. It dropped and rolled a few feet away. My father, standing next to me at first, laughed in his throat as the pitcher fetched the ball.

"That's okay, Mr. Daniel," someone said in the silence. But my father already knew that. He smiled and laughed, and his laugh said, *Hey, what a game, we're sure having a good time here, aren't we?*

⁘

This evening, after shifting the furniture around for an hour—each writer who lives here reconstellates the furnishings—and deboxing my books onto shelves, I'm fiddling with my instruments. The guy who didn't want his solitude regimented by a clock somehow has ended up with three—one was here, one is my usual travel clock, and the third is a gift from Marilyn. It too is a small travel clock, but this wonder of Chinese technology tells not merely the time but the month and date, the day of the week, and even—in Fahrenheit, to the half-degree—the temperature. I was going to cooperate anyway, but Marilyn wanted to ensure that I had no excuse to miss making my weekly call or my twice-weekly calling availabilities. I'm pleased to have her clock. It's almost like having a sentient being in the house, a disciplined companion very good at knowing what it knows and discreet enough to announce it, silently, only upon request.

This talented clock, with a fresh battery just installed, will be Greenwich standard. I've spent the last half-hour synchronizing the other two clocks to it, within one second, and checking its thermometer function against the new German mercury-column thermometer—thank God for *something* not digitalized—I'm going to install outside the kitchen window. The clock thermometer reads one degree higher, which annoys me, but considering the disparity of the source countries, a degree of difference isn't bad. As a son of Franz Emil Daniel, bearing "Franz" as my own middle name, I trust the Germans—in technology and music, anyway. The Germans will tell me the true temperature of my Klamath Mountain ecosphere. The Chinese will tell me, perhaps a degree overheatedly, whether to shove another log into the Fisher stove.

November 25

I've learned three things. One, I don't seem to have forgotten anything major. There are things I'd like to have—a wooden salad bowl, a magnifying glass, half a bushel of good apples—but no ruinous oversight. I did blunder badly when I tossed cross-country skis into the truck, because the skis I tossed—a sign of the tizzy I was in—were one of mine and one of Marilyn's. Doesn't matter, I'm telling myself. The skis are to get me out of here if necessary, over the pass where I had the trouble getting in, which most winters bury pretty deep in snow. Hiking fourteen snowless miles up the Rogue River Trail is my other exit route. I don't expect to have to use either.

Two, I've learned that I didn't leave music behind when I declined the Discman. It smuggled itself in. Various scraps of melody and swatches of lyrics are playing in my head incessantly. I came here for silence, but either I'm one of those people who receive radio through their dental fillings or something in my psyche is fighting silence tooth and nail. It's not even whole songs, which might be tolerable, but a jukebox of song shards. It's especially maddening when one of them plays over and over like a stuck record. Yesterday it was a line from "Dixie"—*Way down yonder in the land of cotton* . . . Earlier today it was part of the refrain from the Beatles' "Lady Madonna," which I can't afford to quote you. Sometimes I don't even know what's playing—it's just scat, riffs, a *doop-de-doop DOOO, doo WAHHH* . . . I didn't reckon on this ragtag band marching in my own mind. Silence, I thought, would be a given. I can see—can hear, that is—that I'm going to have to cultivate it, which is one reason I'm meditating every morning.

And three, the dirt rats are not to blame. Neither is the grouse, who has wisely disappeared. The devourer of my carrot tops and whatever else she can get her beak on is a wild turkey, a lovely female with a blue fuzzy head, a bit of red on her throat, and a gorgeous gold, brown, and black-barred carapace of feathers. She slips blithely through the bear fence into the garden every morning, then again in the late afternoon before she shuffles up the drive to her roost in the woods. The rest of the daylight hours she spends in a leisurely circuit of the cabin grounds, pecking such morsels of bug or grass as she can find, which seem to be plenty. The grass around the cabin and garden was mowed all last spring and summer to reduce fire danger, and now it's a rich veldt of short green, while all the rest of the meadow is overgrown and sere.

I'm pleased to share the veldt, but not the garden. I'm eating from it every day and intend to eat from it right through to April or May. When I see the turkey down there *in flagrante delicto* I yell from the deck, which causes her to pause in her shredding of broccoli or cabbage and lift her head thoughtfully, as if perhaps she has heard something. My next move is to grab some kindling sticks and clomp down the path launching missiles in her direction. She clucks nervously—*Oh dear oh dear oh dear*—and trots away from the vegetable beds. With the third or fourth kindling stick she reluctantly, and with laborious effort, flaps herself over the bear fence to safety.

I have told this bird, out loud, her jeopardy. I came here prepared to hunt, and wild turkey is one of the critters I am prepared for. Thanksgiving has passed, but Christmas is less than a month away. I have four cans of whole-berry cranberry sauce on the Warhol Wall. I expected, of course, to hunt my turkey in the woods. I didn't expect to find one parading so close I could shoot it through a window from my La-Z-Boy chair. This bird has made a bold gambit. In the woods, wild, she would have been at risk; but she has made herself domestic, and so she travels under a letter of transit written by my human sentimentality. She gets the best food in the Rogue Canyon, including carrot tops, and sees not a glint of my shotgun's barrel. Not yet, anyway.

I haven't hunted in a long time, not since the fall of 1962, when I was fourteen. My parents had bought a cabin in northern Virginia, tucked into a hollow at the base of the Blue Ridge, and we went there for weekends sometimes. My parents' marriage was well on its way to wreckage by then, so "we" usually meant one parent and me—my brother Jim, three years older, having by then a compelling weekend social life. My father was no longer hunting in 1962, but he kept two double-barreled shotguns and two .22s at the cabin. I was a passionate fisherman, and when I developed an interest in hunting my father encouraged me. He was tickled when I came back one day with a squirrel I'd blasted out of a tree. He skinned and cleaned it for me on a stump behind the cabin, then soaked the little carcass overnight in salt water to take out the gamey flavor. In the morning he cut it up, rolled the pieces in salted and peppered flour, and fried them in bacon grease along with some sliced green tomatoes. The meat still had plenty of gaminess. It tasted *alive*. Sweet, but with a rankness like old leaves.

Once at the cabin I asked my father why he had quit hunting.

"Oh, I don't know, Johnny," he said. "You get to an age when fall rolls around and you just don't think of it." He was in a sad mood and didn't want to talk.

My father was fifty-eight then. He'd been forty-four when I was born. As I was growing up it sometimes seemed as though everything he'd done was in the past, was locked up there in some kind of vault, like his coin collection in his safe at home. That vault was where he went, I had a feeling, in his long brooding silences.

I came here prepared to hunt because I'm a dedicated if not entirely comfortable carnivore—omnivore, actually, but a man who much enjoys meat. I grew up on my father's grilled sirloin, my mother's pot roast and meatloaf, on lamb for Easter and turkey for Thanksgiving and roast beef or ham for Christmas, and Swiss steak or hamburgers anytime. Even liver—I liked it fried crisp with onions and ketchup—and tongue of beef, which, once I got past the *idea* of it and slathered it with enough horseradish, tasted fine.

I drew the line, and still do, at brains, sweetbreads, and kidney. A brain isn't food. A brain is a thinker, a smart sponge. Nature wouldn't have encased it in a heavy-duty cranium if it were meant to be eaten. (Nature's intentions, I'll acknowledge, can be hard to read. Certain North American cannibals have interpreted the human cranium as a convenient pre-loaded roasting vessel.) A sweetbread, that lovely word, is the thymus gland of a calf. No gland should be eaten. Glands should be interred discreetly with the bones and brain, not dressed up with a euphemistic name that suggests pastry and served with scrambled eggs. And kidney? Kidney, when my parents made me try it, tasted like piss and no doubt still does. What would you expect from a kidney?

But flesh, good cleanly muscle cooked to a juicy turn, is good to the teeth that chew it, good to the tongue that savors it, good to the gullet it goes down. Why *wouldn't* I eat of a choice haunch, a toothsome fowl? My parents did, and their parents before them. I would lay odds that every ancestor in my lineage ate meat, when meat was to be had, clear back to those apelike hominids who descended from African trees to try out life on the ground. It's not pretty to think of, but our early ancestors made their living by killing other animals and enjoying their flesh. There was at least one parallel hominid species that didn't eat meat. It hasn't been heard from for several million years.

My discomfort as a carnivore comes from the distance we have interposed between ourselves and the animals we eat. "Animal" comes from the Latin *animalis*, meaning "living." But for us it's dead, it's hunks of matter we lift from chilled counters at Safeway, neatly packaged in Styrofoam and cellophane, or elsewhere, for a higher price, custom wrapped in tasteful brown paper. The only hint of its origin occurs once in a while when the packaging leaks blood on the checker's hands, or on our own hands at home when we lift our meat from the bag. And so I've set a standard for myself: I should be willing to kill the flesh I eat, and I do kill it at least once in a while. If I can't do that, I'll have to make do with rice and tofu, and that is a future I cannot face.

I considered shooting a deer, and I still could. Two or three of the bucks amble past the cabin almost every day, pausing to eat fallen apple leaves not fifty feet from the deck. In the other room, nestled in a closet with the water tank, is a 30.06 and a supply of shells. (Not mine. The Brothers have thoughtfully provided this weapon, and a .22 as well, so that residents can defend their privacy against bears, river rafters, and other intruders. The Brothers' faith is not a pacifistic faith.) I could sit very still in my rocker on the deck one morning, bundled against the cold in an earth-tone quilt, and slowly slide the deer gun's barrel over the railing, fix the scope on the head or shoulder area of a young buck who has lived a good wild life, and squeeze the trigger and turn the whole thing over to ballistics.

But then I would have, at best, several scores of pounds of fresh venison and no way to preserve it—my little freezer compartment is full—

and only possibly an appetite to eat it after gutting and skinning the carcass, which I don't know how to do, and hanging it in the entry porch, where I would need to elbow it aside as I entered and left the cabin. At worst, and it was the possibility of the worst that decided it, I'd have a head-grazed or gut-shot deer to track and lose somewhere on the steep and thicketed sidehills of the Rogue River Canyon.

So, smaller game. A bird, perhaps. A bird in hand . . .

November 27

Is there a job of work in all the world as satisfying as splitting firewood? One swing does it with these rounds I'm working, if my aim is true and my maul stroke crisp. What was whole springs apart in halves, each with a fresh bright face, ready to stand again on the block and divide once more with another clean shout. The product of my toil rises around the block, tangible and fragrant, each new split piece making a happy knock and rattle as it strikes the pile and finds its place. There is, of course, the occasional knotted round that will separate only on its own perverse and protracted terms; and the occasional piece that won't stand straight for the maul because I didn't buck it straight with the chainsaw; and the occasional errant swing that produces not identical twins but a grazed round and a stick of kindling. But these trials merely add dramatic texture to the serene unfolding of the story.

I'm splitting madrone, a Pacific coastal hardwood that burns long, hot, and virtually poplessly. The flesh of the wood is pale and often tinged pink, echoing in a muted way the outward beauty of the standing tree. Madrone trunks—a tree might have two or three—curve and wander, their sapwood densely muscled beneath thin, papery bark that can be bright olive green on young growth and red-orange to cinnamon on more mature trees, darkening to rich brown and flaky gray on the lower trunks of the veterans. Bark in the red range peels from trunks and limbs in delicate flakes, as if the tree had suffered a voluptuous sunburn, and in long curling strips that look like oversized cinnamon sticks. Madrone is the only tree I desire to *eat*.

It flourishes here, developing trunks up to three or four feet through and eighty to a hundred tall. Down on the Rogue River Trail there's an ancient specimen, still very much alive, that must have measured six or seven feet in diameter before half of it split away. The name *madroño*—strawberry tree—was given by homesick Californian Spaniards for the tree's resemblance to one of its cousins in their native land. And madrones do bring a Mediterranean sensuality to this forest, which is dominated by straight and spartan Douglas firs, western hemlocks, sugar pines, ponderosa pines, and other rough-barked needle trees. But there are other broadleafs too, a welter of them—tanoaks, white oaks, black oaks, bigleaf maples, golden chinquapins, Oregon ashes, bay laurels, Pacific dogwoods, and several more species. The forest of these Klamath Mountains, David Rains Wallace writes in *The Klamath Knot*, is the most diverse in the West and in all of North America except for a few pockets in the southern Appalachians. Wherever I run my vision along the meadow's borders, it touches a variety of forms and textures and shades of green—even now in late fall, because several of the broadleafs, including madrone, are evergreens.

The vitality of this forest is something almost palpable, an exuberant aura, and yet it's a diminished forest. There are ghost trees here. When Mother Margery and the Doctor bought the homestead from Bill Graiff's heirs, the timber had been separately sold. The property was logged, selectively but intensively, in 1968. Leave the meadow in any direction and you find Cat roads, grown over with brush and young trees now, that lead past some impressive stumps. Below the property, in the public forest, there are some old-growth giants, Douglas firs over 150 feet tall and six feet through. The homestead had a few of those too. But that's all done. There will be no more commercial logging on Dutch Henry Homestead, due both to the tenets of the Brothers' faith and to their scenic easement agreement with the Bureau of Land Management. The homestead forest is healing well, which is more than can be said for some of the steep logging sites outside the canyon. Aerial photos show, to either side of the sinuous swath that is the protected wild Rogue corridor, the surrounding forest riddled with a patchwork of clear-cuts and squiggly logging roads that look like insect borings. My winter wilderness, like all American wilderness south of Alaska, is a remnant.

November 28

All writers have been comforted to learn, over the last few decades, of the brain hemispheres and the distinct ways they work. We know well—too well, some of us—that to invigorate the subconscious springs we must spend time away from words doing physical, spatial, right-brain things. Washing the dishes, say, or sweeping the floor, but those appeal little to either hemisphere. Here at Dutch Henry there's always more wood to split, but that's maybe a shade too analytical. There's the hour a day of caretaking—mowing, bolstering the bear defenses, maintaining trails, skimming scum from the newt pond—the Brothers exact for use of their hermitage, but tomorrow is usually a more promising day for that. There's this, there's that, but sooner or later there is only one question: When shall I go fishing? And the answer, sooner or later, is now.

That was my answer today. Twenty minutes down the trail and there was the Rogue, its graceful green self, sliding and roiling translucent between riffles and brief white rapids. It was running at about its summer pace and level, but the boulders close along both sides, which in summer are scruffed with nondescript brown and dirty-blonde matter, have been wakened by the few fall rains to date. They now wear thick green pelts, some velvety, some feathery, some a limish green so bright it shouts, some in richer and darker shades that make me want to sink my fingers into them. The boulders altogether form a verdant retinue flanking the steady, spirited progress of the river. What is this stream, if not the very river out of Eden? The flowing, swirling, churning, soothing, glistening mystery itself, the voice and vessel of possibility.

The only discordant possibility was that raftfuls of human beings bundled in bright, space-age materials might appear in my paradise, as they do by the hour during warmer months. I don't mind rafters. Some of my favorite friends are rafters. I am a rafter myself on occasion. But for the tenure of my winter sojourn I want none of them. I have vivid proprietary feelings about this reach of river. Until April it belongs to me. I've never much believed in multiple use, except in places I don't go.

But no rafters, as it happened, just me and the osprey who nests in a broken-top snag on the other side. I was glad for his companionship, but for him I was one too many. He flew up and down the river uttering agitated cries. I felt less of an extremist to learn that someone around here is even more averse to human company than I am.

Maybe the bird understood, in his osprey way, that my arrival had brought a rival. On a cast to quiet water across the river I had a hard strike and suddenly felt that exhilarating connection to an unseen life that I hadn't experienced for more than a year. Before long I was swinging onshore a lively little steelhead and trying to grab him as he thrashed on mossy stone, his accustomed supporting medium suddenly separated to solid rock and resistless air. He flailed in my hands, one hard arching muscle. I knocked him on the head a couple of times with a rock and he quivered still. I watched his spotted, violet-green iridescence begin to fade. But then, a minute later, he was flopping again on the moss patch where I'd left him. I whapped his head twice on the bare crown of a boulder. He quivered and died.

They aren't called steelhead for nothing. I need to do better. If I'm going to kill the creatures of Eden, the least I owe them is a quick clean end.

In the next hour I missed two and landed one more, a fine spate of fishing. I had expected the river to skunk me a time or two before permitting me a catch. I was a fishing enthusiast in my youth, but in midlife my faith lapsed. Brother Frank, the older of the Brothers, has tried in recent years to rekindle it. I felt his blessing today. Brother Frank is an elder of the Salmon Way. Outsiders know little of the workings of the Way, but some say that Brother Frank is its highest priest and practitioner. When the Brother's line is in the water—usually a fly line, though he does fish by other means—he enters a trancelike state, totally attuned to the river's multifarious energies, a slight twitching of his formidable eyebrows his only outward animation. He does not fish. "To fish" implies a subject-object relationship. He enters that deeper metaphysical condition of being in which river, fish, and fisherman are one, a single fluxful stream of pure potential that resolves, to the eyes of observers, in the manifestation of fish after fish at the end of Brother Frank's leader.

He is generous with his gifts. I have seen him, on a small coastal river, step with spinning gear into the midst of a group of anglers who've been thrashing the water all morning to no avail, cast two or three times, eyebrows homing in, and suddenly his familiar mantra: "Fish on!" As the others cleared their lines from the river, Brother Frank thrust his doubled, dancing rod into the hands of a very surprised novice, then coached the novice as he struggled against the bulldog runs of a very large fish very displeased about its detention, charging upriver and down, screeching line off the reel. The novice had never felt such a power. I know this because I was that novice. Eventually the bulldog tired and submitted to the net, revealing himself as a thirty-pound chinook salmon. I was a quivering puddle. Brother Frank remarked, "Good action," and went back to casting his line.

The steelhead I caught today are of a small variety known only in the Rogue and Klamath Rivers—young fish that, for reasons best known to them, return from the Pacific after only six months rather than the usual two or three years. They'll spend the winter in the river and ship out next year for the rest of their ocean hitch, after which they'll return once or maybe twice to spawn. Though sexually immature, these fish, like the young of many species, are jazzed and ready to dance. If they can't have sex themselves, they want to hang around where sex is being had or has been had or possibly could be had. They are commonly called half-pounders, which is far too pejorative. My two are each about sixteen inches, a pound and a half. They look a lot like rainbow trout, which is appropriate because they are rainbow trout. A steelhead is a trout with a taste for seafood and a willingness to travel. In January and February the grown-ups will arrive, the five- and seven- and ten-pound lords of the Rogue, the kind that turn your knees to putty if you're lucky enough to connect with one. We'll see then what kind of fisherman I am.

In the twilight, as I was cleaning my catch while humming along to "Clementine"—one of the top ten hits on my inner radio—I glanced up at the right moment to see a whiskered head gliding downstream along the mossy far bank, scarcely rippling the surface. An otter, so at home in the river that he *was* the river, as much as any roil or riffle or laughing slosh. He was, as Thoreau said of the fish in Walden Pond, "animalized water." He glanced once my way and slipped on.

Dusk turned to dark as I climbed the trail. I had my headlamp in necklace deployment, ready for duty, but found I didn't need it. The trail was indistinct, but clear enough for my plodding pace. (What takes twenty minutes down takes thirty or thirty-five up.) Where the forest opened slightly, I noticed that my body cast the faintest of shadows. No moon or stars, only the residual light of the thinly overcast sky. At the cabin, after using the headlamp briefly to find my down booties and a beer, I reclined in the La-Z-Boy and enjoyed, in the darkness of my home, the luminosity of early night, now with an evening planet in the west. Conifers stood around the meadow in their various heights like a solemn council holding session in silence, their lower portions blended in shadow, their points and upper reaches sharply silhouetted against the pale glowing sky.

November 30

The fishing went so well, I thought I'd try grouse hunting. I returned with no grouse but with a theory of grouse.

They are such sensitive students of the human footfall, my theory holds, that they can tell if the human is lugging a gun. This explains why on weaponless walks they've thundered out of cover ahead of me, easy shots, and why this afternoon they showed and sounded not at all. My theory further propounds that it may not be the additional weight of the gun the grouse detects in the footfalls, but rather the subtle or not-so-subtle swagger in the hunter's gait, the ready-to-blow-something-away exhilaration with a lid of self-control half on it. It's there, from the hunter's avid eyes right down to his boot heels. *I* was aware of it, a dull-witted human, so why wouldn't a sharp-sensed bird pick it up? I bet they can even distinguish the swagger of a greenhorn, such as me, from that of an experienced hunter. So why then stay in hiding? Because, the cultural traditions of grouse are careful to teach, greenhorns have been known to get lucky.

That explains, I believe, why grouse hide when a hunter is about. But why do they explode from virtually under the feet of unarmed walkers? Simple. To scare the hell out of them.

But that swagger, I recognized it right away. When I was a teenager, the Virginia cabin became a hangout and party haunt for me and my brother and our friends. It was far enough from home—fifty miles—to escape the meddlings of adults, to play music as loud as we liked (that cabin, unlike this one, had electricity), and to drink to the point of collapsing in the yard under a spinning night sky. And to shoot guns. By day we shot beer cans. By night, some of us who fancied ourselves marksmen set a lit candle in the ground fifty feet or so from the cabin, then sat on the porch with .22s trying to shoot the flame off the wick, drinking more beer to improve our aim. This pursuit was inspired by a story about my father. Once—long ago, of course—he had shot a stick match off a fence post at fifty feet. "Aw hell," he is supposed to have said. "I was trying to *light* the damn thing."

I remember one fall day at the cabin with my brother and three or four of his friends, the bunch of us tramping through woods and fields talking and shooting at birds. Not hunting, just taking random potshots at crows and blackbirds. We were kids from the suburbs, from middle-class white and white-collar families, but looking back now I don't see much to distinguish us from an inner-city gang, except that nothing we shot at was going to shoot back. My brother and his friends were discussing girls, which ones would do what, and colleges they might attend. I was tagging along. The talk about sex was remote to me, a realm I despaired of ever reaching, but carrying a rifle with the older guys made me feel capable, even tough.

From my earliest years in school I had shied away from roughhousing and fighting. Because I was tall for my age and wore glasses only part of the time, I wasn't automatically classified a sissy, but if another kid pushed me I didn't stick up for myself, I just walked away. In this I was no different from my friends. We were the grinds of grade school and junior high, the teacher pleasers, the college-track students who took Latin and got As and stayed away from the tough kids who took shop and heckled us in the hallways. We sat near one another on the bus and played at each other's houses after school.

In 1958, when I was ten, our family had to leave our house in Bannockburn, which my parents had been renting. We moved across MacArthur Boulevard to Glen Echo, which was close by and meant no change of school but culturally was a different world. It was not a recent suburban development but a long-established blue-collar town in which most residents attended the Baptist Church and had not attended college. In a way it was a kid's paradise, because next to the town was Glen Echo Amusement Park, which then boasted the second-tallest roller coaster in America. In summer we could hear the coaster's free-fall rumble and associated shrieks from our front yard. I didn't like to ride it—it turned my stomach—but loved to apply myself to the quieter pursuits of Skee-Ball, pinball, miniature golf, and my single favorite food in the world—fat, greasy, salted French fries liberally dosed with mustard in a paper cone.

Thousands of visitors came to the amusement park every summer day, and it never occurred to me that every one of them was white. It did occur to the recently formed Student Nonviolent Coordinating Committee, under the leadership of Stokely Carmichael, and in the spring of 1960 the park opened to a revolving line of singing and chanting pickets at the main entrance. Ours was the only family in the town of Glen Echo to join them. Some of our neighbors were among the gallery of grim-faced onlookers who issued loud cracks and catcalls. A few of them cheered the counterdemonstrations of George Lincoln Rockwell's Nazi brigade, well turned out in their khakis, black ties, and swastika armbands. They marched in their own quite disciplined picket line up the trolley tracks from us. Their only excess was in their signs, which, as my brother remembers, blared thoughtful sentiments such as "Back to the Trees, Boogies" and "Do You Want Niggers in the Tunnel of Love?"

Neither catcallers nor Nazis worried me. I was excited to be walking my first picket line, following in my parents' tradition. I came on my red J. C. Schwinn bicycle one day and circled with a small sign in a line of my own, basking in the attention of my fellow protesters. I knew without question that we were right, that we were wiser and kinder than the displeased gallery and those park goers who sneered at us and walked on in. The shortest person around, I felt superior to just about everyone.

My mother and brother and I picketed Glen Echo. My father was in California most of that summer, trying to organize farm workers for the AFL-CIO. One weekend when he was home he joined us on the line. We'd been there only a few minutes when a D.C. Transit bus pulled up to let out passengers for the park. As my brother recalls it, our father left the line and strode to the bus with his sign on his shoulder. He planted his large frame directly in the path of the exiting passengers, pressing his sign practically in their faces. The picket captain, a young black man, rushed over. "Sir," he said, "sir, please return to the line. We aren't here for confrontation."

"Well, what are you here for? What the hell do you think a picket line *is*?"

"Please, sir," said the captain.

My father came back, marched for a while in glum silence, and left. He didn't join us again. The new age of nonviolent protest must have seemed an effete thing to him, just as later in the sixties it would come to seem that way to many blacks and some radical whites. Union picket lines in the thirties and forties had not been merely informational or symbolic. Any scab who tried to cross could expect to be met with the moral witness of a forearm to the face. My father had come to the labor movement by way of religion, and his work in the movement was essentially a calling of faith, but it wasn't the faith of Gandhi or Martin Luther King. It was a religion of righteous wrath, which did not hesitate to return blows or to initiate them in its own just cause.

My father considered racial integration a just cause, but I didn't know until three years ago how far he had traveled to reach that judgment. His earliest adult letter that I've found, written probably in the early 1920s when he himself was about twenty, shocked me when I discovered it in the archives of the Walter P. Reuther Library in Detroit. In Demopolis, Alabama, recuperating from a foot wound sustained while working on a surveying crew—a summer job, I think—he wrote his mother about hearing "a nigger preacher harangue from the bandstand on the square." The preacher used "the nigger form of intonation which consists of singing the sentences," and his listeners responded. "They are purely emotional beings with a sense of rhythm that dominates everything," my father observed, parroting the standard racial stereotypes of the time.

In the very next sentence, though, the superior young racist is suddenly an envious would-be orator: "I would give anything and I really am risking my reputation for sanity by trying to learn their method of talk when in this emotional state." He goes on to place himself among the "minority" who believe education to be a good thing for the Negroes, and asserts what would become the central belief of his career: "The one thing fundamental that I think is necessary is to raise them to a position of economic independence," he writes, even though to do so "means that for the happy, care free nigger with never a thought for tomorrow, the trait that makes them lovable and unique, we will substitute a being with the worries and responsibilities of our kind."

It's disconcerting to read this letter, with its signs of social progressivism all jangled up with thoughtless racist canards. But there it is, an honest account of a young mind doing what a young mind must if it's to grow—taking in experience, sorting it against received beliefs and understandings, and working this flux, with all its incongruities and discords, into provisional patterns, trying without knowing one is trying to constellate a sense of self. I would be doing the same when I was twenty, a little less confident, no less mixed up, and nowhere a manual to guide the way.

⌘

The protest worked. Glen Echo Amusement Park announced that it would open the next summer for whites and Negroes alike. In the town of Glen Echo, neighbors stopped talking to us. A high school kid wrote NIGGER LOVERS with soap on our blue, big-finned Plymouth. My brother, Jim, handled the hostility better than I did. He had a few friends in Glen Echo, and he was willing to fight the guys who got in his face. I responded to taunters by ignoring them. I kept walking, my eyes on the ground, and their nigger-lover talk turned to chicken talk as I showed them my back. I tried to swallow it into my sense of moral superiority, but it didn't go down.

Two of the taunters rapped on the door one afternoon in late fall. I'd just gotten home from school. I was surprised to see them, and see them smiling.

"Hey," said one, a stocky crewcut kid named Johnny Espinoza. "Sorry we gave you a hard time. We wanna smoke the peace pipe."

Johnny extended his hand, and when I took it he gripped hard and spat in my face. His pal spat too, from the side. I slammed the door, clawing at the warm spit. There was a lot—they'd been saving it. I washed my face three times with soap. Then I started my homework and didn't get up from my desk until it was done.

I didn't tell my parents. I wanted to erase it from history, not write it in.

Sometime that winter, a bright cold day, I was building an igloo in the front yard, packing wet snow into blocks and molding the blocks into walls. Two kids stopped on the sidewalk and smirked, hands in their pockets. "What's that you're makin'?" said one.

"It's a fort," I said.

"That ain't no fort," the second kid said. "That's a nigger camp," and with that they vaulted the brown picket fence and kicked down my igloo. I made a weak attempt to defend it, pushing one of them on the shoulder, but they just shoved me off. I was taller but they were tougher. I retreated to our doorway, tears starting.

My father threw open the door, a book in his hand, and roared. "Get the hell out of here, you little bums!" Which they did.

"Do you know those boys?" he asked me.

"Yeah . . . Not really," I said.

"Damn it, Johnny, don't let 'em do that to you. You've got to fight back."

"I tried," I said, hating the whine in my voice.

"Look," said my father. "If you don't fight back they'll keep pushing you around. You've got to draw the line on 'em."

"Well, it's not *my* fault," I half yelled at him. "Why can't they leave me alone?"

My father made the small grunting noise in his throat that meant his point had just been proven. "They never leave you alone. Life comes at you, my friend. You can't dodge it."

I ran through the open doorway and up the stairs to my room. As I shut the door I heard the creak of my father's rocking chair as he settled back into it with his book.

❦

My father, I now know, fought back from the beginning. He may have inherited some of his spirit and toughness from his grandfather, the original Franz Daniel, known in the family as Grosspapa. A saddler in the Prussian army, Grosspapa came over in the 1860s and became, for sixty years, the town harnessmaker in Osceola, Missouri. ("CHEAPEST HOUSE IN SOUTHWEST MISSOURI," his advertisements claimed.) He was a severe man, very possessive of his Germanic identity. The wife he brought with him from Germany died after bearing one child, and so Grosspapa sent for her younger sister, who came reluctantly—she had a beau in the Kaiser's army—but decades later would say it had all been for the best. My only living connection with them was through one of their daughters, my father's aunt Agathe. I remember her, over ninety at the time, saying grace in German with clicking dentures at a Christmas Eve dinner sometime in the 1960s.

George Hugo Daniel, my father's father, was born in 1869 and had an uneasy relationship with his father. He ran away to St. Louis in his early teens, staying three years, and upon his return he spurned Grosspapa's business, apprenticed for the law, and established a very successful practice in Osceola. In 1890 he married Josephine Ney, from Indiana, and they wasted no time having children. The first four were girls—Berthe, Frances, Josephine, and Agathe—and Grosspapa grew so disgusted with Josie Daniel's inability to produce a grandson that he refused to accompany Grossmama when she went to view the latest female baby. His luck changed on the fifth attempt, and Grosspapa was so pleased that he gave Josie a twenty-dollar gold piece. "There came to remain with us this morning a boy," George Daniel wrote one of his sisters on April 4, 1904. "Born at 9:25 A.M. and he seems to be all right, judging by the noise he made." The boy would be named Franz, after his Grosspapa. The four girls were delighted to have a little brother. Eight-year-old Frances wrote an aunt, in expansive penciling: "The boy is so very sweet that I hate to leave him. Mama said we are going to spoil him. I wish you could see him. He made a waterfall, he made it long! Mama just laughed."

A second son followed, Little Jim, and two more daughters, Margaret and Georgia, and the family was complete. My father's generation, the second to be raised in Missouri, was pretty thoroughly Americanized, but not thoroughly enough to suit all neighbors. During the First World War, when my father—in his early teens—led the milk cow home from pasture after school, kids threw rocks at him because of his German name. He threw the rocks right back. When an unwise boy called him a Kraut and asked how the Kaiser's boots tasted when he licked them at night, my father knocked the kid down and then ran home to ask what a Kraut and a Kaiser were. So the stories go in the family; I never heard them from my father. Grosspapa, for his part, did not improve the Daniel family's standing in the community when he erected in his garden, for an undignified scarecrow, a perfect effigy of Uncle Sam.

But those troubles amounted to little compared to others my father had to face as a boy, troubles he couldn't handle with fists or stones. When Little Jim was four, he took my father's dare to stand beneath a downspout during a wet winter storm, and within two weeks he was dead of diphtheria. In 1917, four years after he had moved the family to the city of Springfield to take an appointment as clerk of the Court of Appeals, George Daniel died of locomotor ataxia, the final stage of a syphilitic infection the family believes he acquired as a teenager during his runaway years and carried in remission through most of his married life. Remarkably, Josie was never infected. Bed-bound at home in his last weeks, George Daniel became belligerently incoherent. He would allow only two persons into his presence: his male nurse, and thirteen-year-old Franz. What the boy was told or what he understood of his father's illness, I have no idea. I never heard him speak of his father or brother. I never asked.

Scarcely a teenager, he became the ceremonial head of the household and, with Berthe and Frances, one of its economic providers. He sat at the head of the table, asked the blessing and served the meal, tended the furnace, took care of the Jersey cow, bought birthday and Christmas gifts for the two younger girls, and took an after-school job as a stock boy in the dry goods store. From the week of his father's death until he left home for good, he was never without at least a part-time job.

I grew up admiring my father's courage as a fighter for economic justice, but I knew only in the vaguest way of his courage as a seventh-grader. It makes sense that he would define life as a struggle, and that he would give himself to an all-involving cause, one that engaged his whole heart and mind—frequently enough his body too—and turned him from his unfightable sorrows. His heroes would be combative crusaders, labor men such as Big Bill Haywood, Sidney Hillman, and Walter Reuther, and passionately partisan intellectuals such as Norman Thomas and Reinhold Niebuhr. He invested his faith and enthusiasm in fighters in the ring, too—Jess Willard, Joe Louis, Sugar Ray Robinson. I know from letters that my father was not only a picket-line scrapper but an impromptu boxer and wrestler with friends even into his forties. Hand-to-hand battle, like political and philosophical debate, fired his spirit.

The day after his first son was born, in Philadelphia in the fall of 1943, my father wrote his sister Margaret about the coming of the child he had so far seen only through a window. Midway through the letter, his exhilaration bursts free: "If his hands are as big as Zil says I hope his knuckles are in line and I'll make a fighter out of him. He may be champion someday. Christ! He *will* be champ."

And a champ little George turned out to be, as well as something of a Christ. He had straight knuckles, golden hair, a solid build, a bright smile, a winning manner, and bad luck. Both parents doted on him, my father especially. He rocked his son on one arm as he prepared formula, my mother wrote in a letter, and laughed delightedly when the baby cracked a toothless smile. He took Georgie to see ducks and sheep in the Pennsylvania countryside, took him to the circus, crowed about him in letters. My mother once told me that little George was the only human being my father ever loved completely, without stay or condition. He died in South Carolina a month after his third birthday, in my mother's arms on the way to a doctor, suffocated by a sudden, rampaging infection of the throat and windpipe. (The doctor, who was associated with the local textile mill, refused to sign the death certificate because he considered my parents Communists.) My father was at work. "I didn't see him born and I didn't see him die," he would mourn over and over to the friends he went drinking with. He left my mother at home with baby Jim, then sixteen months, and Berthe, his oldest sister.

My father must have felt a grim sense of completion when Georgie died. While still a child he had lost his one brother, a death for which he must have felt responsible. While scarcely more than a child he lost his father, torturously. And now his firstborn son, three years old. As I grew up I was aware of my other big brother who had died, but not of Little Jim or my long-gone grandfather. My father had more to brood on than I knew.

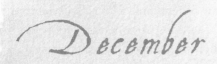 December

But alone in distant woods or fields, in unpretending
sproutlands or pastures tracked by rabbits, even in
a bleak and, to most, cheerless day, like this, when
a villager would be thinking of his inn, I come to myself,
I once more feel myself grandly related, and that cold
and solitude are friends of mine. I suppose that this
value, in my case, is equivalent to what others get
by churchgoing and prayer.

—H. D. THOREAU, *Journal* (1857)

I danced in the morning when the world was begun,
And I danced in the moon and the stars and the sun,
And I came down from Heaven and I danced on the earth:
At Bethlehem I had My birth.

"I DANCED IN THE MORNING," AMERICAN SHAKER MELODY

December 5

Distraction is pretty much the norm around here. Wrens and squirrels, as I've observed them, lead lives of nothing but one distraction merging into another, a continual twitchy vigilance accompanied by profuse vocalizations. I notice them, I realize, usually when they feel threatened, usually by me. I'm not privy to their presumably more relaxed moments with family or friends, or as they pursue their hobbies. The deer are not much less distracted. They keep their muzzles to the grass no longer than two seconds before snapping to upright attention for five or six seconds. The grass, I suppose, is the distraction; alertness to danger is what they are momentarily distracted from.

For my turkey-in-residence, it's no more than a single second at the ground—one peck, maybe another quickie if the first is a miss—and her blue head is up and watching. She doesn't have to turn it much. I've learned from my copy of *Hunting in North America* that her walleyes give her a field of vision of almost 300 degrees. Can't be much acuity to what she sees, but enough to pick up motion, such as a kindling stick hurtling from my hand. She departs under the distraction of my barrage, but returns undeterred later in the day. So now I'm trying positive reinforcement. If I notice her when she first comes down the drive to begin her rounds, I say, "Anywhere but the garden, darlin.'"

We'll see if this turkey's trainable. I know she's edible.

Hunting in North America has not yet bagged me a bird, but I'm still hopeful and am glad to have this informative book. I bought it at a large bookstore in Eugene, along with two others: *The Art of Wild Game Cooking* and *Basic Butchering of Livestock & Game*. The latter, which is in its twenty-third printing, has, understandably, no cover art, though it's quite amply illustrated with helpful diagrams within. A look of such distaste came over the face of the young woman who rang up the sale that I felt suddenly mortified.

"Look," I wanted to say, "I'm not some brute. I'm a poet." Perhaps wisely, I said nothing.

But I've gotten distracted from my topic, which is distraction. Amazingly, it appears that I'm the most relaxed creature on this homestead, except for the flies and wasps when they're torpid in the morning after a night in the thirties, the fire in the stove gone down to ash and feeble coals. When I've stoked the fire and the cabin's joints are creaking as they take in the warmth, a fly or two wakes up and begins to buzz from one place to another in the main room. These I swat. They've become distractions, but it's also an act of mercy—I'm delivering them from lives that can only amount, at their most realized, to a frenzy of distraction. No one deserves that, not even a fly. The yellow wasps are few and only bumble about indolently, even when the cabin is warm, so I generally spare them. Occasionally one will bump repetitively against a window pane, a yellow metronome. Those I dispatch with the swatter, improving the wasp gene pool with every swat.

I take these lives without remorse because it's December, for God's sake, when flies and wasps should by all rights be dead. They persist only on account of the artificially mild climate provided by my woodstove. They are mere hangers-on, welfare sucklings, having split no firewood themselves.

It's a pretty serene life, except for the pieces of unbidden song still polluting my inner quiet, and except that I'm beginning to imitate the deer and the turkey. I'll be reading in the La-Z-Boy, or writing, as now, in the Route 66 Distinguished Chair at the French Provincial Formica table, and involuntarily my head will snap up, not wanting me to miss a critter that may have come into view through a window. Usually I see only the grass, trees, fence, and drive that are always there. Nature excels in empty scenes. The ongoing action is in those vast sectors we can't see—miles of fungal filaments pursuing their commerce in any ounce or two of forest soil, the prodigious traffic of food and fluids in the xylem and phloem of trees, the manifold borings and diggings and chewings and excretings of various hidden insects, and of course the arcane doings of bacteria and other tribes of the Very Small—if we could just see the tribes within our own bodies, we'd need never watch another World Series game for entertainment. But in our ordinary visual range, it's slow going. Usually.

In the late spring of 1994, I was driving in to Dutch Henry after a shopping day in Grants Pass, singing along with Merle Haggard on the radio, when, just a couple of miles from the homestead, a god leapt out of the young woods on the left, instantly *there*, running ahead of the truck, his long and hefty brown tail virtually grazing the grille—ran easily, just fast enough, looked back once, and slipped into tall brush and small trees to the right of the road. By the time I got the truck stopped and Merle Haggard turned off—it seemed disrespectful—and myself out of the cab on trembling legs, he was long gone. Probably. A mountain lion who has just encountered a motor vehicle is not likely to hang around, but I was spooked, as if he might have been staring from the brush. "Thanks," I said, weakly, and re-entered my capsule of steel and glass.

Some Dutch Henry residents have seen a cougar, some haven't. Brother Bradley, the younger of the Brothers, is a luminary of the Cougar Clan and encounters them here routinely. "You'll see a cougar this winter," Brother B. told me as my sojourn was about to begin. His medicine is strong, and I'm grateful for his assurance, yet I also regret it. It dangerously swells my hope. I yearn to see another big cat—or the same one, for that matter—without a windshield and a four-cylinder engine between us, and I worry I won't. Such worry is a distraction. How many hundreds of times in these coming months will I jerk my head out of a perfectly good book or sentence-in-progress to stare out the window into an empty meadow?

As for the distractions I've renounced in order to come here, good riddance. It's very possible I could still drive out—there's been no serious storm since my arrival—but I'm not tempted. At home I'm addicted to the newspaper. Here, it's a great pleasure to begin my morning with Thomas Merton or Thich Nhat Hanh or Shunryu Suzuki—my meditation gurus—instead. Or Henry D. Thoreau, whose *Walden* it seems appropriate to reread while I'm here, along with parts of his *Journal* and Robert Richardson's biography. Thoreau specifically advises not to read newspapers, on the grounds that they peddle the old masquerading as new. He's right. There are newspapers here, several vertical feet of them ranging back a couple of years, and before crumpling a few pages to start a fire I scan them, sometimes read a piece that grabs my attention. The pages tell of attempted or accomplished murders, rapes, kidnappings, molestations, arsons, thefts, and various accidents in which people have perished miserably or been maimed—"Fuzz and Was," as a journalist once characterized the grist of his livelihood. Nothing new in any of that, only a mild titillation, a little buzz of adrenaline.

Between nations it's the same: war, warlike acts and posturings, terrorism and the same in return, banal policy statements from world leaders and large gobbets of insincere, sanctimonious, or bellicose rhetoric. In Thoreau's time the United States warred with Mexico and prepared to make bloody war with itself. Now, having refined the practice, we are careful to keep our warring to other continents. We launch missiles from afar or bomb from altitudes at which the bombers are immune from fire, then dutifully regret the inevitable "collateral" casualties and after a while declare victory. And we too make war on ourselves. The richest country in the world, we destroy our homelands in the name of economic growth. We perpetuate poverty among our own. We still indulge in racism, still exploit the lesser-educated and lesser-skilled. And we spend fortunes on an obsessive War on Drugs, as if such a phrase or such a war made a nickel bag's worth of sense, and build prison after new prison to house the ever increasing numbers of the war's mostly nonviolent "enemies."

There is other news in the papers, of course. At home I look for it every morning—the odd piece about someone's heroism or lovely eccentricity, the success of a good cause. But there is much more news of business, especially the various businesses of making, promoting, and selling new technology, all of which I find dull. Fuzz and Was and Zzzzz . . . In the mid-nineteenth century, it was the railroad and telegraph that were getting the googly-eyed hype of the boosters. Now it's computers and cell phones and high-definition TVs, relentlessly urged upon us to speed our already speedy communications and bind us still deeper in our electronically induced trance. Thoreau's hundred-and-fifty-year-old commentary in *Walden* is still precisely to the point: "Our inventions are wont to be pretty toys, which distract our attention from serious things. They are but improved means to an unimproved end, an end which it was already but too easy to arrive at . . ."

Nothing new in politics, either. I thought I'd be curious to the point of distraction about the election, and I was—for two or three days. I do care about it. That is, I cared about it, and no doubt will care again when I'm back in the world. I found enough differences between the two principals to prefer one distinctly over the other, but I had little enthusiasm for my candidate. The campaign was a dull clash—that's too lively a noun—between two carefully constructed and maintained public personas, each with far more platitudes than fresh thoughts, and neither evincing more than an occasional glimmer of a true calling for leadership. Whoever prevailed, whether Bush got Gored or Gore got Bushed, it's lovely to have them out of my mind.

December 9

Thoreau's on my mind, so maybe it's time to deal with him. He who quickly tired of society and even human company, who "never found the companion that was so companionable as solitude," might have been interested in this experiment of mine. If he were to spend five minutes in downtown Portland or Eugene, he who found the *nineteenth* century altogether too "nervous and bustling" would pray to come with me, though it would have meant riding shotgun in my pickup at seventy miles an hour down a busy freeway. (He would smile at that term, "freeway," by which we denote a rigorously constrained course of travel.) He would admire these forested Klamath Mountains, which might remind him of mountains in Maine. He would be an eager student of the woods. (I would love to show him madrones—and sugar pine cones, which can grow a foot and a half long.) The river, I'm sure, would exhilarate him. He would want to know more than I could tell him about its fish and birds, its otters, the bears that lumber down to its banks, and the rare and furtive cacamistle. He would ask how it is that I can live here and not spend at least half the daylight hours walking, as he did in Concord.

As for the homestead, Henry would appreciate that I, in his tradition, have the benefit of my place without the entanglements of ownership. He squatted on Emerson's land; I squat on the Brothers'. Surely he would savor the silence. The occasional drone of a small plane or faint rumble of a high jet liner is all I hear of the human world. Henry, one of his century's leading critics of the railroad, lived at Walden Pond only a few hundred yards from a rail line. Probably the least convincing passage in the book comes in the chapter "Sounds," when he exclaims, "I am refreshed and expanded when the freight train rattles past me . . . " and goes on to enumerate with forced Whitmanesque enthusiasm the pleasures given off by its various cargoes, "reminding me of foreign parts, of coral reefs, and Indian oceans, and tropical climes . . ." Right. I'd ask him if he really meant that, and I probably wouldn't be able to resist bragging on my purer silence and solitude here at Dutch

Henry, and that would likely be the start of our troubles. Thoreau had a contrary streak. Some say he had an agreeable streak, the rest of him wholly contrary. My friends say the same about me.

"It was not my intention to seal myself in a bottle, no matter the bottle's beauty," I can hear him tartly replying.

The trouble would get worse when we entered the cabin. He'd want to know if I had built it, and now *I'd* be on the defensive. He'd wonder what a single occupant could possibly need with four hundred square feet of living space in the three main rooms, plus loft, deck, galley, and entry porch. His home at Walden was ten by fifteen, plus a tiny garret and potato cellar. Of the appliances, Thoreau would be drawn to the Fisher woodstove, a plain steel box with the feet of a lion (or, I suppose, a fisher). Next to that is a Cribben & Sexton "Universal" wood-burning cookstove ("Guaranteed Best on Earth"), a resplendent piece with white and blue enameling and chrome trim. This stove must have been manufactured several decades prior to the Fisher, but to Henry, I have a feeling, it would look too gaudy and futuristic. And he would ask, inevitably, why the two? Would not one stove alone furnish heat as well as cooked victuals?

It would, I'd acknowledge, but I don't have much experience with the Universal, and out in the galley, you see, there's a propane cooking stove, a *gas* stove.

"Ah," Thoreau would say in his most clipped manner. "*Three* stoves."

What he would make of the propane refrigerator is hard to know. *I* don't know what to make of it. By what beneficent magic can you light a flame and get cold beer and keep butter all winter?

I'm confident that any man or woman of the nineteenth century, even a technological conservative such as Henry David Thoreau, would adapt very readily to running water and a flush toilet. And *hot* running water. Henry would easily grasp the operation of the solar panel, if convection was understood in his time, and would laud the economy of the coiled piping in the Fisher stove that also produces hot water. Of the few pieces of furniture, he might appreciate the French Provincial Formica table on which I write, but probably would find it cold. He might roll around happily in the Route 66 Distinguished Chair. He might ask if the

La-Z-Boy were to sit, sleep, or die in. He would put its name, likewise the term "queen-size bed," to sardonic use in his journal.

As for household objects, the cast-iron skillets and Marilyn's pewter candlesticks he'd find familiar and pleasing enough, and perhaps a few others, but Henry would be quite repelled by the sheer cumulative mass of items he encountered as he drifted around opening cabinets and inspecting shelves: kitchen utensils, cookware, eating ware, toiletries, knickknacks, fishing tackle, three clocks, cleaning agents and implements, paper clips, Post-it notes, Ziploc bags, two fire extinguishers, various cans containing this or that or nothing but dust, a wealth of empty jars and plastic containers with or without lids, assorted poisons and repellents, three straw hats, seven walking sticks, a rubber iguana, and a dispersed clutter of still weirder geegaws and esoteric items left by ten years of writer-residents, such as a jar half-full of dead wasps labeled "Squeeky's Bugs" and a set of inflatable kids' boxing mitts called Sock 'em Boppers™.

Henry Thoreau would be nothing less than horrified, or at best vastly amused, at the absurdity of trying to simplify one's life amid such a welter of *things*. This is a man, after all, who hurled out the window in disgust, when he found himself troubling to dust them one morning, three small pieces of limestone he'd been keeping on his desk.

Well, I take your point, I'd acknowledge with great forbearance, but here's the paradox. You have succeeded beyond your best hopes. You are and will remain among the great American writers. A century and a half from its initial publication, *Walden* is available in umpteen editions. A proliferation of environmentalists and nature writers pay you continual homage. You are read, in excerpts at least, by every high school student in America, yet America has evolved exactly as you hoped it wouldn't. We've *got* more things, bushels and bales and tons more things, we're half buried in things, and so now when we simplify we keep more things. It's all in proportion, you see. This really isn't a lot, by present standards. And not all these things are bad.

But look, I'd go on. The truth is that my aim is less ambitious than yours. You were living a manifesto. You were making a very public statement, to all in Concord and New England and America who would listen, that they had allowed their economic and social practices to enslave them, and that they could free themselves if they wished. I'm just holing up in a quiet place I love, to see what a long, unbroken stretch of solitude is like and to write a book.

"And what is the nature of the book you are writing?" he would ask, naturally.

And I, regretting by now the whole discussion and wishing that my visitor, as much as I admire him, would saunter back to his solitude at Walden and restore mine at Dutch Henry Homestead, would tell him. He might possibly be interested in the parts about the homestead and the Rogue Canyon, the history and natural history, possibly in my thoughts on solitude and politics, but of course he would question the writing about my childhood and my father.

"Well," I'd rejoin, "*you're* the guy who wrote, 'I should not talk so much about myself if there were any body else whom I knew as well.' I've silently thanked you many times for writing that sentence."

"You are welcome," Henry would say. "But I addressed my current experiences—my life at Walden Pond, my excursions to Maine and Cape Cod—in the belief that they warranted the utterance of my thoughts. I would not have thought that the experiences of childhood meet that standard."

What would I say? I might, I suppose, try to establish a literary context for such writing by sketching for him the advent of psychology, of Freud and the unconscious and the loosely shared understanding that adults become the particular adults they are in part because of things they have experienced in childhood, things involving their parents. I might say that writing about those experiences, remembering in language the story one is in, can yield a clearer self-awareness—maybe even a more vigorous self-reliance, in the Transcendentalist mode— and that readers, some readers, sometimes find their own experiences clarified by listening to a writer think out loud about his . . .

But I wouldn't answer that way. I would try to meet his candor with my own. I'd say, "I'm writing about my father and my younger years because that part of my experience seems incomplete. It's in the past but I haven't finished living it. I'd like to do that if I can."

December 10

It's not the song-bit jukebox anymore. The selections are longer, *and they're coming from outside my head.*

I'm not kidding. It started a few days ago at the river. My hearing somehow warped the concert of its slides and laps and rushings into the melody of Beethoven's Ode to Joy, played by an organlike instrument and at times a string section somewhere just out of sight up the river. I love the tune—would rather have it playing and playing and playing than, say, "Louie, Louie"—but it wasn't coming from me and I couldn't switch it off. I sang along for a while to overpower what I was hearing, and it faded as I hiked up into the quiet of the woods.

I should have welcomed Beethoven, begged him to stay. Yesterday I was stream walking, making my way in hip boots up the mossed and ferny ravine of Meadow Creek, when somewhere behind me and up the steep slope to my left, in old-growth timber, I heard bagpipes set in with a spirited rendition of the Marine Corps Hymn. I knew there were no pipers up there, but the sound was so clear and vivid that I stopped and looked. After a while they gave way to the Army song—*As the caissons go rolling along*—sung by a military chorus to the accompaniment of a brass band, and after a while *that* slipped into "Anchors Aweigh," the Navy song, with women added to the chorus, then the Marine pipers again, and I was caught in a continuous medley of the kind you might hear at a Memorial Day concert on the Capitol Mall. I noticed it, forgot it, noticed it, ignored it, and still heard it all the way home. The Marine hymn is playing at this moment, in this cabin, off to my right this time. Evidently I'm awash in military fervor. Thank God I don't know the Air Force and Coast Guard anthems.

I've been hearing other things, too. I'll be standing at the stove in the galley, the wall lamp giving out its low rumbly hiss, and I'll very clearly hear the drone of an engine in low gear, as if someone were driving down the lane to join me. For an instant I'm exhilarated and scared to pieces. Sometimes I hear my name spoken, or someone laughing, or some other scrap of human voice. Such hallucinations are only to be expected, I suppose, for a man who's been three weeks alone, and even the military tunes kind of make sense. The Marine Corps Hymn was the first and only melody I learned to play on the piano. My brother taught it to me when we were living in Bannockburn. He and his friend Peter Lizdas were young scholars of World War Two, which was only ten years past. They knew what ack-ack was, how far a trench mortar could lob a shell. They read and informed each other and argued about Tarawa, Iwo Jima, Guadalcanal, about the end of the war's beginning and the beginning of its end.

I had little grasp of that history, or of the Korean War, which had only just ended. What I knew of the Korean conflict I got from certain comic books full of dogfights between American pilots and slant-eyed Commies, the latter in planes with a single red star on the brown fuselage. The Commies were brave, but crazy brave. The American fliers won when it counted. *VROOOOM!!* went the fighter planes, banking and diving, then *KA-ZAAM!*—a yellow-red sunburst on a fuselage, maybe a wing blown off, and another Red fighter spiraled earthward trailing thick black smoke.

I only knew that wars had always been fought, that nations had grown or busted up or disappeared in wars. Books were written about war, movies made, songs sung. Soldiers fought and died. Some became heroes, others at least became men. I wondered if I would have to fight someday, and if I would have the courage to do it.

I didn't like to think long on that subject, but I did like to play war. Jim and I and some of our friends spent our allowances at the D.C. surplus stores on fake M-1 rifles and olive-drab helmets, dank with a canvassy smell, that had belonged to real soldiers. Sometimes we found a name black-inked on the sweatband. I thought we were wearing the entire piece of equipment, exactly what soldiers had worn in combat. It would be years before I realized that we had only the helmet liners, absent the heavy steel shell that might actually deflect a bullet.

There weren't any rules. We made up sides, dispersed throughout our placid neighborhood, and set about stalking and laying for one another. We hid, whispering our plans, behind forsythia bushes and cars parked in driveways. We slid on our bellies behind low hedges and little kids' playhouses, dashed from the corner of one neighbor's home to the corner of the next. I remember the intense alertness, the way I willed my black canvas sneakers to step silently.

When firefights broke out—an ambush, a sudden encounter of armed patrols—we let out with shrill sound effects. *Blam blam blam!* For a submachine gun, a quick-paced *buhbuhbuhbuhbuhbuhbuh*. And another sound, an unwritable rough-edged palatal blast, like hawking up a big one with an amplifier in your mouth—this when one of us tossed a plastic grenade and exploded it by voice before the enemy could snatch it up and heave it back at the tosser, in his nest behind someone's side yard azaleas.

We argued bitterly about who had been killed.

"I got you, man!"

"You just winged me."

"I *got* you, man. I put holes in you."

To be killed was a disappointment but also a dramatic opportunity. Shot clearly in the open, plugged by a sniper with no chance to return fire, no argument possible, I made the slow and splendid most of it. I staggered, the rifle slipping from my hands as I clutched at the wound and let out a clenched cry, then slumped to my knees and pitched forward in an eloquent sprawl, one arm extended, clawing for life, cheek and nose pressed hard into a neighbor's fragrant, fertilized, carefully mown lawn.

I remember my parents arguing when we moved to Maryland in 1954. I knew, hazily, that my mother hadn't wanted to leave Denver, where we'd lived for only a year. She loved the Rockies. She was also, I learned later, tired of moving around. My father was somewhere on the road when he learned that Walter Reuther, president of the CIO and his admired friend, had made him a field assistant and would soon have a prominent place for him in the new AFL-CIO. He called my mother in a burst of elation, she told me years afterward, telling her to start packing for Washington, D.C. They argued, and she almost had a breakdown. "Buck up," my father said to her. "Don't let my friends see you like this." And I guess she did buck up. Back in the thirties, when they had talked of getting married, my father had made clear to my mother that the Work, the labor movement, would always come first. And she, who shared the Work at the time and believed in it as intensely as he did, said of course it would.

My bedroom in the Bannockburn house was just off the living room and kitchen. As they argued I'd lie very still and alert. I couldn't hear many of the words or phrases. I followed the tone, the shifting dynamic. Voices tightening and quickening, falling off to short silence. A new flurry of exchanges, my father shouting, slapping the table. My mother: *Keep your voice down.* My father: *Don't you tell me what to do . . .* I worried most when my father got up, the hardwood creaking with his heavy steps. I froze, then thawed with relief when I heard the refrigerator door, the crunch and rattle of ice cubes pried loose in a metal tray. I never heard my father hit my mother, but many nights I thought I was about to hear it.

I knew, I suppose, that their fights were fueled by liquor, but I liked my father to drink. Often it put him in the mood to watch baseball or to play cribbage or head-to-head poker. I think he let me win at poker, but he gave pointers and made a pretty good player out of me. Those were nice evenings—him exclaiming, "Why you little son of a gun! Where the hell'd you get that third jack?" as I raked in another rich pot of pennies. If his mood was more solitary, my father would sometimes spend an evening drinking with Beethoven. The Eroica, the Fifth and Seventh, the Violin Concerto, and the Emperor Piano Concerto were his favorites, and he liked them loud, the hi-fi hissing and popping as the Great Man stormed and soared. In his rocking chair my father would stab the air, stroke the music with his hands, nod violently at *sforzandos,* tilt his head back with closed eyes when a sweet melody lifted off, sometimes straining after the violins with his own off-pitch voice.

If I was around he might try to draw me into his rapture. He couldn't speak the beauty he was hearkening to, so he pointed to it: "Now listen, Johnny . . . the strings, *there*—do you hear it? Do you hear?" Sometimes I did. In the second movement of the Seventh, especially, I heard and felt something I knew was important, not happiness or sadness but a blend of both, something vast, majestic, and true. That *Allegretto* is still my favorite passage of symphonic music, because of what Beethoven made and what my father tried so hard to touch.

Other times his listening was subdued and somber—Beethoven or Brahms or an opera as brooding music, or Dylan Thomas, rattling the windows with his ringing declamations accompanied by scratches on the record that sounded like snapping twigs. The brooding was okay, too, because it usually came after a fight, not before, or else it occupied my father sufficiently that a fight was less likely. But the weather was unpredictable; it could turn at any moment. One night in the Bannockburn house—I was either eight or nine—my parents went out for the evening and came home not late but loud. I was watching television in the basement. I heard shouting, my father's footfalls, the sharp reports of my mother's heels. A door slammed. After a while my father came down the stairs, a bottle in his hand.

"Johnny, you better get to bed," he told me. His face was grim, more his hangover look than his drinking look.

Upstairs, my mother was running dishwater in the kitchen sink.

"Zilla," I said, "is Franz gonna sleep downstairs?" My parents had raised Jim and me to call them by their first names, thinking this would encourage the four of us to relate as individuals.

"I don't know, John. Franz will sleep where he wishes to sleep."

Later, in bed, I heard my mother and brother in the hall. My brother went down the stairs to the basement while my mother waited, then came back up. I heard him go to his room. My mother, after stirring around a little, went to bed.

I let a few minutes pass, then slipped out of my room and down the stairs. I peeked around the brick corner into the rec room, where a light was on. My father, wearing his hat and overcoat, lay on the floor. He was slumped half on his side, his head propped against the front of the sofa, his face sagging against his chest. He was breathing heavily. I had never seen him passed out. Over in the corner his safe was open, a paper or two scattered on the floor in front of it. That gave me a clue. I knew my father kept two pistols in the safe, one of them a .45 with the serial number filed off that had come his way in the 1940s.

I learned more of the story in the months that followed, mainly from eavesdropping on conversations. I heard my father rail to a friend about the "pipsqueak jerk" my mother had "run around with." I guessed who the man might be—a guy I'd seen at the house a couple of times, and who once in the library parking lot had leaned against the open car window and spoken in a low voice to my mother. Over time I inferred that he and my mother had done whatever it was that husband and wife did, that my father had found out about it—my mother, a direct woman, may well have told him—and had intended to threaten or kill the guy.

Whiskey, luckily, settled the issue. My father had been drunk when he came down to the basement, and he drank more there. Once he was still my mother checked on him, but she worried about what might happen if he should wake while she was taking the pistol from his overcoat pocket. Knowing he would never harm Jim, she sent him down to lift the gun.

Late the next morning, a Sunday, I saw my father in his robe at the kitchen table eating milk toast my mother had made him. Milk toast was his hangover food. He called it graveyard stew.

December 13

Wednesday night is a pretty big deal here at Dutch Henry Homestead. It's like prom night. Starting around supper I get all stirred up, listing things I want to be sure to say and glancing often at the clock by the phone, though I've already set its alarm—set it at breakfast—to go off at 9:58 P.M. I fret that the phone might not work, though of course it always does, and I worry that I'm not using the right radio lingo with the mobile operator, the one human being I converse with, briefly and formulaically. So far she hasn't corrected me or even sounded exasperated, so I guess I'm giving my unit number and requesting my call and signing off tolerably well, or else she's just going easy on a greenhorn. I give her the number to call, she says "Stand by," and within a minute it's ringing, always four times, and lo! I am greeted by my own stupidly cheerful voice: "Hello! Please leave a message for John or Marilyn after the long tone!"

I do, barreling ahead at a smart clip because our answering machine, which dates from the Late Archaic period, will sometimes unaccountably cut off with a screech. Some callers with a lot to say have had to call back not once but twice to get it said. So far, perhaps because it recognizes my voice, the machine has been politely receptive to my calls. I spill out my little casket of news and well-wishings and occasionally a message to forward to someone, then express my undying love, say goodbye, and tell the operator I'm done, unit 7796 is clear. I keep expecting her to say, "None of my business, sir, but isn't it kind of weird to call your own house every Wednesday at 10 PM and talk to your message machine? You could like call at a different time, you know, when your wife might be *home?*" But she is a paragon of professionalism. She says, "Thank you, Medford's clear," and keeps her opinions to herself. So do all the mobile telephone users in southwestern Oregon who may be monitoring their units at the time. This is radio, after all, one big party line. I wonder if my weird weekly ritual is attracting an audience. Maybe I should start a call-in show.

Marilyn, suspecting that left to my own devices I would give only a terse "Everything's cool" each week, made it clear that she expected some details, some news. Which I happily provide, though sounding pretty silly to myself as I do. Afterward I feel deflated, out of sorts, wondering why I've put myself in this isolation ward. The little weather of sociability has passed. It wasn't even sociability, just me talking into a phone. To tell the tape machine about the deer I saw or the salmon I caught or the exquisite movement of mist in the canyon is nothing very close to sharing those joys with my wife in her person. I miss that. It takes some of the luster off my fun, especially because a lot of it is domestic fun—baking a great batch of biscuits, being a human laundry agitator in the utility sink, returning from a walk and sighting the cabin with its welcoming plume of woodsmoke. The kind of fun Marilyn particularly likes, and which we are used to enjoying together.

Beyond that, it's not outright loneliness I feel, but a vague ache. Not a hearty appetite for company or even an honest hunger, but an irritable craving for it—or for tidings, at least, of friends and family and community. Letters. Gossip. Email. I feel hung between worlds, as if I haven't quite found my way to solitude yet.

Two of my more spiritually attuned friends warned that I would probably have to endure a rough patch at some point. One spoke of a dark night of the soul, the other of being ambushed by personal demons. This doesn't have the dignity of a dark night. It's demons, maybe, and they've conspired to torture me by Muzak. Yesterday the theme was Big Endings, coming in a sort of surround-sound from everywhere. It began with Beethoven's Fifth, of course, the finale with nine lives—"You sink ziss iss it? Ha!"—and verged seamlessly into Mahler, the swollen tympanic grandeur ending his Third, or was it his Fifth? Then Brahms's First, Rachmaninoff—one of the piano concertos—something that sounded like Sibelius, and then, God help me, Richard Strauss, "Also Sprach Zarathustra." These and others I couldn't identify surged and subsided in a continuous medley, the Ending with no end.

What if it *doesn't* end, I thought, with a flash of real fear. What if one of these days I have to drive, ski, or hike myself out of here to the nearest psychiatric unit?

The silence here, when my noisy head lets me hear it, is overwhelming. I stand out in the meadow in the light of a first-quarter moon, the council of trees around me, the distant wash of the river drifting up from below, and I feel huge and small at the same time, utterly privileged to be alive in this ancient presence so thoroughly oblivious to me and to anything human. I want to meet that silence, honor it, with an authentic silence of my own, and I don't know if I can. I don't know if I'm worthy of it. I've been here not even a month, and the four months yet to go look like a very long time. I can do it, I think, but I don't want to just tough it out, just run out a string of days. I guess I came with a bigger ambition than I admitted to myself. I want to break through into some new state, some new seeing, some certain realization to take me through the rest of my years, and I'm afraid it won't happen.

I found in one of my dictionaries this morning a surprising dimension in the word "solitude." It comes from the Latin *solus*, alone, but *solus* itself is of murky origin. It may share kinship with the Greek *holos*, meaning whole, entire. That's the solitude I haven't yet found.

December 15

It hardly sounds like my mother's voice, which I recall most clearly from her last years when it had slowed and softened. The enunciations so crisp, the phrasing so lively. The tape is a quarter-century old. She visited in the summer of 1977, a year after my father's death, and agreed—readily—to talk at length about him, their careers, their marriage. She was sixty-nine then. I find myself groaning out loud at times as I listen. I wish I had asked better questions, followed up those I did ask. But mainly I'm glad we talked, glad I had the sense to get her on tape well before Alzheimer's, or a series of small strokes, first nibbled then gulped her memory.

"Oh yes, Franz meant to shoot him," she said of the pistol incident. "No question about it." She and her lover wisely ended their relationship. My mother moved out of the house for a few days, then moved back for the sake of me and Jim. She went to a psychotherapist and persuaded my father, not a believer in such stuff, to go with her to a marriage counselor. All they did, as she remembered it, was sling resentments at each other. The counselor told them, after a few sessions, that their differences were insurmountable and they really shouldn't be married. My father, who was capable of considerable paranoia, accused my mother of having "gotten to" the counselor. The one success of these adventures was that my father agreed to get rid of his pistols. He took his sister Margaret with him and threw them off Chain Bridge into the Potomac River in the middle of the night. "There was nothing small about his gestures," my mother mused in our interview.

Nor about hers. It was she who pressed for a divorce, and her forum for announcing that wish, and for telling my father that she no longer loved him, had been a dinner party with friends. My mother, up until her very last years, had a fiery, rebellious temperament and a flair for the dramatic. From the beginning of the relationship, she had been the goad and impetus. In 1930 she broke off her engagement with another man when she met the handsome and intensely charismatic Franz Daniel. "I decided I'd go after him," she told me. As their romance bloomed she sat literally at his feet at parties, wept at his eloquence when he spoke at rallies. It was she who initiated their sexual relationship, which was her first and his second. "He consented," she put it in our interview.

My mother wrote their wedding vows, working in some verses from a labor movement poem about storming the Battlements of Wrong and marching as long as they had breath. "We were just tremendously involved in the work," she recalled. "We thought the labor movement was going to save the world." As they pursued their organizing for the Amalgamated, usually on different campaigns, they sometimes spent weekends together, longer periods when they could. They agreed—I didn't ask her, but this too must have come at my mother's urging—to go their own ways in sexual relationships when they were apart. My mother did so, with several men. My father, she thought, probably didn't. He definitely did raise hell, despite their agreement, when he learned of her liaisons. They settled into monogamy, and my mother, who turned thirty in 1938, was ready to have children. My father, though, worried that he carried the syphilis that had killed his father, and that he could transmit it to offspring. Only after much coaxing and multiple medical tests—and after my mother agreed to quit her own unionizing career, a lively and notable one in a time when few women were doing that work—did he consent to father children.

My mother had affairs with men. My father's affair, of some fifty years' duration, was with the bottle. It was not a problem in their early years together. My father drank, my mother drank, their friends and comrades drank, and it probably made them more effective organizers. Like many who joined the labor movement in the 1930s and '40s, my parents came to it not as wage workers but from the universities—"God-damned college-graduate intellectuals," as one textile union official grumped. These men and women, who felt blessed beyond deserving by their own modest advantages, brought a major infusion of idealistic energy to the movement and helped it achieve respectability in the eyes of academic and political leaders. But the cultural and economic divide between them and those they tried to organize was considerable. A tee-totaler such as Walter Reuther could become a brilliant national leader, but for organizers in the field it had to have been an advantage to be able to—to *want* to—hit the bars when the workers got off their shifts and knock back shots and beers with them.

In 1939 my father's habit caught up with him. He was drinking, my mother estimated, as much as a quart of whiskey or white lightning a day, maybe more. He suffered an alcoholic collapse. The Amalgamated arranged for him to enter a sanatorium in Milwaukee, where he stayed for a month or six weeks. The union sent my mother to be with him for most of that time, and kept both, to its everlasting credit, on full salary. A doctor at the sanatorium told my father not to touch another drop of beer or liquor and not to return to the South, to make a fresh start somewhere else. My father returned immediately to the South, where the labor movement needed him. My mother objected, mildly, the first time he opened a beer, and he curtly brushed her off. "From then on I knew," she said. "But I didn't want to see it, so I put it in the back of my mind."

One way my mother coped with my father's drinking was to drink more herself. They had good times together. From the South they moved on to New York City, where the Amalgamated was trying to establish a laundry workers union, and left within a year for New Orleans on the same mission. The union shuttled my father around, and frequently loaned him to other unions, because he was a rallier, an inspirer, one of the best speakers the Amalgamated or any union had. My mother had a miscarriage in New York, recovered from that and a deep depression in New Orleans, then got pregnant again shortly before they moved on to Philadelphia, where George was born. My mother hoped they would stay in Philly and raise a family—Jim was born there in 1945—but it wasn't to be. In 1946 the CIO tapped my father to become its director in South Carolina, one of the leaders of its postwar Operation Dixie organizing drive.

George died two months after they moved. I don't think either of my parents ever recovered. Every year on the anniversary of the death, for decades, my mother ritually relived the experience with a female friend. My father did his grieving alone or with friends in bars. He was arrested for drunk driving a short while after Georgie died, and my mother had to chauffer him around for six months. He kept a bottle in a drawer in his Spartanburg office. "We couldn't communicate about it," my mother told me. She felt there was much territory in my father she never got to know.

Still, the late forties was probably their happiest time. They had two healthy little boys—I came along in 1948, in South Carolina, a pinch hitter for little George—and a circle of like-minded bon vivant friends. There were barbecues, watermelon parties, trips to the mountains, the Carolina coast. Operation Dixie foundered—the South was and would remain the most union-hostile region in the country—but my father's star continued to climb, unhampered, it seems, by his weakness for the sauce. His staff admired him and worked their hearts out for him; leaders continued to tab him for tough assignments. In 1950 we moved to Charlotte, North Carolina, where my father directed both Carolinas for the CIO. In 1953 it was on to Denver and the CIO's Rocky Mountain region, and within a year came the call to work under Walter Reuther and assume a position in the new AFL-CIO.

Even in the D.C. suburbs we didn't stay put, living in four different houses in the space of five years. When we moved to Glen Echo in 1958, my father was fifty-four, my mother was fifty, and they were buying their first house. They would share it, more or less, for six years, by far their longest tenure in one home. But for my mother, by then, it wasn't about staying put anymore. It was about escaping. And for my father in those years, it was about trying to hold on—to his marriage, to his career, and finally to his dignity itself.

December 17

Why is it sixty-four degrees a week before Christmas? I've got dande-
lions blooming beneath the apple trees, and in the garden the old rose-
mary bush has popped a few blossoms. Some kind of tiny midge has
hatched in prodigious numbers, wafting like motes of dust in the afternoon breeze. I built a little fire this morning to take the chill off; half
an hour later I was opening windows to cool the place down. One bear,
at least, is convinced it's spring—unless rafters are growing claws, I saw
his tracks in wet sand by the river. And now, absurdly in the bright sun,
my sole local frog, who lives in a little mire down by the turnaround, is
giving voice—a more vigorous voice than I've heard from him during
mist and rain, which he properly should celebrate. He is either a very
confused frog or else a prophetic frog, a frog of the future, a frog to lead
his lineage through the balmy doom of global warming.

I'm out for air—maybe a tan as well—and to apologize to the wild
multitudes for having defiled their vernal peace for the past hour. My
ears are ringing so loud I can't hear the drift of river sound from below.
Under the cabin, which is built on stilts against a hillside, is a gas-
powered Honda generator. Now and then, to charge the battery that
powers the radio phone, it's necessary to crank it up. This can be a very
enlightening experience if undertaken with full mindfulness. I recom-
mend it to all.

First, you must fill the generator's tank with gas from a five-gallon
can, inevitably spilling some on your boots, and check its oil, inevitably
getting black grunge under several fingernails. Then set the choke, give
the starter cord a smart pull, and bring the beast to life. It will sound like
a hundred-and-forty-pound lawn mower. Now come into the cabin,
flipping on the battery charger as you pass it on the entry porch. In the
main room, place a small electric light on the French Provincial Formica table and plug it in. A lava lamp is perfect. Position the La-Z-Boy
by the woodbox, as close as possible to a point directly above the generator beneath the floor. Now, stretch out comfortably in the La-Z-Boy
and begin the Fossil Fuel Meditation of the Threefold Way. With your

eyes, focus on the lava lamp as it stirs to life. With your ears, attend to the loud, continuous, blapping throb of the generator. With your nose, take in and smell well the rich combustion vapors seeping up through the floorboards.

Practice thus for half an hour at a time and you will begin to realize the original true nature of "electrical power." You will have restored to that abstract phrase its sensory vitality. Now, when you flip a switch at home, or when someone else does, you will alertly watch, listen, and sniff. If you fail to detect even one of the threefold sensations, you will know that you have lapsed into illusion. Repeat the Fossil Fuel Meditation as necessary to dispel illusion and remember the truth. Persevere in this practice. At the very least, you may discover that lava lamps are pretty cool after all.

This time, I'll confess, I got distracted. I had not a lava lamp to focus on but an even more compelling appliance. My longhair days being twenty years behind me, I needed some way to trim my locks during my solitude. I figured I could do a good enough job with scissors and comb, but Marilyn settled the question by purchasing an electric clipper with plastic guides for cutting hair at various lengths. I chose one-half inch. That went so buzzingly crisp and quickly, and evoked such a vague warm aura of barbershop memories—from back in the days when I used to converse with human beings—that I changed guides and took it down to a quarter-inch. This gave me a GI look, which seemed not entirely inappropriate, but I still had momentum and a powerful instrument in my hand. What the hell, I said. I've never seen my naked scalp, and when will I have a better chance?

The result is a dome of stout, sandpapery stubble maybe a thirty-secondth of an inch tall. I like it. My head's got grain, texture, and it isn't gray. It feels buoyant as a balloon. My hairline, now for the first time fully revealed, comes to a distinct point atop my forehead, in line—fortunately—with my nose. I look purposeful, resolute. I need only follow the arrow that I am. Otherwise, sadly, my scalp turns out to be unremarkable. I was hoping to find something shocking—an embedded microchip, say, or a birthmark in the form of the number 666, something that might sell this book. Failing that, maybe a stamped product code with instructions for obtaining a manual. It would be nice to know how best to use this large, well-lit, air-conditioned skull.

I look monkish, which is also not entirely inappropriate. Every morning, before coffee or breakfast or reviving the fire, I bundle up in sweatpants and sweatshirt and climb the fold-up ladder to the loft to meditate, sitting on the edge of a folded futon. I've been a dilettante meditator since the late 1960s, several times starting a practice then getting impatient and ditching it. If I can establish a practice here, maybe I'll keep it up when I rejoin the world. I need a vessel to carry back with me the stillness and clarity I'm beginning to know, for moments at least, and the vessel can only be me, a part of me that the world can't push or pull out of shape and that might help me know how best to lead the rest of my life—which, I must reluctantly acknowledge, at fifty-two years and seven months, has quite possibly passed its halfway point.

I'm following a Zen way. Zen attracts me because it's so thoroughly centered on practice, on doing something. My teachers are Thich Nhat Hanh, in *The Miracle of Mindfulness*, and Shunryu Suzuki, in *Zen Mind, Beginner's Mind*. They make a good pair. Nhat Hanh is milder and more sensuous, more attuned to integrating meditation into one's life in the world and one's social values. Suzuki is more trenchant, a bit crisper in elucidating the practice itself. Each has a sense of humor and engages the beginner without talking down to him; neither hands you a suitcase full of theology or tells you to put down your own baggage. Both direct you to sit and watch your breathing, which doesn't seem too much to ask. It's about awareness, not belief.

And so I sit on the futon and learn every morning anew how ridiculously hard it is to stay aware of my breathing for a sustained period of time—thirty seconds, say. It's remarkable, the mind's yen for distraction. Ships of thought are leaving home port all the time, and though you've reminded and reminded yourself that this time you're there only to watch and wave, not to travel, you always end up *on* one of the damn things, halfway out of the harbor before you look back and realize you're not standing on the dock anymore. *Oh yeah* . . . The mercy of the method is that you don't berate yourself or mortify your flesh for messing up, you merely call your consciousness back to your breathing and start over. You're not out to eliminate your thoughts. You're trying to recognize that your thoughts are a weather moving in the sky, and that you are the sky as well as the weather, and that it's important to experience yourself as the sky.

Some mornings I'm really engaged for most of the half-hour or forty minutes—I don't time it—and, if I think of it, glad to be there, even with the cramping contortions required to weave my legs into a quasi-half-lotus position. (The full lotus? Not in this lifetime.) Other mornings I'm just putting in the time, my mind lunging ahead like a dog on a leash toward coffee, oatmeal, the pleasure of reading about Zen instead of the difficulty of doing Zen, and whatever work or hike or fishing or hunting I've planned or haven't yet planned for the day. All I've achieved so far is a continuity of daily attempt and a renewed suspicion, which first came to me when I took LSD in the 1960s, that normal workaday consciousness is a kind of sleepwalking, punctuated erratically by wakeful moments. Dire illness will do it, or the death of a loved one, a scare on the highway, a new love or the end of an old one, the birth of a child. Otherwise, we're driving or working or conversing or eating or distracting ourselves with ourselves, our *selves*, only vaguely present.

One cold rainy morning I watched a wasp climb the inside of the galley window screen. Clamber, really—he was so torpid with cold he could lift only one or occasionally two of his six single-jointed legs at a time. Each leg moved in slow motion, stiff as a stilt, wide from the wasp's body, feeling for purchase on one of the tiny open panes of the screen. He was making one-and-a-half inches per minute. After watching for a while I went on with whatever I was doing, frying corn meal mush for breakfast, I think, then eating it with maple syrup, drifting on into my day. When I remembered the wasp and realized that he was me, my practice, I went back to the window and he was gone.

December 18

Early in the monumental journal he would keep from the age of twenty until his death at forty-five, Henry Thoreau wrote long passages almost in the voice of a literary drill sergeant, going on and on about the vital need to summon soldierly bravery into one's life. This seemed odd to me at first, coming from an essentially gentle man who quit his teaching job rather than cane his students, and who would soon come to despise his country's military adventurism. It certainly elicited some rhetorical grandiosities: "Waterloo is not the only battle-ground: as many and fatal guns are pointed at my breast now as are contained in the English arsenals." Sure, Henry. But then I remembered that the author, wise and great as he would become, was at the time a kid fresh out of college. He was, in his way, feeling and expressing what every young man feels—the need to try his courage, to prove himself and be recognized. He was reaching around in language to locate his necessary battleground. Even at twenty he knew that letters would be the field of his striving, and even then he was setting to work with a warrior's discipline. (Robert Richardson, in his wonderful *Henry Thoreau: A Life of the Mind*, recognizes something always overlooked with regard to Thoreau's famous dictum about marching to a different drummer. Different indeed, notes Richardson, but the fellow *is* marching to a drummer. Thoreau defined himself in that soldierly way.)

I would be close to thirty before I dared even to begin to think of myself as a poet or writer, but I did tab myself early on as a student. I found that I could excel in school, and so I did—partly because I actually liked books and writing and learning things, and partly because by getting good grades I won the praises of the adults in my life, particularly my father's. I knew I wasn't pleasing him as a fighter, and in those moments when I looked for my future, nothing I could imagine doing came close to matching the deeds of his heroic past. But I could bring home As and the praises of my teachers, swinging my lunch-box like a worker at the four o'clock whistle. From grade school through junior high and on through high school, that's what I did. More of a manufacturing enterprise than a battleground, it took no bravery, only time and work.

My father, like Thoreau, found his theater of action early. Maybe he found it at age eighteen, with the strike at the Frisco shops in Springfield. He had certainly found it five years later, in 1927, when the legal drama of Nicola Sacco and Bartolomeo Vanzetti came to its climax. Working at home that summer, his B.A. from Wisconsin in hand and a place waiting for him at Union Theological Seminary in the fall, he followed the case closely. The two Italian immigrants, a fish peddler and a shoemaker, had been convicted of the 1920 murder of a Massachusetts shoe factory paymaster and guard, and the theft of the company's fifteen-thousand-dollar payroll. No evidence directly linked them to either crime. Both were anarchists, accused during the height of the Red Scare that followed the Russian Revolution; both had evaded the military draft during World War I; both professed their innocence. The judge, who referred to the two outside his court as "anarchist bastards," sentenced them to death. As their appeals failed over the years and the execution date drew nearer, Sacco and Vanzetti inspired demonstrations of outrage and support across the United States and Europe. Even the Pope appealed on their behalf. It was the most famous, or infamous, capital criminal case in American history. Sacco and Vanzetti died in the electric chair on August 22, 1927. My father's sister Margaret remembers him listening for news that evening on the radio, pacing the house, extremely upset. At dawn the American labor movement had two of its most renowned martyrs, and my father had not slept.

"They were railroaded," he told Margaret. "They didn't kill anybody. They stood for a radical cause and they were put to death for it."

Symbolically, my father would declare his battle charge two years later, at Union, when the seminary community woke up one morning to discover the Red Flag flying on the flagpole. No one confessed to the prank or was disciplined for it, but everyone who remembers it claims it was common knowledge that Franz Daniel had done it. (As a representation of my father's ideology the flag was a blunt instrument; he was even then a passionate anti-Communist, and would remain so throughout his career. American Socialists and Communists were com-

mitted enemies in those years, regularly disrupting each other's meetings, rallies, and organizing activities. Communists considered Socialists sell-outs to the capitalist order, working for meager reforms rather
than true revolution. To the Socialists, Communists were more interested in ideology than in justice, cared too little about individual free-
doms, and had too keen an ear for orders from overseas.)

The battle was fully joined by 1930, when my father, twenty-six and
organizing for the Socialist Party in Philadelphia, living mainly on discarded vegetables from the docks and "borrowed" milk from doorsteps
in the blue-blood districts of town, appeared perhaps for the first time
in a newspaper photo, under arrest and not submitting quietly, a peace
officer on either arm. The best story from that time, though, came from
a different arrest. As Missouri labor historian Neal Moore tells it, my
father had been busted for holding a rally in a park without a permit—
though in fact he had secured the permit—and was thrown into a paddy
wagon with various drunks and vagrants, the pick of the day. He had
managed to keep a sheaf of handbills with him, and so—ever the organizer—he set his companions of the moment to folding the handbills
and sliding them out the ventilation slots on the sides of the paddy
wagon. "And I can visualize the wagon," writes Moore, "all the way to
the police station, the folded handbills coming out of those slots and
fluttering down to the streets of Philadelphia—announcing the next
meeting!"

Battlegrounds . . . I did like sports, and I played pretty well in pickup
baseball and football games. When I was going into the tenth grade,
my father told me I ought to go out for junior varsity football. It meant
cutting my summer short, but I liked the prospect of being the only kid
in my Advanced English class to also play football. Surely it would make
me irresistibly attractive to all the right girls. I decided to do it.

Practices were long and grueling. We ran laps in the sopping late
August heat until I was sick to my stomach. The coach was a florid little man who liked to stick his face up to yours and scream, "Are you
here to play FOOTBALL?" He and his assistants ran around in shorts

screeching on their whistles like berserk camp counselors. Whatever they had us doing—hitting the blocking dummy, running sprints, scrimmaging—they'd yell *FIRE OUT!* and *GO-GO-GO-GO-GO-GO-GO!* as if the secret to everything was in those two commands, if only we would just *get* it.

A couple of weeks into practice, the coach gathered us around him on the field one afternoon and raised his hands for quiet. He looked down at the grass. When we had achieved the proper hush, he looked up and said, almost in a whisper: "Fellas? The *cream* . . . will *rise* . . . to the *top*."

It did, and without me. I made the team, as a tight end and defensive end, but it was clear that I wouldn't play much unless a first-stringer got hurt. Since playing football, the game, had been the main attraction, and because I was out of my element among shrieking coaches and blue-collar teammates, a month into the school year I decided to quit. I had my mother prepare my father for the news. The official line was that practice was taking too much time from my studies. He was raking leaves in the side yard when I came home from school. I headed for the front door, hoping he wouldn't see me, but he stopped his rake and looked over.

"Did you quit the team?"

"Yeah," I said.

And he went back to working the rake with his thick hands and arms, his graying hair rumpled, his mouth downturned in the pouty expression that meant he was disappointed and nothing could be done about it. I walked on into the house, staring at my shoes.

My brother was the better athlete, and he was also better looking. He had the unforgivable attribute, from my point of view, of dark hair with a slight wave that could be combed, with application of sufficient Vitalis hair tonic, exactly in the manner of Elvis Presley's. I had dorky brown curls, which looked even dorkier slathered with Vitalis. Jim did air-band imitations of Elvis, using a broom for a guitar, to amuse our parents. He was an actual musician too, a drummer, and played in a few bands while we were growing up. One of them, the Reekers, cut a single titled "Don't Call Me Flyface" that got some air time on D.C. radio stations. Despite these glamorous involvements, he was very tolerant of his younger brother. He played his new Little Richard and Chuck Berry singles for me, taught me to jitterbug, and let me tag along sometimes when he and his friends went duckpin bowling or to the newest Elvis or James Dean movie.

My father got more of a fighter in my brother than he got in me. During the Glen Echo hostilities, Jim stood up to his taunters and tangled decisively with Thor Olson, the guy who wrote NIGGER LOVERS on our Plymouth. Jim also stood up to our father. They engaged in some hot jawboning about hair length, use of the car, school performance, staying out late, and other issues central to the growing-up experience in the American middle class. Our father, for all his early radicalism and continuing activism, was temperamentally quite conservative. He was very concerned with appearances, dressing respectably, doing things right. Perhaps because he'd been saddled with unexpected responsibilities in his own teenage years, he had little tolerance for aimless fooling around. He believed in the virtues of discipline, felt it built character for young people to involve themselves in organized activities—he was, after all, an organizer. *His* main idea with regard to j.v. football, I see now, was that it would help me mature.

I did spend some time on a real battleground, but it was somebody else's. Early in high school, when my friends and I were into folk music and blue work shirts, a few of us joined the Washington chapter of the Student Nonviolent Coordinating Committee and took part in some rallies and demonstrations. At meetings we sat on the floor around the fringes, quiet as mice, usually the youngest in the room and the only whites. Once in a while Stokely Carmichael dropped in and said a few words, which gave our suburban liberal hearts a buzz. I did some leafleting for SNCC in black neighborhoods of Northwest and Southeast D.C., handing out notices about an upcoming rally. My strategy was to stand outside grocery stores. If an emerging customer at first didn't take the notice I offered, I walked alongside talking continuously about the rally until he or she did. I thought I was getting good at arousing interest, but most of my marks, surely, took the thing just to get rid of the yacky white kid who had accosted them out of nowhere.

I went door-to-door in the projects once, spreading the word about a planned mass demonstration at the District Building for better housing and a welfare system that didn't leave people hungry. The folks who opened the doors were surprised, courteous, and usually pretty baffled. I remember one middle-aged woman with straightened hair who answered my knock and stared at me intently through her glasses, wiping her hands on her apron, as I gave my spiel.

"Now tell me again what you want?" she asked when I was done.

"Well," I barreled along at a world-saving pace, "it's about being hungry, you know, and not having a good place to live, and—"

"Good Lord, honey," she interrupted, "do you want somethin' to eat? Come in, we got plenty."

"Oh . . . no, no . . . ," I stammered, suddenly aware of the rich smell of frying chicken wafting from the apartment, "it's not me, it's . . . Here," I said, thrusting a leaflet toward her and beating a mortified retreat.

But the demonstrations were spirited and fun. They were here and there, one agency or another, a segregated business or suburban development. Most of the demonstrators were SNCC people, black college students. As at the amusement park a few years before, we walked in a long revolving line, waving our signs and singing:

Ain't gonna le-et no-o-bo-dy
Turn me round,
Turn me round,
Turn me round,
Ain't gonna le-et no-o-bo-dy
Turn me round
Keep on a-walkin',
Keep on a-talkin',
Walkin' up to Freedom Land . . .

And "We Shall Overcome," of course, which I knew in an earlier union version as the less emphatic and more proletarian "We Will Overcome." It must be like singing hymns in church, I imagined. We were a kind of impromptu fellowship. We didn't all know each other—my friends and

I knew hardly anyone—but we believed in justice and fairness for black and white together, and we were out there marching and singing for it. It felt good, like maybe the best thing I'd done in my fifteen years.

But a year or two later my view of race relations, and of myself, took a jolt. Four friends and I, tanked up on beer on a Saturday night, decided to go hear Martha and the Vandellas at a Northeast club. We were way into the Motown sound, along with most other sounds on rock radio. We found the place, parked, and joined the long line in an alleyway, chattering happily. The first sign of trouble was not that everyone else in the line was black, because I think I realized that only later. The sign was a hand feeling for the wallet in my hip pocket. I turned and took a hard punch in the pit of my stomach. Without wind and suddenly quite sober, I lunged off along the alley toward the nearest cross street. Three of my friends were doing the same. For a scant second I saw the fourth friend lying on his back on the cobblestones, unconscious, blood drib-bling from the corner of his mouth. In the crowd behind us I heard older voices scolding the kids who had mugged us.

The cops arrived almost instantly, it seemed. We were all okay, including the friend who'd been knocked out—no thanks to the rest of us. I and two of the others ended up riding home in a cop car. One of the cops was white and one was black.

"What were you boys doin' over there?" the white cop said.

I was buzzing with anger and leftover fear. "We went to hear some music," I said. "What's wrong with that?"

"You were in the lion's den, that's what. That's not your part of town."

The black cop turned his head to look at me. I thought I saw—prob-ably imagined—the glimmer of a smile on his face, and something pulled loose in me. It came out without thought, sounding to my own ears as intensely unreal as getting socked in the stomach had felt. "We were minding our own business," I said to the black cop. "It was *your* kind that caused the trouble."

The black cop looked away, scowling. "Shut up, boy," the white cop said. "You're a goddamn fool."

December 19

When I wondered whether the turkey was trainable, I should have asked, "Which one?" The turkey on the ground continues her usual rounds, pecking up bugs, grass, cabbage leaves, rutabaga greens, and such other delectables as catch her omnivorous fancy. She seems to have the turkey in the cabin pretty well trained. He keeps the .22 leaning in the corner by the bathroom door. When he spies the other turkey in the garden he grabs the gun, takes to the deck, and commences fire across her stern. She flutters into the air, agitated, as if this has never happened before, runs around a little, and eventually, after several more shots, launches herself over the fence to feed somewhere else. She doesn't come back to the garden for at least an hour.

What the turkey in the cabin *ought* to do, instead of shooting his beets and cabbages full of holes, is kill the turkey in the garden and eat her for Christmas. Eat her for Christmas week. He may have to kill her if he wants to eat from his garden, else he won't have a garden—it'll have grown feathers and wings and moved on up the canyon. Ecologically, of course, the outdoor turkey could argue that it's a square deal, since in exchange for her garden withdrawals she deposits rich and copious droppings. I'm not impressed—with the greenish droppings (that green is *mine*) or with the ecological logic. That's the trouble with ecology. It's always singing, "Every life has its place in the balance! It all evens out!" without regard for any *particular* poor slob who's getting his *particular* carrots clipped. I need that garden. I don't know how long I'll be in here, and I don't want my diet to come down to canned corned beef and pinto beans.

The turkey in the garden can't win the ecological argument anyway, because she's not native to these mountains or even this region. She belongs, unfittingly enough, to the Rio Grande subspecies of wild turkeydom, introduced here through the wisdom of wildlife managers for the benefit of—who else?—hunters. She is present by the artifice of man, an artifice intended to make her available to the full effect of a 12-gauge shotgun such as mine. Q.E.D. Except, of course, that the turkey wielding the gun can't win the ecological argument either. He too is an introduced exotic—he introduced himself—having been born and bred even farther away than the Rio Grande. And the plants he so aggressively protects? Kohlrabi, Romaine lettuce, and Kyuna Mizuna mustard are no more native than the bird who is shredding them for her daily coleslaw, and are artificial—products of human artifice—in the very arrangement of their genes.

So both turkeys and the garden we both covet are unnatural here, but we in turn could argue, if we wanted to, that the nature into which we have brazenly intruded, though on maps it's called a wilderness, is itself unnatural. Much of the forest surrounding us, for instance, does not look as it did two hundred or even a hundred years ago. It's so choked with small, sun-starved trees that in some places only mushrooms will grow on the bare needle duff beneath them. This artificial condition has been caused not by something humans have introduced but by the absence of something we have removed. Prior to the twentieth century, periodic fire was the housekeeper here, the light-giver, the regenerator of these woods and all western forests. Since their frequency prevented major buildups of brush and fallen wood, the fires were generally of low intensity. The Indians here, as in other parts of Oregon and the West and most of North America, abetted this natural process by firing the landscape themselves to keep it productive of game and edible plants.

This meadow, and others nearby, are vestiges of the much more open, fire-conditioned forest of the past. Both Dutch Henry and Bill Graiff followed the Indian way, regularly torching the meadows to freshen the grass for their horses and mules and keep the surrounding woods at bay. Now, with fire absent from this meadow for more than half a century, sun-loving Douglas fir seedlings are relentlessly encroaching. To thwart their hordes, Brother Bradley assigns to every writer-resident the Walking Meditation of Meadow Mindfulness, which is best performed when the soil is moist in the spring. After clearing his or her mind of sentimental thoughts about little Christmas trees, the meditator slowly paces the meadow perimeter, eyes on the earth, aware of each footfall, each breath, and uproots the invader seedlings one by one.

When four have been gathered, the meditator faces the forest and chants: "*We . . .*"—and flings the first seedling—"*slaughter . . .*"—the second—, "*your . . .*"—the third—"*children!*"—and hurls the last of the bunch at their parents' feet—. To save time, the meditator is permitted to hurl all four at once along with the entire mantra.

In this way we strive through benevolent artifice to purify the homestead of malign artifice, using a thorn, as it were, to remove the thorn that injures us.

It may be that only the essential topography of this landscape is thoroughly wild. This pleasing array of steep-sided ridges and ravines must have looked to Peter Skene Ogden in 1827 much as it looks to me today. The mountains continue to rise, streams continue to dissect their flanks and feed the river, the river continues to keep pace with the general tectonic uplift by wearing its channel deeper. But the river, the coursing soul of this land, may be its most humanly altered element. When I go down to fish I walk over broad terraces that the river did not make. Gold miners did, carving into the banks with high-pressure hydraulic hoses and water cannons. Here and elsewhere in the Rogue Canyon their pipe and winches and cables remain, rusting into the landscape. Even the watered channel itself is far from virgin. When rafters and kayakers shoot the rapids they know for certain they're involved in a wild river, but they may not know that its wildness is humanly influenced. From the 1920s into the 1940s, an enterprising guide and boatman named Glen Wooldridge dynamited practically every significant rapid on the Rogue to make the river more congenial to boat passage. The Forest Service supplied the powder; Wooldridge and his crews grew expert in teaching boulders to fly. In some places he shifted the main channel clear from one side of the river to the other.

Other unnatural changes have come to this stretch of the Rogue from higher in its watershed. Dams constructed in the 1970s now regulate its flow, preventing flood disasters in populated areas but also denying the ecological benefits of flooding to the entire lower river. Floods, which clear spawning gravels for fish and enrich streamside soils, are to rivers what fire is to forests. The river carries sediment from logging operations, as well as various pollutants from agriculture, industry, and urban runoff. Eighty-four miles of the lower Rogue, including my winter park, have been protected since 1968 under the federal Wild and Scenic Rivers Act. Its water quality was deteriorating before 1968 and has continued to deteriorate since, though maybe at a slower rate. Salmon and steelhead runs, with sporadic annual exceptions, have declined more sharply since 1968 than they were declining before. When Mother Margery and the Doctor were first practicing the faith at Horseshoe Bend in the forties, and even into the sixties, when Brothers Bradley and Frank were taking their vows and learning the various ministrations, the Rogue River teemed with wild steelhead. Now most are hatchery bred, diluting the genetic heritage by which the wild fish have finely tuned themselves to the particular waters of their birth, and even the hatchery runs are much sparser than the native runs of the past.

So, my Eden is no Eden. Like all rivers, the Rogue embodies a complicated truth, partly fallen, partly pristine, entirely itself. Thirty-some years ago, when I was first hiking and climbing in California and the Northwest, I knew precisely what was natural—the wilderness areas where I liked to lose myself—and what was not: any place where people lived or cars could drive. The older I get, the more it seems that the human and the natural interfuse, and need to interfuse. We are daily demonstrating the futility and danger of imagining ourselves outside of nature. I believe in preserving wild landscapes where no humans live, but ultimately, the only way we can protect nature is to rejoin it, and the only way we can rejoin it is to define what we can legitimately take for our own sustenance and what we must give back in return. We have begun, haltingly at least, to do this. The Rogue River, though it reflects every ill we humans have visited upon it, is beautiful, relatively unspoiled, and still robust. It reflects our love and good intentions even as it reflects our carelessness and disrespect.

I'm not sure *what* Madam Turkey reflects, besides the metabolized produce of my garden, but she too, in her homely way, is beautiful. She is often the first thing I see in the morning when I look out a window, pecking on her rounds below the cabin. She will sometimes pass behind the cabin as I meditate, moving at her accustomed deliberate pace, statelier and more substantial than my own passing thoughts. She has about her, when I'm not shooting at her, an equable temperament. She is humble in the literal sense—close to the ground, the humus. She does not put on airs. Ben Franklin was right. This creature would have made a fine national bird. The one we chose instead is a loafer and a preener, a scavenger of wounded ducks and spawned-out salmon. A jackadandy, a bird in a suit. Fitting, I suppose, for a society sold down the river on glitzy appearances. This turkey, this plodding plucker of bugs and greens, would better betoken our better selves.

There's not a chance I'm going to kill this bird, is there. The only turkey at my Christmas dinner will be me.

December 21

I wasn't looking for it. I was reaching into the cupboard in the galley for some fresh D-cell batteries for the flashlight. The beam of my headlamp, lighting the motley hoard of junk behind the batteries, caught the black, rectilinear corner of something. A transistor radio, I knew instantly. *Leave it,* my higher self commanded. My right hand reached. *Smash it,* my higher self screamed. Probably doesn't work, I mused. What's the harm? I grabbed two Double-As along with my D-cells. *Leave it and get back to work, you poor weak fool,* hollered you know who.

I've been writing hard, I said to myself. I need a little break. I sat with the radio at my little red-blanket dining table. Yup, two Double As. Always satisfying, slipping fresh new batteries into a chamber sized precisely to receive them. *Don't do this! Don't wreck your solitude!* Now, click it on, just to see . . . Nothing, as I thought. Piece of junk.

But look, here's another switch. A rather complicated little black box—a "Dynamo and Solar Radio," made in Hong Kong. Henry Thoreau should have seen *this*. Now . . . life! The sudden, boundlessly spacious staticky field of AM radio at night, the white noise of everywhere in the American land, the anthem of countless nights I've spent driving long and far across the West . . .

I knew my danger. But surely, it occurred to me, this would constitute not a mortal or deadly sin, but only a slight sin such as any merely human being might commit. No pride or covetousness or lust or anger or gluttony or envy or sloth, just . . . curiosity. If my fingers should turn the dial and happen upon a station, what harm? It's lonely here. Rain has been drumming the roof all evening. A bit of news, that's all, such as used to flow from radio or TV when I was a boy—Edward R. Murrow, Robert Trout, Walter Cronkite, those fluid baritones, those comforting intonations, whatever they said. To me they said, This is our family, this is our house, this is the news of the day . . .

You . . . idiot.

My fingers, with their own bit of brain, their own will, turned the dial. My higher self, with its slightly stronger will, made my fingers *keep* turning the dial, not stopping at any of the quick blips of voice the dial now and then cut through. At the end of the dial my fingers turned it back to the other end, blipping through the stations and back again, and again, a kind of Hong Kong roulette without ever pulling the trigger. Ah, such a drug is adrenaline. Only once did my fingers happen to pause at a station long enough for an entire word to reach my ear. The word, spoken by a man with a nasal voice, was: "—physically—."

I screamed and flung the radio across the room. Without intending to, no doubt because my suburban American upbringing taught me not to break useful appliances, I flung it toward the La-Z-Boy, and in the La-Z-Boy it landed. Before it landed I had already clapped my hands over my ears, because I realized that I hadn't moved the dial when I'd let fly. So now, presumably, a man's nasal voice was speaking from the radio in the seat of the La-Z-Boy, the ruin of my experiment in solitude if I were to hear it—and how to turn it off, without use of my hands? I thought of kneeling and clamping the radio with my teeth—I have a big mouth—then elbowing open the sliding glass door and dropping the evil thing as if vomited off the deck. Too risky. The voice too close to my ears. I briefly tried to move the dial with my elbows, but they performed like the blunt instruments they are. And so—brainstorm!—I sat on the thing, yelled continuously to drown out any unmuffled noise, fumbled for the controls and switched it off.

Whew. For something substantial, maybe—Bach's B Minor Mass, an evening with my wife, Willie Nelson in concert, maybe even a pint of Ben & Jerry's—but for late-night radio *news*? My higher self is not inevitably wrong. I removed the batteries and returned the infernal black box to its cupboard. *Smash it*, said my higher self. *The hammer's on the shelf.*

No, I replied, nobility surging. A future resident may wish to use it. This will be good for me. I'll be Odysseus lashed to the mast. I have my own radio theater without need of a radio, and tonight the volume is down at least a half-turn from its accustomed level, exactly as if a radio were playing softly in the next room. What's more, with a humane sense of occasion, it's playing some of my favorite carols: "Adeste Fidelis," "Little Town of Bethlehem," "O Holy Night," "The First Noel." I scratch with my pencil scarcely noticing, and when I do hear it, I'm kind of glad it's on.

December 23

Some days this just feels *hard*. Why have I chosen to exile myself? I miss Marilyn, miss my perfectly lovely home on an acre in the country, miss the good smell of my leather writing chair, miss my friends, miss the Christmas season, miss the movies, miss *carne asada* burritos at Burrito Boy, miss pints of excellent beer and good conversation in Eugene's brewpubs, miss the Jim Lehrer News Hour and Charlie Rose, miss English Premier League soccer at two in the morning, miss making small talk with grocery clerks at Ray's and with Helen and her crew at the Elmira post office, miss the Eugene Symphony, miss 49er Flapjacks at the Original Pancake House, miss Merle Haggard and Jimmie Dale Gilmore and all the other great singers I've left at home, miss the little seasonal stream on our property that's probably running by now, miss double short lattes at Starbucks . . .

So why am I here?

Because you're a complicated person, a writer.

My writer friends aren't here. They're sharing their complications over food and drink.

Because you've wanted to do something like this since you were fourteen.

So I'm a fifty-two-year-old fourteen-year-old? *That's* a good reason?

Because you need silence to settle yourself.

It's quiet at home. No sirens, no car alarms. Wind in the trees, the lilt of the creek . . .

Because you want to conduct an experiment in solitude.

Right, and why? Because I'm a misanthrope. I'm missing Christmas at home just to prove how little I need people.

You hate Christmas.

Do not. I hate shopping.

You're here because you hate shopping.

That's a completely dumb reason to be here.

And you're a completely dumb person. You're here because you're here. Get on with it.

December 25

Christmas Day came clear and bright, and I went down to see the river after three days of rain. It was up a few feet but still its translucent green self, sliding and roiling with its complicated singleness of purpose. I sat on a rock about twenty feet from the water. I was still in a dejected mood, my own sense of purpose murky and dispersed. I half-hoped a party of holiday rafters would float by, solitude be damned. Gradually, as my thoughts turned in a slow eddy, I became aware that I was hearing the song of a bird, had been hearing it for some time. An ongoing series of flutey trills, grace notes, serene warbles. It seemed not to repeat but to keep making itself anew. Then I realized that I could see the bird—a water ouzel, now usually called the American dipper, small and charcoal gray, on a flat-topped rock I had several times fished from. He was doing the quick knee bends characteristic of his kind, and with some of his dips he was turning a few degrees on the rock, as if desiring to deliver his song to the many directions. In the five minutes or so that I watched and listened, he made several complete revolutions, pouring forth silvery music all the while. Then two alarm calls—*tseet! tseet!*, like a policeman's whistle—and he was slanting off upstream across the river.

I hiked up the trail feeling a little happier. Purpose is hard to identify, and probably always complex. It's said that birds sing to attract a mate and establish territory. They might well, but they might have other purposes too, or none at all. I know the ouzel had a song to sing, a beautiful song, and piped it with all he had. It sounded celebratory, it sounded noble. I don't presume that he was singing for me, but neither do I presume he wasn't. He was singing; I heard him. I know more, a little more, about my own motivations. I went to the river to see if it was up. I went to the river because it was Christmas. I went to the river because it was sunny after three days' rain. I went to the river half-hoping for human company. I went to the river for air and exercise. I went to the river because I was blue. I went to the river for medicine, and found it where it found me.

I believe in chance, I believe in what C. G. Jung called synchronicity, I believe in what some Christians call providence, and I suspect they are three angles on the same bird. Every moment is an intersecting pattern of events. At times we're aware of some portion of the pattern we're involved in, and it has meaning for us. What interests me is not a name for that, but that it occurs. I can't imagine it, but I suppose there could be a universe without awareness, without singing, without meaningful patterns. There could be a universe without beauty. There's beauty in this one, and that's a generosity. As I broke out of the woods into Dutch Henry Meadow, luminous peach-colored clouds were glowing in the western sky.

Dinner was a small lamb roast; rutabagas from the garden, cubed and steamed with some of their greens, buttered, salted, and peppered; and a salad of romaine, arugula, and Red Giant mustard, all from the garden. Fresh greens at the nadir of the year—a guy could feel lucky, if he let himself. And a bottle of good merlot, which was on hand not by chance or synchronicity or providence, but by wise human forethought.

Then I opened the boxes, marked "Do Not Open Till Christmas," that Marilyn had produced as I did my final packing on November 19th. She made me load them early, so that if something didn't fit it wouldn't be those. She had been conspiring, I now discovered, with our friends and with her parents in Seattle. The boxes yielded an extravagant potpourri of edible delicacies, homemade preserves, wines and liquors, and books, candles, a harmonica, even a pair of fingerless gloves for winter fishing. There was a sheaf of email greetings that Marilyn had solicited or extorted—that's why she asked for my password, to get at my address book—and several cards of Christmas and Solstice greeting. A guy could feel *very* lucky, and this guy was. The best gifts were a picture of a bear from my three-year-old friend Schuyler, and a photograph from Marilyn, of herself, in black, emerging from the dark hollow trunk of a huge redwood tree. It has to be from our trip to San Francisco in August. Whoever took it obviously has a genius for photographic composition, and had a beautiful subject to compose.

Christmas was getting better and better, and it wasn't done. A bit overwhelmed, I left the wrapping-wreckage on the floor, took the bottle of merlot, and sat in the rocker on the deck, wrapped in the down comforter from my bed. The wind had kicked up. It was rushing in the treetops, whistling under the eaves, streaming and surging in long currents across the darkened meadow. *Spiritus* was on the loose. It blew, hovered, ran somewhere else and came again. From the river in its canyon to the high ridgetops, it was touching everything. I imagined it ruffling the fur of the deer where they lay in the woods, lifting the turkey's feathers in her roost, stirring the waters where steelhead held in slow pools, dark in the dark flowing river. It seemed to burnish the fierce Hunter in the southern sky. My small breath went out to meet it. There *is* a birth, and I believe in it. There is born in Bethlehem and the Rogue River Canyon, in all times and all places, a miraculous life. It belongs to none of us. All of us, all beings, belong to it.

For the first time in my life I celebrated Christmas. I felt my father and mother present, my two brothers, my niece. I greeted and thanked each, then watched and listened for I don't know how long. Out of nowhere, no intention to speak, I heard myself ask aloud, "How long do I have?" The "v" of "have" was still on my lower lip when a streaking star blazed above Rattlesnake Ridge and left an afterimage in the sky.

January

What a man wants to do in his life, he does it.

And that isn't easy.

—Uncle Ray (Eugene, Oregon,
philosopher of the streets, c. 1920–1988)

Morning is when I am awake and there is a dawn in me.

—H. D. Thoreau, *Walden*

Just being in the woods, at night, in the cabin, is something
too excellent to be justified or explained!

—Thomas Merton, *Raids on the Unspeakable*

January 1

It was New Years, 1965, when my father cracked up.

He drank his way to his downfall fair and square, but there's more to the story than his weakness for whiskey. It can't be understood outside the context of a larger story he was part of, the history of the American labor movement through the heart of the twentieth century. My father's career and the career of organized labor followed the same arc.

Unionism faltered in the South in the thirties and forties, but in the Northeast and Midwest it was a different story. By the mid-thirties it had become clear that the American Federation of Labor, with its guildlike unions of plumbers, carpenters, and other workmen organized by trade, was not inclined and not competent to organize the nation's burgeoning industrial workforce. In auto plants and steel mills, as well as in clothing and textile mills, it made more sense to organize all workers, regardless of their specific jobs, into one big union. The most dynamic champion of such industrial unionism was John L. Lewis, the oratorically thunderous president of the United Mine Workers of America. Enraged by the AFL's timidity, and emboldened by New Deal legislation that for the first time gave workers the right to organize and bargain collectively, Lewis ripped his Mine Workers from the federation in 1935 and cofounded a new national alliance, the Congress of Industrial Organizations, which united major new unions such as the United Auto Workers, the United Rubber Workers, and the United Steel Workers of America with older unions such as the Amalgamated Clothing Workers.

CIO people considered the AFL staid and elitist, too cozy with the bosses, prejudiced against blacks and lesser-skilled whites. The AFL establishment saw the CIO as too politically oriented, too far to the left, too enamored of the volatile masses. Both federations prospered, though, as the economy began to recover from the Great Depression and Americans united in the common cause of a popular war. When the war years ended, the AFL, which dated back to 1886, had ten million members, and the CIO, little more than ten years old, had five million. Their member unions represented altogether more than 35 percent of the civilian American labor force, a fivefold expansion in only twelve years.

But as workers responded to the union gospel, business and its political allies reacted. In 1947 a Republican Congress overrode Harry Truman's veto to pass the Taft-Hartley Act, which revised New Deal labor law to make it harder to organize in the workplace, and, with the coming of the Cold War, red-baiting once again came into fashion. In 1955, with both Congress and the presidency firmly in Republican hands, labor leaders regrouped. The AFL, under former plumber George Meany, and the CIO, led by United Auto Workers zealot Walter Reuther, decided to link arms in a united labor movement. Meany became president and Reuther a vice-president of the AFL-CIO. It was a moment of high enthusiasm, despite past antipathies, and it must have been an exciting time for my father, Reuther's field assistant and a CIO man from the beginning. Reuther first suggested that he head the AFL-CIO's political action committee, whose task would be to pressure Congress on issues important to labor. My father said he could do that, but he wasn't enthusiastic. Both men knew that Franz Daniel was not a lobbyist but an organizer, a field man who worked best in the rough-and-tumble of unionizing at the ground level.

He became assistant director of organization for the AFL-CIO. He would be a troubleshooter and pinch hitter, working for any member union that needed him anywhere in the country. He would continue the vagabonding in the cause of labor he'd practiced for twenty-five years, and now with the backing of the national leadership of American labor's new united front. It must have felt as though his team had come from behind in the middle innings and now was poised to take the lead. The CIO's mission to unionize America's industrial base was far from accomplished. The time was ripe for bold new organizing drives.

The fifties waned, and those drives never came. The AFL dominated the leadership of the merged federation, and organizing had never been an AFL priority. George Meany, who had never led a strike or walked a picket line, was of the philosophy that workers, the right workers, would come to unionism when they were ready for it. Meany and his executive council treated the Department of Organization with condescension and funded it poorly. Jack Livingston, the department director, was a listless and unimaginative leader. Hundreds of organizers working for scores of member unions were eager to take the field to build a broader movement, but the manager and coaches kept them cooling their heels on the bench.

It had been the CIO's practice to hold its major meetings in various industrial cities—Pittsburgh, Chicago, New York. The AFL, and the AFL-CIO under George Meany, convened its twice-yearly meetings, even as the economy lapsed into recession and unemployment climbed, in such places as Bal Harbor, Florida, and San Juan, Puerto Rico. At the 1958 winter meeting, Walter Reuther, uncomfortable with the semi-tropical venue but powerless to change it, proposed an AFL-CIO-spon-sored march on Washington to pressure Congress and President Eisenhower to do something about unemployment. The media got wind of the proposal and had much delicious fun with the irony of it—an unemployment protest hatched by a cabal of overweight men in swim-ming trunks smoking cigars on the beaches of Puerto Rico. The march, in any case, was not approved by the executive council.

A breakthrough seemed to come in 1959, when Reuther and other progressives persuaded Meany to launch a drive to organize farm workers in California. For the next year and a half my father was closely involved in getting the Agricultural Workers Organizing Committee started and supervising its operation for the AFL-CIO national office. He spent more time in California than at home, exhilarated to be doing once again the real work of the labor move-ment. Organizing farm workers was an enormous challenge and enor-mously necessary. At a time when unionized industrial workers were earning seventeen dollars a day, workers in the blue-sky sweatshops were making an average of six. Entire families were living in cars and squalid camps, putting in long, back-torturing days with no minimum wage guarantee, no child labor regulations, no unemployment insur-ance, not even a right to organize under the National Labor Relations Act. The United States was the only industrialized nation in the world without a well-established union movement among its agricul-tural workers.

"Money, equipment, and manpower will be needed in stupendous quantities," my father said in a 1960 speech, "but more important than material things is the need of spirit. A union can't be bought into being. It has to be built. The problems of organizing farm workers are formidable. They can be solved."

Privately, I suspect, he was not so optimistic. The Agricultural Workers Organizing Committee found the going tough. Growers refused to negotiate and hired scabs. Police used snarling dogs and phony disorderly conduct charges to intimidate and jail the pickets. AWOC became the target of an intense flurry of lawsuits seeking to enjoin organizing activity. Most crippling of all, growers were entitled under law to hire half a million Mexican nationals as guest workers and to pay them even less than they paid domestic workers, easily circumventing the law's provision that domestics be hired first. This program, begun during the war to remedy an actual labor shortage, lived on in the sixties as a huge windfall subsidy for the growers.

Still, over the course of two years, AWOC made gains. Here and there throughout the Central Valley, organizers were able to get the Mexican nationals removed and replaced with local workers who had been available all along. Though the union was not recognized, its actions and the threat of actions won modest wage increases for union and nonunion workers alike. Publicity from the drive, aided by the airing of ABC and CBS television documentaries on migrant labor, resulted in improved living conditions in many camps. Church groups, urban unionists, civil rights leaders, even the American Veterans Committee enthused about the drive. AWOC's director reported that the union was on the verge of winning recognition from several big growers.

And then, at the AFL-CIO's December 1960 meeting in Miami Beach, Meany and the executive council decided to terminate the AWOC pilot project, citing a reason any corporation would have understood—insufficient funds. The real reason, my father and many others knew, was that the national leadership had never viewed the drive as anything more than a sop for the CIO crowd. It had written checks but had never backed AWOC with the full power of its bully, united-labor pulpit in Washington. The AFL-CIO had the capacity to raise funds if it wanted to, from its member unions and through national appeals. Public concern about farm workers was at its height, fueled by the TV documentaries and the interest of such eminent progressives as Eleanor Roosevelt.

Failure was possible, of course, even likely. The history of the labor movement was replete with failures. But to begin a good fight, an important fight, and to pull out before it had a fair chance to succeed—that, to my father, must have felt like betrayal. In the summer of 1961, as an act of protest, he stayed on in California two weeks beyond the date he had been ordered to return to Washington. He spent time with the many AWOC organizers who intended to stay on the job as volunteers when the national funding lapsed. They had been making only seventy-five dollars a week in any case. My father's loyalty was to them, not to the higher-ups in D.C. In a speech that summer he said these words, which could not have been well received if they came to George Meany's attention:

> From time to time one hears the creaking joints of our labor movement. And creaking joints are symptomatic of a congealing brain and a hardening heart. There is a specific for this disease. It lies in doing once again what we did in our youth. The imagination we once had, the willingness to experiment, the ability to break with the tyranny of sterile tradition—these are ours if we will but make the effort to re-establish them.

January 2

My father would have loved it here. These steep green Klamath Mountains would have reminded him of the Smokys, which he and my mother knew well from their work and travels in Tennessee and the Carolinas. He'd enjoy the garden, this miraculous winter garden still giving me lettuce in January, well worth the trouble of tarping the beds every clear night against frost. He'd like the firewood routine, the nights in the high twenties or low thirties, the days nippy-to-mild, the mist drifting in the canyon. He with his Germanic sense of order would probably get right to hoeing weeds in the garden and pruning the fruit trees and setting the cabin to rights and other jobs I haven't done. He'd like to sit in the rocker on the deck on warmer afternoons, reading and smoking. He'd like playing cribbage with me.

He'd like it here, and in a week or two he'd be ready to leave. He'd want to get back to his work, to friends and parties and ball games and betting on horses, or to the pursuits and diversions that kept him even more variously active in his retirement than during his labor career—correspondence, writing book reviews for the paper, serving on civic boards and commissions, coin collecting and woodworking, leading a Unitarian fellowship, and following the news. Especially the political news, in which he never lost interest. In the last month of his life he was a delegate to the Democratic National Convention in St. Louis, where he supported the consensus choice of a Southern governor named Jimmy Carter. The Republican convention was in progress when he entered the hospital. The day before he died, he learned that President Gerald Ford had selected as a running mate the senior Senator from Kansas, a conservative *and* a Jayhawker. My father's last recorded words were: "Oh my God, it's *Dole*."

His life was thoroughly engaged with people, human institutions, and the issues of his time. He wouldn't have cared much for my experiment in solitude. To him it would have smacked of my dropout disaffection of the late sixties and early seventies, which troubled and pained him. I told him then, and anyone else who inquired, that I needed to find myself—a cliché of the times that had, like any cliché, its core of truth. To my father it looked like aimless, disinvolved drifting. He wasn't entirely wrong, and who's to say he'd be wrong about my present pursuit? I can imagine—with extreme discomfort—trying to explain Zen meditation to him. "You cross your legs and listen to yourself breathe?" I can hear him saying. "What the hell *for?*"

Indeed. What exactly *am* I here for? Seems like I ought to know, seven weeks along. To write, of course, but I've never been a writer who needs to go off to colonies and retreats. It's true that the phone doesn't ring here, friends don't visit and I don't visit friends, there's no TV or movies or concerts or ball games, so I do get more done. But what does it say about me that to get more done I have to take refuge from a life in the world that bears very little burden of the kind of engagement and commitment that my father considered essential to *any* meaning-ful life? Even in the decades when he got tuned up every day and stag-gering-drunk too many days, he served. He put his time and body and spirit and finally his career on the line to contribute, by his lights, to a better world.

We do different work, of course. I like to think that in the long haul writing helps make a better world, or at least that it's essential to any good world, but that's a pretty hard claim to defend. It sounds suspi-ciously like a rationalization for doing what I want to do anyway, make satisfying wholenesses out of language and get some attention for it. God knows I'm not in it for the money, but still, serving Beauty or Imag-ination may just be a dressed-up way of serving myself. At the very least there's a considerable self-regard implicit in it—what I have to say is important, and so I will spend my life discovering what that is, and say-ing it, and you, if you have taste and judgment, will listen. And buy my books. I like Chekhov on this subject: "The minute the writer takes up a pen he accuses himself of unanswerable egotism and all he can do with any decency after that is to bow."

Nature and environmental writing might have a better claim as to serving the cause of a better world. It certainly serves the cause of a *bigger* world, a world more various than the human. It is saying things that need to be said, attempting to restore a perspective of human belonging to nature that's been lost for centuries. Whether many are reading it, outside of a limited audience of the already converted, is another question. Whether it changes any unconverted minds it does reach is still another, and the answer is probably very few. There is also the problem of the too-easy piety nature writers sometimes indulge in, our tendency to locate all good in what is natural and wild, all bad in corporations and government agencies and rural resource workers who don't agree with us. We like to identify ourselves as the prophets of this moral drama, defending nature as if we were the only ones entitled to speak for it—as if it were our private colony—all the while paying scant attention to our own economic involvement in the evils and injuries we decry. Sanctimony and green-colored glasses do not necessarily make for a better world.

But writing aside, or writing included, it seems I'm still doing at fifty-two what I was doing at twenty-two—trying to discover who I am. Progress? Well, I've holed up in the backwoods of southwestern Oregon for seven weeks and discovered that I am . . . myself! The same guy who inhabits the world—same mood swings, self-doubts, peeves, petty thoughts, brief epiphanies, hurting back and ankle, sudden cravings for raspberry jam—the whole package, including drinking too much over the holidays, thanks to a bottle of Baker's bourbon and another of some luscious equivalent of Bailey's Irish Cream, supplied among my Christmas booty by friends who either know me too well or not well enough.

I had hoped, assumed, that this far into my sojourn I would have found a me I haven't seen before, some major reconciliation with living and dying and being who I am. A breakthrough. Hasn't happened, so I'm disgruntled. Disappointed? Seems ungrateful to say so, given the rare privilege of such a time in such a place, but yeah, a little disappointed.

Maybe it's just the winter blues. Or maybe it's an accumulation of sheer loneliness bending my spirit, like a young fir tree weighted with snow. The homestead is an empty island these days. No deer since well before Christmas. The only four-legged creatures I see evidence of are the craven little dirt rats who are gnawing my beets to nothing, the cowardly way, from underground. If I could see them I'd shoot them, and just having something to shoot at would make me less lonely. I haven't seen the turkey for over a week. Got tired of me warming her tail feathers, I suppose. Hard on her blood pressure. She was trainable, all right, but not the way I'd hoped. She's lost her free lunch. I've lost the pleasure of her company *and* the possible pleasure of her roasted flesh. How did I arrange to lose twice in this deal?

Yesterday evening I walked up the drive to a spot near the Brothers' cabin where I like to watch mist in the canyon and the array of ridges to the south. As I stood, I heard from the nearby woods the sound of a smallish tree or snag falling over—groan and crackle of fiber giving up, pop of small branches breaking, concussion of the trunk hitting ground. The air was still, not a breath of wind. Amazing, I thought. This particular moment as I'm standing here, some wood-chewing bug takes a crucial last bite, a fungus dissolves a critical fiber, a bird lights almost weightlessly—something, and a tree topples. It seemed like a Zen koan, its significance hovering just out of focus.

Too far out of focus.

"Wow," I said aloud. "I came to the woods, and I heard a tree fall." I turned and walked back to the cabin.

January 6

There's pleasure, even when I'm feeling low, in tending the garden, splitting and stacking and lugging in wood, even in sweeping the floor (occasionally) and washing the windows (once, so far) and doing my laundry. Or not pleasure, necessarily—it's not pleasant to flail the maul at a knotted hunk of oak or to hustle down to the garden and drag tarps over the beds by headlamp with frost already forming—but even then, beneath my hurry and annoyance, there's a certain satisfaction I know only faintly in my doings in the world. Filling a cart at Safeway or writing a check to the power company isn't the same. My life here is hardly self-sufficient, and in a few months I'll be back in the aisles at Safeway, but for a time at least I'm tasting the sanity of working directly, physically, to sustain my life. I'm remembering some of the daily rhythms of wholeness.

For my mother, in her last years, the loss of such work was a sorrow and a frustration. Physically too feeble to wash dishes or sweep floors, mentally unable to pursue sequential activities of any complexity, she drifted between bedroom, bathroom, and eating table, her hands empty or wringing a tissue. She lit up when I had laundry for her to fold, strawberries to de-cap. It was as though I had offered food to a hungry wanderer. She was literally dying for lack of authentic work. Many of us are. As we rid our lives of meaningful labor, we slip deeper and deeper into a profoundly distracted boredom known in previous centuries only to the aristocratic classes.

The great success of the Industrial Revolution meant, of course, the dissolution of domestic economy. Division of labor and the factory system of production yielded vast efficiencies, an abundance of goods, and great wealth for some, but also forced men and then women out of the home, turned labor into repetitive, dehumanizing chores, abolished economic independence for many, and piqued desires for material possessions as compensation for what had been lost. Thoreau saw this happening in America and hated it. As Robert Richardson observes in his biography, "Thoreau's whole experiment at Walden is a protest against the dogma that the division of labor is beneficial to the individual." Or, put positively, it was a public demonstration that a life of self-reliant wholeness was economically feasible, physically practicable, and spiritually desirable.

The mission my father and mother and their kindred pursued in the labor movement helped American workers in real ways. Families ate better, jobs were made safer, retirements were secured, working men and women gained self-respect. Nothing the labor movement did, though, addressed or could have addressed the alienation inherent in industrial wage labor. Whatever it might pay, not many human beings are likely to find working a machine in a textile plant a fulfilling way to spend forty years. Given other choices, few would seek in such work their uniquely creative way of belonging to the world. It is progress, by one measure, that relatively few Americans still find themselves forced to work such jobs, but the work, of course, is still performed. We have shipped the sweatshops and their messy labor and environmental problems beyond our borders, to countries where our industrial history of a hundred years ago is now recapitulating itself—twelve-hour days, six-day weeks, wages of pennies per hour, and a record of many deaths from factory fires in buildings with locked exits and no sprinklers. We rationalize this as part of what poor countries need in order to "develop," as we enjoy the products of these foreign sweatshops at bargain prices.

Work that can't be exported and few Euro-Americans are willing to do—picking our crops, cleaning our homes and offices, bussing and washing dishes in restaurants, tending our gardens, even raising our young children—is performed by poor immigrants, many of them here illegally. We depend upon these workers even as we decry their presence, while scarcely slapping the wrists of the many employers who illegally hire and often exploit them. More than a fourth of the food on American tables is raised in the Great Central Valley of California, and almost all of it is cultivated and picked by Mexican-Americans, Mexicans, other Latinos, and Filipinos. We get the fruits and vegetables; they get the meager wages and stooped backs, they breathe and absorb the pesticides of which we consume only traces, and they get the cancer.

I made a brief acquaintance with this work in the summer of 1968, when I had dropped out of college and was trying to find a life to live in San Francisco. The shape-up was at a certain corner a few blocks south of Mission Street. I arrived in the gray light of 5 A.M. and joined a crowd of mostly older men, some of them nipping on bottles, some of them sitting asleep against the building fronts. The Latinos in the crowd were alert and watching. Every little while a bus pulled up and a man shouted from the door in English and Spanish. The crowd pressed toward the bus and filled it, and the bus drove away. The first few times, I tried to listen to what the contractor was shouting and was too late to get on. When the next bus came I just pushed ahead and thrust myself inside.

Somewhere out past Stockton in the hot valley flats we bounced into our destination, an orchard of dark-leafed cherry trees. I got my ladder, my buckets, my punchcard, and set myself up on a huge spreading tree full of fruit. Shady work! I couldn't believe my luck. The heavy clusters of Royal Annes slipped easily off their stems into my hands. I filled two buckets quickly and hurried to the dock where crates were being filled.

"Jesus, kid! The stores don't want those cherries," said the sneering man in a baseball cap who took my buckets. "The stem comes *with* the cherry, get it?"

He dumped the buckets into an empty crate and punched my card, scowling at the quality of help he'd been sent.

The picking went a little slower after that, but even being careful to get the stems I was plunking cherries into my buckets at a good clip. The tree was immense and it was loaded. A Mexican, a wiry man with a mustache, walked up with his ladder.

"Un palo grande, no?"

I smiled.

"Con permiso?"

I smiled again and the Mexican raised his ladder and almost sprang into the tree. It was phenomenal to watch. His hands moved before him in a liquid stir, cherries traveling almost unbidden from boughs to bucket as his feet stepped up and down the rungs as casually as they might step along a sidewalk. It wasn't picking so much as an incantation. He had two buckets in the tree and two more on the ground. He left for the dock with all four of them full, two in each hand, and was back almost instantly. I hadn't halfway filled my second pair.

The Mexican never flagged, and by noon the tree I had expected to sustain me all day was bare. As he departed, with a cheerful call, I couldn't be angry. He was masterly. He belonged in the best tree. I traipsed around the orchard the rest of the day looking for another mother lode but finding only worked-over trees abandoned by other pickers. My pay came to seven dollars and change.

That was my best day. The next time out they brought us to a trampled, torn-up tomato field, stripped of all but some rotten remnants. We were picking not for fruit but for seed, the contractor explained. Each of us moved in a stoop along a row, gleaning every red glob we came to, slowly—very slowly—filling our buckets with tomato slop. The overripe smell welled up and enveloped me, rank and thick, the plum tomatoes squishing in my fingers, a steady cramping ache in the small of my back. I had to quit now and then and walk away from my row, breathe air a little less putrid with tomato at six feet than it was at three. The field stretched perfectly flat ahead of us to where cars flashed in a shimmer of heat on a distant highway. My pant legs were smeared and crusted with tomato, my hands etched red for days.

On my venture out I listened to the contractors as they yelled their work and terms at the shape-up. I chose apricots, thinking shade, thinking upright picking. But the apricots were green, some of them hard as walnuts. I picked a bucket of the ripest I could find, and the foreman bawled me out for picking too green. I picked another bucket, working several trees for almost an hour to fill it. I filled my third bucket with green fruit and a layer of blushing ripe ones on top. The foreman was distracted and didn't catch it. I picked another bucket and he gave me hell. I set the bucket down, walked half a mile to a little store, spent all the money I had on two sixteen-ounce cans of Hamm's beer and a bag of potato chips, walked back to the orchard and sat in the shade of an apricot tree and drank my beer.

One of the contractor's men walked by. "Won't make a wage that way," he said brightly.

I only smiled. Nobody was making a wage that day. There were no virtuosos, no incantations. Everyone was grousing, everyone was getting screwed, probably the contractor too. When the men and women brought their buckets, complaining of the thin picking, he snarled.

But everyone worked on, everyone but me. I began to understand something about privilege that afternoon. I was close to broke that summer. My parents didn't have a lot of money, but I could write them if I had to. I could shoplift ground beef from Safeway and get away with it. I could let my roommates carry me for a while. I could get another job, I could go back to college on my parents' money or a loan and make everybody happy. I could set down my bucket and drink my beer in the shade and wait for quitting time.

But what if I couldn't?

The AFL-CIO's decision to drop the California agricultural campaign brought a fusillade of angry, incredulous letters and telegrams from labor leaders, liberal politicians and public figures, clergy, and rank-and-file union workers. A woman from Walnut Creek, California, spoke for many when she wrote this to George Meany: "If the founders of the American labor movement had given up as quickly as the AFL-CIO did with the farm workers, I am afraid there would have been no unions. . . . The rank and file of union men are quite disappointed by this action. They are not quitters and they do not want their leaders to be either."

Within the AFL-CIO leadership, Walter Reuther led a vigorous effort to keep AWOC going. The letters and lobbying worked. At its 1961 winter meeting, the executive council reversed itself and re-funded the drive. My father lived in California through most of 1962, getting AWOC reorganized to Meany's satisfaction, but the new commitment from Washington proved no more substantial than the old. As AWOC made small gains in the field, its director, Al Green, practically begged for more financial support so that they could build on the gains. Meany and his council ordered a downsizing instead. Green wired back: "CUTTING AWOC BACK AS PER ORDER LEAVES 4 PEOPLE ON PAYROLL IMPOSSIBLE TO OPERATE." So it went for three years, the hamstrung operation limping along on the dedication of its staff.

In 1965, during a series of Central Valley grape strikes, AWOC joined forces with the recently formed National Farm Workers Association, led by a young Chicano named Cesar Chavez, and the events were set in motion that would lead to the grape and lettuce boycotts, the first major agricultural contracts in American labor history, and the establishment of organized labor as a fact of life in California agribusiness. AWOC and the National Farm Workers merged in 1966 to form, under Chavez, the United Farm Workers of America, an AFL-CIO affiliate with some 50,000 members today.

My father, semiretired in Missouri when the United Farm Workers met its triumph, applauded from afar. He admired Chavez and understood, I suspect, that the movement couldn't have succeeded without a Latino leader, and without a leader of such charisma and moral gravity. He surely wished, though, that the AFL-CIO's original drive had been given a chance to succeed, or at least to better prepare the ground.

But my father by then was circling in a quiet eddy, far removed from the mainstream of organized labor. In 1963, the agricultural drive for the moment revitalized, the AFL-CIO had undertaken a second major organizing campaign, this one on more traditional turf. At the urging of Reuther and others, the executive council approved a massive multi-union drive in the growing heart of the Sun Belt, Los Angeles and Orange County. Forty affiliate unions were involved, from bakery workers to the aircraft industry, with the joint goal of enlisting half a million new members. The AFL-CIO's role was to coordinate the effort, backing it with staff, publicity, and limited funding. It was the biggest recruitment effort the labor movement had launched since the 1930s. My father was tapped to direct it. It was a big job, just the kind he'd been wanting. His drinking problem was no secret, and was spoken of, I'm told, when he received the assignment. He needed to stay sober and on track.

I wish I had a clearer grasp of what happened. My father moved to L.A. in January of 1963, got an apartment, wrote letters to friends and his sisters about the happy work of getting the office set up and the drive under way. According to his reports to Washington, the organizing went modestly well, though it quickly became evident that the target of a half-million new members had been wildly optimistic. I don't know what my father did day-to-day, besides chair a meeting here and give a press statement there. Time alone in distant cities seemed always to return him to the same old trouble. I'm told that he fell in with another alcoholic, the drive's publicity director. Word got back to D.C. over the spring that my father was off the wagon. George Meany flew to L.A. to assess the situation and meet with him. My father didn't show up. Maybe he was drunk, or hung over. My father disliked Meany, and he felt—with what justice I don't know—that the man had been out to get him from the beginning.

In early summer my father appointed as a subdirector a person from one of the local unions, a man bitterly disliked by the AFL-CIO leadership. This appointment violated explicit instructions that subdirectorships were to be filled only by AFL-CIO men, and it seems to have had the effect of placing national funds to some degree under local union control. I don't know why my father did it. He may have been acting out his resentments toward Meany, or he may simply have appointed the guy he thought best for the job. I do know that he wouldn't have done it if he hadn't believed it would help the drive. My father trusted the local unions. They were made of the men and women who had built the labor movement, not the cigar smokers in swimming trunks who put their money on the table one month and might well pull it off the next.

Jack Livingston, my father's immediate superior, removed him as director and ordered him home. My father stayed on in L.A. as my mother and brother and I drove cross-country in June—a trip already planned—and spent a few days with him before the four of us turned around and drove east. I have only one clear memory of the visit. After dinner at a restaurant one evening, my father took Jim and me—my mother went back to the motel—to a park where leftist speakers sometimes soapboxed, as he had done in Philadelphia back in the thirties. We listened for a while to a man with a strong accent who spoke the word "capitalistic" a lot, sliding quickly through the first three syllables to the fourth.

My father, cheerfully well lubricated, interrupted. "Friend," he said, "look here. You tell me where Karl Marx uses the term 'ballistic.'"

The guy stared a few seconds at my father, then continued his spiel. My father turned to me, laughing lightly in his throat, as if he had scored a decisive point. I was ready for the motel.

On the drive east my mother and father squabbled and pouted about the route we should take and where we should stay. The drama occurred the day after we got home to Glen Echo in late July. Waiting in the mail was a letter from Jack Livingston. It said, in two terse sentences, that not only had my father been removed as the Los Angeles–Orange County director, he was terminated from the AFL-CIO. My brother happened to be in the living room when he opened the letter. Our father stood for a long time, staring and staring at the brief typewritten text.

According to a memorandum in his file on George Meany, Walter Reuther intervened with Meany at the AFL-CIO executive council meeting two weeks later, questioning the fairness of summarily dismissing a man who had contributed twenty-nine years to the labor movement and was two months short of qualifying for an enhanced pension under the new AFL-CIO retirement plan. Meany agreed to put my father back on the payroll long enough to qualify for the pension. The next morning, though, as Reuther ate breakfast with A. Phillip Randolph and others, Meany approached the table "and made all kinds of gestures, stomped his cane on the floor and began to shout at the top of his voice—creating a scene." Meany renounced his and Reuther's agreement of the night before, said that Jack Livingston had documentary proof that Reuther and my father had had phone conversations—*phone conversations!*—and demanded a list of all persons who had spoken against the firing of Franz Daniel. There had been many, Reuther told him, and asked if Meany would be good enough to leave the table and discuss the matter under more suitable circumstances.

I don't know what further talks ensued, but Meany seems to have stuck to the agreement after all. My father would qualify for his pension. Meany would not rehire him into the AFL-CIO Department of Organization, but he wasn't out of work long. By the end of 1963 Walter Reuther had found him a post in the Industrial Union Department, Reuther's power base within the AFL-CIO, and my father went back to troubleshooting here and there for various unions. But the blow had landed, and everyone in the labor movement knew what it meant. Franz Daniel, though he would be treated deferentially by those he worked with for his seniority and legendry, would end his storied career as little more than a staff organizer.

He pretty much dissolved in drinking. On the advice of his close friend Newman Jeffrey, a recovering alcoholic, my mother left Alcoholics Anonymous literature around the house. She soft-pedaled her pressure for a divorce while my father struggled. She also discovered Adele Davis—a health-food guru—about this time and began putting brewer's yeast and wheat germ into everything we ate or drank, hoping thereby to mitigate all ills. Her concern seems poignant now, but she served some truly horrible dinners. My father ignored the AA material. My mother went into one of her own heavy drinking phases, and their arguments escalated. By her own account, she goaded him into fights. He hadn't hit her before, but he hit her now. She slept on a cot in the basement. He barricaded the basement door. I did my thing at school. Jim was attending Montgomery Junior College.

In 1964 my father stopped coming home to Glen Echo when he returned from trips. He stayed with Margaret and Georgia, his two younger sisters, who lived across the Potomac in Arlington, Virginia. Jim and I saw him there from time to time when he was in town, but he was on the road almost continuously. Over the holidays that year, he stayed in the Arlington house while Margaret and Georgia vacationed in England. He threw a New Year's Day party, which Jim and I attended briefly before lighting out to our own celebrations. Our father, already three sheets to the wind, was pouring entire bottles of various liquors and a few incidental flavorings into a punch bowl, stirring up a concoction he called Fish House Stew.

A day or two later his sisters flew in to National Airport and called him to pick them up, as planned. He said he couldn't. Annoyed, they took a taxi home and found him in a state not far short of delirium tremens. It seems he had been drinking, with little food or sleep, straight through from New Year's Eve or before. The sisters got him into George Washington University Hospital, where he was treated for alcohol poisoning, and within two weeks he was on his way to Men-ninger's Clinic in Kansas.

I have a small photo of my father taken at Menninger's, a head shot. His face is ashen, sagging. He is not looking at the camera, not looking at anything. His eyes are blank, lightless, thoroughly defeated.

January 10

Clear nights, brilliant glittering stars, hard frost every morning. I don't know why, but on brittle cold nights the ghostly river sound, the blending of all the rapids in this reach, whispers out of the canyon twice as loud.

I'm jumpy.

Earlier tonight I spread tarps over the garden beds in the dark and was walking up past the lower corner of the cabin when something moved to my left. My left arm shot up to shield my head, cold panic—and I saw my shadow, cast by the soft spill of propane light from a window.

Inside sometimes, reading, cooking, a small quick motion catches the fringe of my vision. Like a mouse, but there are no mice. The Brothers deal fairly with mice. Periodically they present a contract, the key clause of which reads, clearly, *Just One Bite*. It's mouse ghosts I'm seeing, little gray specters, protesting. They freely took the bite, and now they want to renegotiate.

But mouse ghosts don't scare me. Last night I woke in pure dark convinced I'd heard a footstep in the entry porch. I froze beneath the covers, filled with pit-of-the-stomach dread. He's found the axe, I knew instantly. Or brought his own. Could I get to the guns in time? Doubtful. Where was my fishing knife? What was here, on the nightstand? An Icelandic novel—a long one but a paperback, no help. Ah! I reached for the pewter candlestick, listening for another step, half-expecting to hear: "You want some *cha-a-a-a-ries?*"

Dutch Henry did live here and die here and is buried here—not the Brothers or even Mother Margery know where—so why wouldn't his ghost be hanging around?

And not just his. I've been poking around at Bill Graiff's place. The rock-and-clay foundation is all that's left of his house, and a little two-burner woodstove in what used to be his cellar. He used it for canning his fruit and bear meat, I expect, and maybe it was involved with his still.

Graiff was in his seventies when Mother Margery and the Doctor started horse-packing into this stretch of the Rogue Canyon in 1946. They had a cabin on a gold claim down at Horseshoe Bend, little more than a mile's hike from Graiff's place here in the meadow. It was there at Horseshoe Bend that they founded the Oregon faith now carried on by the Brothers, though Mother Margery—and the Doctor too, who died in 1993—would say that they simply absorbed the faith from the river, the canyon, and the assortment of reclusive sourdoughs, including Graiff, who'd come to scratch for leftover gold in the gravel bars and tributaries of the Rogue.

Mother Margery and Brother Frank remember Bill Graiff as a wiry, tough little man who spoke in a high, squeaky voice with a strong German accent. When he came down to visit at Horseshoe Bend he would wait around in the woods until someone noticed him and hailed him in, often for drinks and dinner. Sometimes Mother and the Doctor hiked up to Graiff's place and brought him a steelhead. They didn't stay for a meal.

"I always eat with you," Graiff would squeak. "How come you don't eat with me?"

Because, they didn't tell him, they didn't want to contract botulism from his canned bear meat.

In 1950, maybe recognizing that at seventy-nine he was getting too old for backwoods life, Bill Graiff sold the homestead to a California movie producer and went to live out his days with family in Alaska and Seattle. But he didn't get along with family, which was why he had fled to the Rogue in the first place. The movie man wasn't making his payments, so Graiff foreclosed and moved back to the place that felt like home.

In the early fall of 1953 he was picking apples in one of Dutch Henry's trees, looking forward to a new batch of applejack, when he slipped and hit the ground. He broke a hip and his pelvis and knew he was in a lot of trouble. There was no telephone and no road then—Graiff packed in horseback what he needed—but he had an arrangement with Deak Miller, a bush pilot who flew people and supplies into the canyon. A sheet or blanket spread on the ground meant that Graiff needed help.

The nearest apple tree is 75 feet from the house. Most of the trees are 300 to 400 feet away, over the crest of a mild hill. He must have pulled and elbowed himself along, pushing with his one good leg, in pain I don't want to imagine. Maybe it took him a few hours, maybe overnight. Did he then have to go *into* the house, up steps, to get the sheet? Maybe he kept one ready outside. However he did it, he got the sheet spread out, then waited two days for Deak Miller to fly over.

Deak Miller drank a lot, and he needed to. There is no place to land an aircraft here. The Rogue River Canyon is called a canyon because that's what it is, but Miller and Graiff had cut a few trees on a steep meadow above the homestead and declared it an airstrip. Miller, who came to hunt once in a while and to bring Graiff some necessaries, landed his Piper Cub heading up the mountainside and took off down the same.

Deak Miller found Graiff alive, took off, and flew in a doctor from Myrtle Creek. They stayed two days with Graiff at the homestead, trying to nurse up his strength for the evacuation. They wheelbarrowed him to the "airstrip"—the better part of a mile, uphill—and had to partially dismantle the Piper Cub's body to get him in. With the patient tied to the floor so he wouldn't slide out the back, Miller got his craft airborne and flew to Myrtle Creek.

The surgeons tried to put Bill Graiff back together, but even his fortitude had a limit. He died in the hospital on October 2, 1953, at the age of eighty-two, of pneumonia and gangrene.

A cautionary tale, which I have now taken to heart. I've known all along, of course, that I could get into trouble here, and the trouble could be bad. I've got the radio phone, but if I broke a leg at the river or on a ramble and couldn't get back to the cabin, I wouldn't be missed until Wednesday at 10 P.M. rolled around. If at the river I'd have to pray for a raft or boat, but very few make the trip this time of year. I've seen none, seen camp sign only once.

I haven't worried about it. I'm pretty steady, I'm not doing foolish things. But my unexpected success with the fishing rod has made me just a hair giddy. A few days ago, on a gray and mizzling afternoon, revved at having caught and released six steelhead, I was scrambling over a strew of boulders to try one more hole when I took a dumb step. Double-dumb, because I saw myself about to take it and knew it was dumb. I put the toe of my right boot on a boulder that sloped at about forty-five degrees, a surface the sole would have stuck to if it were dry. It was wet. My foot shot out from under me and I landed hard, full body against the sloping rock.

My right hand, after dropping my fishing rod, must have broken my fall. I looked at it and saw the end of my experiment in solitude. The little finger was dislocated at the knuckle, the butt of the finger bone protruding grotesquely under stretched-out skin. On an impulse at once reflexive, therapeutic, and aesthetic—the finger was *ugly*—I grabbed the right hand with my left and the bone popped back into place. I got up and critically compared my two little fingers. The right was numb and tingling, the nerves buzzing crazily, but looked nearly as straight as the left. Feeling came back, with growing pain, as I worked the joint.

Relief! To have had to return to the world early because of a dis-jointed pinkie would have been, to say the least, embarrassing. More embarrassing, even, than having a play-for-free jukebox in my head.

I praised my right hand for its resilience, and for dropping the rod and reel in a way that did them no damage. To prove to myself that I was okay, I went back to the little beach where I'd left my pack and made a few casts. Wham! I hooked and landed my seventh of the day, a lively eighteen-incher which I killed and cleaned for the barbecue. (I carry a sixteen-inch driftwood stick for the killing. A few words of thanks, then one whack does it.)

Up at the cabin I read in my first aid book that a dislocation that slips back quickly is called a subluxation, and it's treated like a sprain. I already had the hand, which had swollen considerably on the right side, in a bowl of ice water. I declared an extra round of grog for all hands present, even disabled ones, and counted my blessings. Since then I've been keeping the little finger taped to its neighbor and some compression taping over the joint area. It's still swollen, but I can write and cook and do most everything else. It hurts mainly when it knocks against something, which is too often.

I didn't tell Marilyn about it in my message tonight. It would only have worried her. I promised to give news, not all the news.

No more dumb steps. No double-dumb steps, at least. And I'll save my major rambles for Wednesdays, and leave a note telling where I've gone.

January 11

I had my first drink of whiskey in the summer of 1964, while I was six-teen and working for a rock wall construction outfit in Maryland. It was a Friday evening. I was riding home in the back of a green pickup with one of the masons, worn out and wondering why the hell I was spend-ing the summer lugging fifty-pound rocks and ninety-pound bags of cement for a bunch of ignorant red-tanned men with hamlike arms who thought Barry Goldwater would make a terrific president and whose remarks to me consisted of one incessant command: "Need s'more mud, boy!"

I was drinking Coke from one of those small, thick-glass bottles you don't see anymore. Don, the mason, leaned over with a pint in a brown sack and poured the half-empty bottle full. "Thanks," I said, wanting to seem grown-up. Don winked. I drank, felt a warmth. Don took a pull from his pint and exhaled loudly.

"You hear about those two ol' boys who went fishin'?" he said.

I shook my head.

"Well, they're on their way to the river, you know, when they spot this snake with a mouse in his jaws, and the mouse is still alive. 'Pour a drop of whiskey in that snake's mouth,' says one of 'em. 'It'll burn him, maybe he'll let go.' Well, they try it and damned if it don't work. The mouse staggers off, just a little bloody, and those boys go on down to the river and get a fire goin'. They get their lines in the water, they're sit-tin' all comfortable, tellin' stories, drinkin' whiskey, and one of 'em feels a bump on his back. He turns around, and what do you think he sees?"

"What *does* he see?"

"Why, it's that snake again, and damned if he ain't got him another mouse!"

For the rest of the ride I was glowing, my weariness and self-pity gone. Everything was perfect. I was succeeding in the best-paid job of my life, had the liking of the masons, had in my shirt pocket a fat brown envelope full of folded money, would be going with friends to the horse races at Charles Town that night, was soaringly high and laved in warm wind in the back of a pickup whizzing down River Road past my high school—ha!—toward home. The word "drunk" did not occur to me. Neither did the word "ecstatic," but ecstatic is what I was.

I've wondered, often, when and how my father started. He did not come from a bibulous family. In Grosspapa's house, my Aunt Berthe once told me, drinking was a concise evening ritual. When the harnessmaker came home from his shop, smelling of saddlesoap and leather, Grossmama produced a whiskey bottle and poured him a short jigger. Grosspapa studied the spirit, took it in tiny sips, and held out the empty glass.

"Another drop, Mama?"

"No, Papa, not another drop."

So it went for six decades. She kept the bottle in the clothes hamper, which of course Grosspapa knew.

George Daniel, my father's father, evidently drank little or not at all. After his death, as my father hit his high school years, his sisters Margaret and Georgia heard rumors that away from home he was "wild." His childhood shyness outgrown, he ran with older friends, the college fraternity crowd. (He was attending a special high school at Southwest Missouri State College.) He bought fine clothes, despite the family's limited means. Margaret recalled him coming home from his summer job at the Frisco railroad shops black from his shoes to the top of his greasy head. Their mother—"Mama" to all her offspring—would have a bath drawn, and an hour later young Franz would go out on the town with his frat-rat pals looking like the son of a banker.

Margaret never saw her brother drunk at home, but surely he was drinking, likely drinking a lot. He had large sorrows that he couldn't well express, responsibilities from which he must have cherished intervals of glad release. He moved in a social set in which drinking was axiomatic. That he took his first tastes in the early years of Prohibition must have made them all the sweeter, a reliable response of the young psyche that lawmakers still don't fully appreciate. If my father wanted a drink while in school in Madison or New York City, drink was available, and there's no question that he wanted it. He took Margaret to her first speakeasy in New York. Phil Van Gelder, an organizer who knew my father from the Philadelphia years on, remembers him ordering over the phone "a pair of overalls"—code for a bottle of bad gin. My father kept himself and those around him well fitted out with overalls. On the day Prohibition ended in 1933 he appeared on the Van Gelders' doorstep with a case of beer on his shoulder and a large grin on his face.

As his sense of vocation bloomed in the 1930s, as the labor movement became the most vital progressive force in American society, my father became an enthusiast, a fiery believer. By then, I have a feeling, he drank not only to drown sorrows. By then he was aiming as a monk might aim, to magnify the presence of his belief and hunger. He was drinking to join Beethoven and Verdi, to touch his own burning ideal of a better world. He was drinking because he loved to drink.

Little belief or hunger was left in him by the time he cracked up. To me at the time, he was simply my father, an old story, a man who drank too much and had gotten in trouble with his jerk bosses. Now, looking at a letter he wrote from George Washington Hospital to Newman Jeffrey, his most trusted friend, I have a glimpse of how it felt to be him: "I've been in the grip of as foul and deep a depression as is possible to imagine. The past six months have been sheer hell with sleeplessness, panic, night walks until exhaustion, booze as anaesthesia, anger, self-pity, worry over the boys, distress over the scattering of my possessions. . . ." His longtime doctor, together with the George Washington chief of psychiatry, convinced him, he wrote his friend, "that I can't rehabilitate myself on a do it yourself basis. They state very bluntly that if I go back to a lonely hotel room and start midnight walks again I'll end up in a half-gainer off a bridge."

And so he was amenable to Menninger's. And while he was drying out and getting himself together there, I was becoming a regular and enthusiastic weekend drinker. In D.C. then you could drink beer and wine at eighteen. I was sixteen, but my brother, having lost his wallet and found it a few weeks later, had a spare driver's license and draft card which he generously bestowed on me. I liked the glow that gathered with a couple of pitchers of beer with friends—the easiness, the ready talk, the way things seemed warm and happy. I was a rather reticent, self-enclosed youth. Drinking opened me up, just as, I'm sure, it opened my father. It probably made me more interesting to my friends. Maybe it made my friends more interesting to me.

I sometimes failed to stop short of that fateful whirlpool of nausea that would toss me out only after I had tossed up the contents of my stomach, and I didn't learn or even try to learn to stay out from behind the steering wheel. Horsing around one night with a friend in another car, I got the jump on him at a stop sign and pulled straight into the path of a car going fifty miles an hour. Nobody was hurt, amazingly, but I had totaled my mother's prized black Studebaker wagon. Her response—she didn't know I'd been drinking—was remarkably tolerant and sensible. She bought cheaper and sturdier cars.

In my senior year we had a tanklike 1960 Jeep wagon, excellent for getting to our cabin in winter as well as for surviving the random collisions of adolescence. Driving with a friend late one night in the wilderness of the greater Maryland suburbs, both of us well-tuned, I took a curve a little wide, saw the rear of a parked car looming, and found it inconvenient to redirect the Jeep. No problem. The Jeep's prodigious front bumper crunched the car forward a few feet, I quickly backed up and peeled out, and my friend and I were laughing safely away before the poor householder had even had a chance to properly wake up. When on similar excursions it seemed necessary to turn around, I sometimes took the cross-country route, swerving over the curb onto somebody's lawn and looping back into the road headed the other way. The Jeep performed this maneuver with unfailing traction, even in the wettest and sloppiest conditions, when it was unfortunately necessary to leave major ruts in the lawn.

It's hard to reconcile that errant vandal with the author of the letters I wrote my father while he was at Menninger's. My mother and brother and I had moved from Glen Echo to an apartment in Northwest Washington. My mother had obtained, or would shortly, not a divorce but a legal separation. (She didn't want to remarry and had never been after support, only freedom.) I had left my public high school in Maryland for a progressive private school in D.C. where classes were small, blue jeans were allowed, and we called our teachers by their first names. I loved it. My letters to my father are windy with talk of grades and

SAT scores, college possibilities, and many not-very-considered opinions on Shakespeare and Shaw, the Russian Revolution, the civil rights situation in America, even Henry David Thoreau, whom I didn't like: "He seems to be an egotistic, loquacious, romantic transcendentalist who wanted something to write a book about so he lived in the woods for 2 years . . . Henry David says early in the book that the old have very little to teach the young, and as far as I can see Henry David has little to teach me."

Spoken like a child of the 1960s. Thoreau had been only in his twenties when he went to Walden Pond, but even the young rebels of the past were way too old for me.

My father's letters to me, as always, were about politics, sports, the weather, and his physical activities. He seemed to be thriving. He split firewood every morning in ten-degree cold, worked out on a stationary bike, spent a lot of time in the woodshop making church furniture and pieces for his sisters' households, attended classes, answered the avalanche of cards and letters of well-wishing he received, and was doing some reading on the history of the Kansas-Missouri border disputes. (He was wryly aware of the irony of a Missourian being institutionalized in the midst of the damn Jayhawkers.) He saw a therapist daily, but that he wrote about to no one.

It's interesting, but maybe shouldn't be surprising, that the man who was so chronically concerned about order and discipline in the lives of his sons was himself the one who most needed order and discipline, whose sense of self depended on tasks, obligations, reliable routines. When he had those, the demons that plagued him during his insomniac walks were vanquished, or at least held fast in a closet. It's also interesting that nowhere in the scores of condolent and encouraging messages he received, and nowhere in his responses that I've found, do the words "alcoholism" or "alcoholic" appear. Surely they were spoken in his therapy sessions, but they aren't in his discourse with the world or the world's with him. The realization that he couldn't pull off a do-it-yourself rehabilitation was a milestone, but the pink elephant in the living room still had not been named.

After two months at Menninger's, in the best physical and emotional condition he'd known for many years—though his liver, he wrote Newman Jeffrey, looked "like an old shoe on a riverbank"—my father went to live with three of his sisters in Springfield, Missouri, where he had done most of his growing up. Berthe, Frances, and Josephine, none of whom had married, had retired or partly retired from their careers and set up housekeeping together. They were eager for their brother to join them. The Industrial Union Department, which had footed the no doubt immense George Washington and Menninger's bills, now created a light-duty position for my father to get him to his retirement four years off. He would consult as needed on Missouri labor actions and do some traveling, not a lot, to western states. Scorned and discarded by the AFL elite, he was treated with vast generosity by what survived of the CIO in the no longer promising new age of the American labor movement.

In D.C. I cruised through my last year of high school, pleasing my teachers, genuinely excited and drawn out by a few of them. I felt myself gravitating toward literature—and, I hoped, writing. I was reading Hemingway, Steinbeck, Thomas Wolfe, Jack Kerouac, full of raptures about the tragic beauty of life and the unfound soul of America. I yearned for travel, adventure. Turned down by Harvard, accepted by Wesleyan, Cornell, and Reed College in Oregon, I had already made my choice. I would be lighting out for the territories, for a state whose name had always entranced me, for mountains and forests and seacoast I had never seen, for wherever and whatever my life was supposed to be.

My father came late to my graduation, missing my valedictory address. He'd been drinking. It was awkward introducing him to my friends and teachers, but I almost didn't care. I was ready to go out drinking myself, with my friends, and I knew I wouldn't have to deal with my father much longer. That was my other reason for choosing Reed. I wanted to leave my split-up parents and their intractable problems far behind.

My final spring in the East had two emblematic moments. The first announced itself one afternoon in May when I found on the doormat a telegram from President Lyndon Baines Johnson declaring me a Presidential Scholar for 1966. This meant attending a ceremony on the White House lawn with a hundred-and-some co-scholars from around the country, a few mumbled words from the president as he handed me a medallion (*What enormous ears,* was all I could think, but Lady Bird was lovely), and a reception with notables such as Edward Albee, Stephen Spender, and Buckminster Fuller—none of whom, sadly, I was capable of conversing with—and Bill Russell and Stan Musial, with whom I did better. It was an exhilarating whirl, a sign, I assumed, of more to come as I rode the escalator of my education into college and beyond.

It turned out to be a sign not of the future but of the past—the payoff, at better than union scale, for my twelve years of lunch-bucket labor in the schools. The sign of the future, the experience that will always mark the beginning of my 1960s, was exhilarating in a different way.

I was drinking beer with my friend and schoolmate Charley Phillips at his mother's townhouse in Georgetown. Charley was a painter, on his way to the San Francisco Art Institute in the fall. He had an interesting, uneasy mind, and one of the things he was uneasy about was his family's money. As we drank and talked he kept looking at a clutch of things his mother had had him assemble for charity—clothing, a couple of small furniture pieces, a color television.

"It's evil," Charley said.

"What's evil?"

"It's like giving them . . . *tuberculosis,*" he said. "I won't do it."

"Somebody can use that stuff," I offered, imaginatively.

"It'll use *them,*" Charley said. "You turn it on and you get toothpaste ads. You get Art Linkletter. You get the fucking war."

I liked his drift. We developed our cultural critique through several more beers, and when Charley stood up, I stood with him. It was obviously a moral imperative for him, and I was his friend. We picked up the TV, a big, boxy set, and carried it to the door to the basement.

"This'll be great," said Charley, and it was. The TV tumbled beautifully, corner over corner down the wooden stairs, going airborne at the last and exploding with a huge gassy boom on the basement floor.

January 15

Almost two months here, and I think I'm on to something. In my morning reading, I came upon Shunryu Suzuki saying this: "Whether you have difficulties in your practice or not, as long as you continue it, you have pure practice in its true sense. Even when you are not aware of it, you have it. So Dogen-zenji said, 'Do not think you will necessarily be aware of your own enlightenment.'"

And here I'd thought that awareness was the whole point! Evidently, that view was unenlightened. It's entirely plausible, according to two Zen masters, that I'm already enlightened. (I'm just the type who wouldn't know it.) I've decided to try out this theory, to live as though I already know everything I need to know. If it pans out, it's revolutionary. It means there's nothing I have to break through to. I'm already there.

I've been observing myself today, and so far the theory holds up. It's beyond dispute that I know how to get out of bed when I'm ready. I know how to put the kettle on, how to spoon coffee beans into the little German grinder, how to crank the handle while standing on the deck looking out on my bright or sodden domain, how to come inside and tell the whistling kettle to be patient as I place a filter in the cone and tap the ground coffee into the filter and place the cone on the thermos pitcher, then pour in the murmuring water from the kettle and smell the good black smell. I know how to half-listen to the coffee drip as I prepare my pan of oats, which I also know how to do. I even know something that I don't need to know—that in his *Dictionary*, Samuel Johnson defined "oats" as a grain given to horses in England and to people in Scotland. This doesn't hamper what I need to know. It only sweetens the porridge a little, like the brown sugar I know how to sprinkle on before I pour the milk.

This may seem a slight, even paltry realization to have attained two months into a solitary retreat, but listen, it's not a buyer's market in realizations around here. This is the one that showed up. Lately I've been mucking around in the Great Dismal Swamp of all that I don't know and do need to know. How to balance my life in the way of those men I admire. How to meditate. How to be less bristly, more emotionally supple with my wife, my friends. How to rid myself of unworthy feelings. How to love, how to be loved.

Whoa, I said this morning, after reading Suzuki-roshi. Why do I keep slogging through this morass? I'm here to *simplify,* for gosh sakes. Henry Thoreau's stated aim, in *Walden,* was to work and wedge his feet down through the shams and appearances of human society to bedrock he could stand on, and he invited his readers along. Fair enough. I'm feeling around through the muck of what I don't know for the sure footing of what I do. I'm upright, so I must be standing on something.

This notion has also been affirmed by the ants and the grouse. I was in the bathroom, on my usual seat, when I noticed a single ant stranded in the bathtub. He wandered, hesitance in every move. Two or three six-legged steps, then a pause. A part-turn left, a few steps right, pause. His two feelers working, scanning, seeking. Over the course of a few minutes he described several erratic circles, crossing his earlier path many times. His behavior showed nothing of the purposeful vigor of the colony of ants I watched a few days ago, as they worked a bonanza of sweet spillings on the kitchen counter. Those ants hurried to and fro along a ten-foot trail hot with pheromones, their only hesitation a brief pause when two met head to head and touched feelers—*yeah, yeah, this is the way!*

Those ants knew everything they needed to know. (All right. They didn't know that I eventually substituted a sweet poison for the counter spillings, but that knowledge would only have distracted them.) The poor lonely ant wandering the white Sahara of my bathtub, on the other hand, needed to know much more. He was desperate for a whiff of something familiar, something *ant.* There was no wholeness to his solitude. It occurred to me—again, realizations are in short supply—that I was not that ant, and that thought was modestly but genuinely comforting.

The grouse, to all appearances, have taught me that I don't know how to hunt grouse. There is strong evidence for this conclusion. I haven't one grouse to show for my hunting. Why keep trying? Well, I like the alertness, the walking up the road carefully, listening and watching. It's different from just walking up the road. And I've noticed some things. A nervous grouse will sometimes hop up into a tree with a brief flutter of wings. So will a varied thrush, and you can hear the difference. The thrush's flutter is lighter, more subtle. A grouse will feed on madrone berries, I've noticed, and will do so for an hour while thirty feet below, on the ground, a man is making a fearful racket splitting firewood. I could have fetched the shotgun and bagged that grouse, but that would have been something less than hunting—discourteous, too, to blast a bird in your own dooryard.

It amazed me that a normally nervous bird would feed at such length in such repose. Then, reading in *Northwest Trees*, I learned that madrone berries are reputed to have narcotic properties. Ha! Since then I've paid closer attention to madrones, looking for the berries that might mean seriously addicted game birds in the neighborhood—or, failing that, I could eat the berries myself and quit worrying about grouse. Very few madrones, it turns out, have berries, and those that do have them high off the ground, which is probably just as well.

I did get off a shot at one grouse—well behind him, the recoil leaving a bruise on my right bicep, which is as close to my shoulder as the stock of the gun got—and followed him into the woods. (I've noticed that a flushed grouse, though he goes in a storm of wings, often doesn't go far.) He didn't show himself a second time. That particular patch of woods I had never tramped in, so I kept going, contouring along the slope, then turned uphill where it steepened below. After a time I came upon a happy surprise, the biggest sugar pine I've seen around here. Its purplish-barked trunk, clear and near-perfectly columnar to a great height, was over five feet thick and might have been six.

That got me thinking that maybe I know how to hunt after all; I just shouldn't prejudge what it is I am hunting. Another day in the same vicinity, I followed no doubt the same grouse again—a real thrill seeker—down the slope this time, lost him, and kept working my way down on deer trails through lovely woods. I happened upon a grassy glade, a moist pocket of the mountainside with a big oak snag, a place I'll visit again in the spring for wildflowers. Long past thought of grouse, the gun on my shoulder, I meandered on down, the going easy, and came out on the river trail well downstream from the places I've fished. Hiking homeward I admired the river's stately, deep green pools, the current moving at about the pace of a man walking. Six mergansers were drifting one of the pools, the females with their russet heads, the males' green.

I woke next morning with those deep green pools on my mind. I had a feeling. I packed a lunch, grabbed my fishing pole, and headed down the trail. I fished the first pool from a rock shelf at water level and quickly hooked three half-pounders, landing one. I cast my copper spoon cross-river, let it swing downstream near bottom with the current, and had started to retrieve when it stopped, the rod arced, and line stripped off the reel against the drag. "This is a bigger fish," I said aloud, calmly and not calmly at all. He made three work-horse runs, staying deep, letting me win some line back between runs. I sensed Brother Frank hovering behind me, eyebrows bristling. Little by little I gained on the fish, or in any case he consented to come closer, then suddenly he dove straight down, screeching the drag. I got the line back and began to wonder how to land him. I worked to my left, toward a little sand beach, the fish generally cooperating.

As he loomed into view, a vague husky torpedo, I must have loomed into his view. He dove again, down where the river undercuts the rock shelf where I'd been standing, raking the monofilament line against the rock. I quickstepped back to my original position, reaching out with the rod to clear the line. We did the same dance three times, me suggesting the beach, him bolting deep, me running after him saying, "Okay, okay." The fourth time I got him near the beach he looked done, slowly fanning in the shallows at my feet. I saw the spots on his long green back, his hooded eyes. He looked all of thirty inches long. All I could think to do was dredge him partway onto the beach and grab him by the tail or gill. As I applied a little more pressure he found one more flurry, a great head-shaking thrash, and the copper spoon popped a couple of feet into the air and landed—*tink*—on a rock. The steelhead hovered a moment in the shallows and was gone in the deep green river.

I dropped to my knees, which weren't holding me up very well. I felt wronged, like a child. Then I felt something else, which I slowly recognized as gratitude. If I had landed that great fish, if I had touched him, I probably would have kept him, and that would have been the wrong end to the story. I closed my eyes and saw again his dark spotted back, his last churning refusal to leave the river, and I thanked him for the privilege. I had every pleasure of him but possession. That evening, as I smoke-grilled two smaller steelhead on the deck, I listened to the river's steady whispering rush. The fish I had hooked belonged to what I heard, and just knowing that was plenty.

January 18

At Reed College I learned very quickly that I didn't know nearly enough. I learned, first, that every student there was as smart as I was, and quite a few seemed smarter. I had always been singled out by my teachers; now I was in classes with peers who sounded like teachers themselves. Reed demanded that I work and think, which I could do, but I was better at playing smart and accepting praise. I responded by shutting up in class, reading hard, trying to write good papers—which had always been my strength—and wondering if something was wrong with me.

I learned, second, that something *was* wrong with me, something big—I had lived eighteen years without knowing who I was and without seeing the world I walked in. I learned this not by reading or attending class but by swallowing a tablet of LSD. Much about the experience was wonderful. The lawns and trees of the Reed campus glowed, as if fired by their own inner light, and the same light glowed in me as love and wonder toward the world. My entire body felt flooded with consciousness, and whatever consciousness was, I knew I was experiencing its wholeness for the first time. I walked along the wooded stream course Reedies call the Canyon as if in Eden, the sweetly tuneful songs of birds resounding through the forest's lit green canopy. Every tree, every leaf, seemed entirely, inevitably its own perfect self.

But what am *I*, I kept wondering, or someone kept wondering. A shadow of fear rose with the question, and I decided I'd better find the answer. I lay down on a patch of grass, shut my eyes, and was in trouble right away. Whatever I was was drifting indistinctly through an expanse as vast as time or timelessness itself. *I'm a student at Reed College*, a voice claimed. *I drove here in my mother's Jeep . . .* And I knew I was, I had, but I was ridiculously more than that. The voice spoke for a small boat, but I was the ocean too, the drifting, swelling ocean that swallowed my chatter and drifted on, as if to say, *Think again, sonny.* I was going nowhere, literally. I opened my eyes, saw trees and sky, with relief this time more than awe. From that moment I was coming down, and glad of it.

But like many of my dorm-mates and other Reedies, like a lot of students across America in that time, I would return with some regularity to that transcendent world I had stumbled into, that world exactly coincident with the ordinary world and immeasurably different. How could I stay away, knowing it was there? My fears lived there but so did beauty, a splendor in all things, a sense of truth such as I had never known. Something had loosened inside me, some small current had begun to trickle over dry stones. I felt as though I'd spent my life in a house of words and taken the house for reality, had scarcely taken a step in the true universe outside. How could I have made that mistake? From going to school, of course. That's what kids did, that was the system. When I asked myself why I was in college, the reasons I could locate all had to do with the desires and expectations of others—my father, my mother, my aunts, my teachers in high school. I could find no reason native to myself. I would last three semesters at Reed College, but my destiny was probably sealed—well before Timothy Leary came to campus with his famous incantation, "Turn on . . . . . . tune in . . . . . . *drop out*"—when I took that first tiny tablet of LSD (made by the renowned chemist Owsley Stanley III), washing it down with a glug of grapefruit juice.

The other big news of that first fall at college came from my mother back east. My father had fallen apart again, this time in Farmington, New Mexico, where the Industrial Union Department had sent him to boost a drive to organize oil workers in the San Juan Basin. I had stopped in Springfield in late August on my way west, and my father and I had driven on in the Jeep to Farmington. He drank beer in the motels at night, not a lot, and maybe a bourbon or two at dinner. Over the weeks in Farmington, evidently, he had drunk himself into a belligerent delirium, at one point wandering into the hotel lobby in his undershorts, wrestling with his demons. He was taken, maybe forcibly, to a detox and rehab center near Albuquerque called Turquoise Lodge.

I wrote him a letter while he was there. I've remembered it as little more than a perfunctory get-well-soon message, but I've got a copy of it in front of me, and I put more into it than that. I address him directly, tell him my unwavering respect, and express an understanding I didn't know I had back then: "I know it isn't that simple, Franz, but if you could just believe in yourself a little more, believe in Franz Daniel, what he is and what he can be, believe in yourself as a human being who never stops growing, never stops becoming until he dies—I may be totally blind in saying this, but do remember that I only say it because I love you so very, very much."

I'm glad my father saved that letter, glad it ended up in his collected papers at the Reuther Library in Detroit, where I came across it thirty years later. To my memory, I never told him to his face that I loved him. I'm glad I at least wrote it, at a time when maybe it helped. And I could be wrong, but I don't think I would have written as openly and directly as I did if I hadn't melted open the vault of my feelings by taking LSD.

My father must have been on my mind that fall, but I don't remember thinking much about him. I was dealing with a new world, stranger and more alluring than I could have imagined, and onward, not back to my past, was where I wanted to go. In 1966 and '67, onward usually meant San Francisco, where the full lush flower of Haight-Ashbury was opening. My new friends and I were drawn like butterflies. Nobody else had a car, and so my Jeep, with its leaks and rattles and incurable electrical system, became our San Francisco shuttle. It held, somehow, up to ten. My name for it had been Cayetano, an unlucky but noble gambler who survives much pain in one of Hemingway's stories. One sunny day outside the old dorm block, several of us painted elaborate red designs on its venerable blue and white body and rechristened it, at someone's suggestion, "The Envy of Sisyphus," because it sometimes started without a push.

In the City we joined the dancing swarms at Winterland and the Fillmore, where Janis Joplin and Jefferson Airplane and the Grateful Dead pierced us through with their long, bending, amped-up licks, sprays of colored light pulsing on the walls as the entire hall stopped and started, froze and flowed in the strobe light's quick blue flicker. Afterward we would wander the city for most of the night, stoned and careless of where we adventured, escaping muggings and worse, no doubt, sheerly by the spell of our blithe innocence. We crashed, when we were ready, on the floor of an O'Farrell Street flat rented by a girl my brother had known in Maryland who had once dated Bob Dylan, and there we laughed and talked in our sleeping bags, comparing the shimmering dope-displays we imagined in the warm enclosing dark.

In the spring of 1967, at the end of my freshman year, I hitchhiked to San Francisco (the Jeep in need of a generator) to look for a summer job. The Beatles' *Sergeant Pepper* album had just come out. With a friend named Evans, who lived at the O'Farrell flat, I went to buy it at Tower Records on Columbus. The two of us hopped on the cable car and absorbed ourselves in the oddball crowd of faces looking out from the album's front cover—Dylan, Karl Marx, Mae West, Paramahansa Yogananda, Sonny Liston, Shirley Temple, C. G. Jung, Marlon Brando, Oscar Wilde, Johnny Weismuller as Tarzan, Mozart, Marlene Dietricht, Edgar Allan Poe, and all the others we didn't know. Inside—it's the open-up kind of album—was one big photo of the four bandmasters themselves in gaudy uniforms against a bright yellow field, intrigues of kindness in their eyes, John Lennon with daisies in his right epaulet. At some point Evans and I hooked arms. As he held fast to the lurching cable car I leaned out as far as I could, snapping the album open in the faces of startled pedestrians until the gripman made us quit. "Here's the news!" we hollered. "Lucy in the Sky with Diamonds!"

At the end of that summer, staying a few days with my father in Springfield, I played *Sergeant Pepper* over and over on the stereo. My father would sit down and listen to parts of it, pulling on his cigarette, frowning. "I don't see what they're trying to get at," he'd say.

"Beats me," I'd reply, and go on listening. It wasn't about explanation. It was what the album *was*, not what it meant. Something in the music of that time, something in the smiles between strangers in the bright windy streets, the spontaneous kindnesses, the beards and long loose dresses and flowing hair, something was abroad that felt to me and I think to many like a magical secret we carried without quite knowing what it was, only that it was new and luminous and alive. It feels ludicrous to say it now, the sixties having been so thoroughly reabsorbed into the culture they bubbled from, but a lot of us back then believed that human society was changing in a sudden, profound, and irreversible way. For many it had to do with politics, but my sense of it was much more Romantic. It was a spirit, a sense of mystery, the glint of beauty and possibility everywhere.

Part of it was just being that age, I suppose. All adolescents on their way to adulthood, especially those like me who take the long route, charge and color their world with an energy that to each generation must feel unique. Part of it, for me, was being an eastern kid on the fabled West Coast, the coast of Kerouac and Snyder, of Robinson Jeffers and Kenneth Rexroth, of the new Oregon novelist Ken Kesey, of Big Sur and Mendocino, of City Lights Books and the Golden Gate Bridge. Part of it, for sure, was the dope and acid and other drugs. And part of it—part of it was the way amazing things just happened.

I remember a St. Cecilia's Day festival at Reed in the spring of my freshman year, a sun celebration after the long gray winter of rain. Games and dancing, frisbees, general cavorting, students and dogs and a few professors milling around, wafts of dope smoke in the air. Big speakers had been set up on the deck of the Old Commons, and the music I remember was Country Joe and the Fish—"Section 43," that psychedelic anthem of guitar and organ and amplified harmonica that leaps, without words, between raucous comedy and ecstatic majestic intensity. I noticed at some point that a pickup had backed under a tree across the lawn and some older Reedies were unloading a bathtub. A bathtub, of course. With the tub on the ground they took watermelons from the truck, dozens of melons, raised them high overhead and smashed them into the tub. My friends and I started over. A guy in a purple t-shirt was pouring liquor into the tub, an upended bottle in each hand, then two more bottles, then more.

A crowd was forming, shouts and laughter. By the time I had pressed in close and managed a glimpse over somebody's shoulder, a beautiful young woman was naked in the bathtub handing out cupfuls of nectar.

She was a student. I had seen her around. But this! She tossed her brown hair and smiled her joy, her breasts glazed with glistening pulp, the pink mash and hunks of green rind stirring around her as she dipped the cups and offered them, one knee bent and raised, her central darkness only a suggestion. I was a sexual innocent, the veteran of a few inept high school dates. I was afraid almost to approach her when my turn came. I found myself dropping to one knee as I took the cup. She smiled at me—kindly, serenely confident, the only goddess I have ever seen. I could hold her gaze only a moment. I heard the music again, soaring exultantly, as I walked away.

Whatever sum of money my parents had to pay for my brief sojourn at Reed College, to drink from that cup was worth it. That cup was news to me.

January 20

Tonight I've uncapped a memento of my father—a bottle of Jim Beam, his brand of bourbon. It's a decent whiskey, nothing special. My own taste runs to more flavorful, more expensive spirits, which to my father would have smacked of snobbery. He was not a pretentious man and had no tolerance for pretension in others, and of course it wouldn't have done for a union agitator to drink fancy booze. It also mattered to him, I'm sure, that his staple drink was inexpensive. Buying a bottle had to have been a conflicted experience for my father. He knew what whiskey could do to him. He didn't need the additional guilt he'd get from lavishing money on high-price hooch.

If he knew what it could do to him, what it had done and surely would do again, why did he keep buying it and drinking it? That was my question as a kid, when I thought about it, and it's a fair question now. After his first breakdown, in 1939, my father should have known everything he needed to know about Franz Daniel and liquor. But he was still a young man then, only thirty-five, with a tolerance for alcohol almost commensurate with his desire for it. What he did, I think, was make an adjustment. He found the limited discipline to go ahead and drink but to stop himself short of dissolution. The responsibility of raising children probably helped him stick to his adjustment, and it worked, more or less, for fifteen years, until his marriage and career hit their troubles. Those he couldn't adjust to except to drink more, and his hard-used body by then was no longer young.

But after the debacle of 1964–65, after Menninger's, after coming so thoroughly undone, he still wasn't ready to quit. I marvel at that. It speaks to the power of alcoholic addiction, but it won't do to gloss my father's story purely as that of an alcoholic or an addictive personality, though surely he was both. Every alcoholic is an individual. He finds his own way to addiction, his own ways of staying addicted, and—if the story ends right—his own way of breaking free.

My father had many gifts. Looks, magnetism, intelligence, cultivation, enthusiasm, conscience, courage, commitment, the power to move people through the spoken word. He projected an aura of confident strength, but he lacked, I think, what I pointed to in my letter from Reed in the fall of sixty-six—confidence in himself. He needed the trust and admiration he so consistently inspired in those around him because he had little of either for himself. And especially he needed the support and praises of his bosses and mentors in the labor movement. Because they believed in him, he could believe in himself. With the merger of the AFL and CIO, for the first time he had a manager who didn't treat him like a star and wouldn't make allowances for his great flaw. It may have been this, more than his personal and political differences with George Meany, that caused him to handle the Los Angeles–Orange County role so poorly and to self-destruct. In the new regime of united labor, his insecurities at last got the best of him.

At the same time his wife, who had made allowances for many years, came to her own limit and would make them no longer. To my father it must have seemed, if he rationalized it at all, that Jim Beam was the only support left. It had been, in its way, an unfailing friend. It had never abandoned him.

My mother, who knew him best and never lost her love for him, told me in our recorded interview, "His spirit was strong within him, but his ego was very frail. So many things *hurt* him." He parlayed this vulnerability, repeatedly rebuffing my mother's concerns and desires by telling her to take it easy, he was going through a bad time just then. He used that tactic on his sisters, too, forcing them to tiptoe around his sensitivities, but for all that, his vulnerability was very real.

I was twelve the first time I was aware of hurting him myself. It was in the Glen Echo house, a period when he and my mother had been fighting for years. When divorce had first come up I had begged them to stay together. Now, a little older and a budding young rationalist reformer, I went to my father one evening on the screened porch and said, "Franz, since you and Zilla aren't getting along, do you think maybe you shouldn't be married anymore?"

I saw right away that I'd goofed. He was taken aback, the contours of injury forming in his face. He stammered, as I remember, and spoke in a formal tone: "Well, Johnny, it's . . . it's a complicated thing, you see. When two people marry, and then the children come . . ."

I took the earliest opportunity to go upstairs and put both of us out of our misery. This was during the time my mother was pushing for a divorce, and it occurs to me now that he may have thought my mother had put me up to it. She hadn't. It was my own little brainstorm—and took, it also occurs to me, a degree of courage to carry out. It hadn't dawned on me that my suggestion might hurt my father.

I wonder sometimes how much he knew of what Jim and I knew. Maybe he assumed we slept through their fights. Maybe, when he was good and drunk, it didn't occur to him that slamming doors and banging tables and shouting to raise the dead might raise the kids in their rooms upstairs. During his spells of heaviest drinking, there must have been nights and days he remembered sketchily or not at all.

I suppose most alcoholics are frail of ego and easily injurable to begin with, and prolonged drinking makes them more so. The medicine aggravates the illness it balms. I think this thought as I pour a third shot of my father's whiskey, which is tasting better. Perhaps it needed to breathe?

He would have cast a cold eye on this particular line of research, but I'm trying every approach. He's a hard man to know. Over the last few years I've tracked down and picked the ailing memories of his labor movement friends and associates. I've been too late for some. I interrogated Aunt Margaret, the last of my father's generation, all through the 1990s, and was visiting her with further questions in 1997 when she fell ill and died at eighty-nine. I've interviewed my brother and mother and cousins. I've leafed and scanned and pored through scores of boxes of correspondence and other papers at the Reuther Library in Detroit and the George Meany archive in Washington. I've gone through my own boxes of letters and clippings again and again, and I've rubbed and scratched and prodded my own memory.

This will be the stiffest test of my new philosophy of sufficiency. What I've got is probably all I will know of my father. Can I call it enough?

Once, just once, I'd like to have gotten thoroughly drunk with him, sailed round the horn of midnight in his company, all sheets to the wind. I'd like to have known the man his friends knew in his prime. Boo Herndon, a journalist and one of my father's best buddies, told me that during my parents' years in New Orleans in the early forties my father would sometimes barbecue a suckling pig or haunch of beef in the court-yard of their French Quarter apartment building. The party would steam all night, music playing on a small hi-fi on a long extension cord with the volume topped out. The records, 78s, needed a lot of changing and turning over to get through a symphony or concerto. One night, Boo remembered, as one of the revelers went to the hi-fi to continue the playing of Beethoven's *Eroica*, my father, basting the roast, interrupted the story he was telling and bellowed, "On your knees, you son of a bitch! That's *God* talkin'!"

Who has that spirit, that enthusiasm? Not me, very often, and not my friends. My father needed liquor to set his spirit loose, but in that he was merely human. Most of us need something. I've appreciated from the beginning that the Brothers affirm strong drink as a sacrament of their faith. They hold long and not at all solemn symposia on the sub-ject. The word "whiskey," they teach, derives from the ancient Gaelic word for "water of life." They point out that "spirit" means distilled liquor as well as the breath indwelling in all things. To take spirits is to be inspired, *inspirited,* and to be inspirited is to achieve the sacred state of *enthusiasm,* for enthusiasm means—literally, *en + theos*—to be filled with the god, or gods, or capital-G God, whichever the celebrant prefers.

Some believe that the Brothers' faith is a North American sprout-ing of a mysterious lineage of medieval rites that derived originally from the cult of Dionysus in ancient Greece. Any who have been around the Brothers, even briefly, find this entirely plausible. Dionysus was the last of the Greek gods to be elevated to the Olympic pantheon, taken in reluctantly and under protest simply because there was no denying him. He rode the populist surge of his reveling devotees, who wor-shipped him with wine, dancing, and ecstatic practices of the flesh. Great festivals were held for Dionysus, poems composed in his honor, and wherever he went he led a retinue of satyrs, maenads, and nymphs. In his sober hours he taught the arts of viniculture and winemaking throughout the Greek world. The grapevines growing in the garden here at the homestead are said to have descended from slips of the original Dionysian rootstock. The Brothers neither confirm nor deny this. The vines, they say, are like the Oregon faith. They are what they are. They speak for themselves.

The cult of Dionysus had its darknesses, of course. Any faith does. Spirited followers sometimes verged from ecstasy into violent excess, tearing fellow humans to pieces and devouring their flesh and blood. Dionysus himself was the only god susceptible to suffering, the only god whose limbs were hacked off like the cut-back grapevine, the only god who could die and rise again—like a Christ, like a hungover drunk taking hair of the dog, like a man who takes a shot in the chest and tells the tale over shots of bourbon, like a man brought low by his own excesses who stands, at last, on the bottom he has hit and makes himself anew near the end of his life.

A man I knew. And didn't know. I imagine us killing this bottle of Jim Beam tonight. I imagine my father talking, me asking questions. I imagine him telling story after story. Who knows, maybe he'd ask questions and I'd tell stories.

As a drinker I couldn't have kept up with him, and I don't intend to tonight. But I won't be driving anywhere (to be double-safe, I've confiscated the keys), I have nowhere I need to walk, I have no pressing engagements on the morrow except with this pencil and possibly with the river, and so I intend to pour one more. I do enjoy drink. I concur with the singer of the 104th Psalm, who in thanking the Lord for all blessings does not fail to thank Him for "wine that maketh glad the heart of man." Had the Psalmist been fortunate enough to have tasted good bourbon, single-malt Scotch, or Oregon beer, I'm confident he would have thanked the Lord for those blessings too. (I wonder how the Woman's Christian Temperance Union deals with that verse.)

Compared to my father's prodigious habit, and compared to my own debacle with drugs at the end of the 1960s, my drinking seems moderate. But I keep an eye on it. As my father's son, I'd be a damn fool not to. I was in my late twenties when I began to recognize him in me. I sit like him, elbows on knees. When I stand in place I rock on my feet like him. I write the cursive capital "F" the way he wrote it. I curse and brood like him when the wrong team wins. I barbecue a steak his way, slap the carving knife on the steel his way. Like him, I listen to conservative blowhards on the radio—his were fundamentalist preachers, mine are talk show hosts. I build a fire as he did, love the music he loved, and I too have trouble, sometimes, with self-confidence.

I do a lot of things like him, but I don't drink like him. I can stop.

January 22

It makes me smile, thinking about the 1960s here at my backwoods commune of one. I stayed briefly at a few communes in those years, declared and *de facto,* urban and rural. I never would have made it as a permanent resident. I'm too brittle, too jealous of my privacy. I need elbow room, mood room, and considerable quiet. I find, like Thoreau, that even the best company can soon become wearisome—not the persons themselves, but the ongoing need to converse, to respond, even to smile and laugh. I better appreciate, after nine weeks here, that to keep up a social face is an exertion for me. It's often worthwhile, an exertion with rewards, but it does take energy that I can gain back only in solitude. There are those who feel most themselves in the company of others, and there are those who feel most themselves alone. No mystery about this boy.

Most of us need some measure of both, but in our culture we tend heavily toward human company. Anthony Storr, in *Solitude: A Return to the Self,* raises an interesting point. Overwhelmingly, mental health professionals measure good health as the ability to form and sustain meaningful relationships with others. Fair enough. But why isn't it also measured as one's ability to spend satisfying time alone? The ability to form and maintain a meaningful relationship with oneself?

I wonder, watching kids at the mall or the movies, how much time they spend alone, and how much of that time amounts to real solitude. I've read that young people spend six hours a day involved with electronic media. Watching TV, playing with the computer, and talking on the telephone can be done alone but surely constitute something less than solitude. Plenty of adults too—many of them the parents of such children—seem rarely out of the company of others: coworkers, friends, spouse, lover, children, or the anonymous company of bar or health club or internet chat room. More and more of us go about our lives with a telephone in purse or pocket or a beeper on the belt, or both, making it still less possible to be alone—less possible, even, with call waiting, to speak merely with one person at a time. We all have our reasons, but surely much of our communicativity is a product of technological availability, and boredom, rather than real need. Addiction thrives in many forms, and not all of them involve the ingestion of a substance.

It pleases me, in my solitude, to imagine Marilyn in hers—in the rooms of our house, in the garden, meandering around the acre as she likes to do. She planned to use the opportunity of my absence to take a semi-retreat of her own, to socialize less, drop the satellite TV service, maybe stop the newspaper too. It'll be baseball season when I'm back home, so we may have to reassess the TV, but maybe I'll take strength from her example and do without. Like any marriage, ours is a region of varied weather, a tidal zone of ebb and flood, an equilibrium never perfected. Solitude, at home and apart, helps us appreciate what is most vital and valuable between us. It makes us wholer partners as well as wholer persons.

There have been moments here, stretches of a few hours, most of a day now and then, when I've been acutely lonely, and there will be others. There were such stretches when I was a kid, too. Sometimes I chose to be alone, but it was often because of shyness, social ineptitude, or an unwillingness or inability to express my wishes—or even to know what my wishes were. There was pain in that loneliness, but I know now that it wasn't a stunting or crippling pain. It contributed to whatever resources of attention, reflection, and creative association I now have, and my patches of loneliness here will do the same. "No man will ever unfold the capacities of his own intellect who does not at least checker his life with solitude," wrote Thomas De Quincey, but it's about much more than intellect. Solitude, says Thoreau, "deepens the stream of my life."

I'm realizing, though, that the kind of solitude Henry David meant is not realized merely by being alone. It's *how* you are alone. Solitude deepened the stream of his life because he was thoroughly and actively present in his aloneness. He attended to, and wrote into notebooks, all the particulars of landscape, weather, creatures, reading, and human society that interested him, which were many, and observed as closely and continually the inner weather of his own thoughts and feelings. The product was his *Journal*, a twenty-five-year, two-million-word chronicle of consciousness he called a "meteorological journal of the mind," from which he evolved *Walden* and his other books, and which itself stands as his greatest work, the record of a life lived as something close to a sustained meditation.

Needless to say, I'm not up to Henry's standard. I need lots of down time—crossword puzzles, reading I don't make notes on, fly-swatting expeditions, cocktail hour, aimless reveries. But I do want to be *here*, I want not to squander this retreat. If I'm sitting at the red-blanket table gazing out at the empty meadow wishing a critter would appear while chewing my lunch of kidney beans and chopped carrot in time to "I've Been Working on the Railroad" playing somewhere behind me, and with half an eye on the unfinished crossword on the table from break-fast, then my awareness is in four places, and since you can't be in more than one place in one moment, I'm nowhere. I'm alone in a backcoun-try cabin, but I'm not in solitude because I'm not whole. To be dis-tracted, I've learned from Thomas Merton, is to submit to a violence. The word means, literally, to be pulled apart.

Better, wholer, to consciously taste the beans and carrot (the olive oil, the cider vinegar, the salt, the pepper), to slow the overeager tempo of my chewing and let the railroad song fade into merciful quiet, to save the crossword for a time when I want to give it full attention—and if a cougar should bound into the meadow waving his tail, to trust that for-tune and my field of still very good vision will let me know. That's what my morning meditations and readings are teaching me. Do what you're doing, do that. As Thich Nhat Hanh said would happen, chores become less chorelike when done mindfully and wholeheartedly. I'm not up to his standard either—he cleans the teapot, he says, as if he were giving the baby Buddha or Jesus a bath—but I don't need to be. I'm a begin-ner. It's enough, instead of fighting the prospect of doing the laundry, and eventually doing it just to get it done, to *do the laundry*—run the hot water, heat more on the stove if there isn't enough, pour in the mirac-ulous slick blue liquid, heap in as many clothes as the utility sink will hold, and slosh and scrub and swirl them in a violent orgy, working up such a sweat I have to open all the windows to let in some forty-degree air. Yes! Then drain the filthy, sweet-smelling washwater. Slosh the load once in rinsewater, and once again, and if that water's still pretty gray? Don't cheat, rinse yet again.

Wringing is hard, especially jeans and sweatshirts, and especially with a sore little finger not keen on gripping, so let the load drain in the sink and take a breather. Forget laundry. Add a stanza of Emily Dickinson or Hugh McDiarmid to the memory hoard, or read out loud a few pages of *Walden*. (I bet Henry David took his duds home for Mom to wash. I know he went home for dinner a lot, though he won't tell you that in the book.)

Then wring, wring big time, wring for all you're worth with not an ounce of you not wringing—keep the windows open—and drop the twisted carcasses of your clothing one by one into the laundry basket. When they're all wrung out, or when you are, heft the laden basket ahead of you up the fold-down stairs, de-wring your pieces of apparel and hang them to dry. The clothespins are waiting on the lengths of white line you mounted on the rafters in December. When you return to the loft the next morning to sit *zazen*, your colorful, fragrant laundry will surround you like so many stiff-as-a-board prayer flags.

This way, this entry-level practice of meditation and mindfulness, lacks the drama and stunning efficiency of LSD. You don't swing for a home run, you just try to get on base, and when you fail, you try again. In its drudging working-class way, though, it aims as I was aiming in the sixties. To rouse myself from the sleep of distraction and habit to the presence of the extraordinary ordinary world. To release my mind from the bare room of its accustomed detachment. "To live deliberately, to front only the essential facts of life, and see if I could not learn what it had to teach, and not, when I came to die, discover that I had not lived."

It's not dramatic, but it just might be sustainable, if I have the discipline to keep it up when I'm back in the world. And it's honest. It does make me smile, watching myself thirty-five years ago. I don't regret taking psychedelic drugs. I'm glad I did. They helped me grow. But that central act by which I meant to declare independence from a soulless, materialistic society was an act entirely characteristic of that soulless, materialistic society.

Don't like the way you feel? Want to see things differently? Here, swallow this.

❦

I know nothing about the treatment my father received at Turquoise Lodge after his breakdown in New Mexico, but it seems that he gave himself to Alcoholics Anonymous while he was there. He didn't stay long, two weeks at the most. The week before Thanksgiving he was back home in Springfield, sober and attending AA meetings every day. When I stopped off to visit in January 1967, between semesters in my freshman year, he'd been sober for three months and seemed happier than I'd seen him in a long time. Beyond the meetings, he was on call to visit members who had slipped and wanted to get sober again. He called them "wandering brethren." "Drunks trying to fly right make for an interesting group of people," he told me. If the one I know is representative, I thought, I couldn't agree more.

The Industrial Union Department treated him with great consideration. His boss, Nick Zonarich, had been candid: they would help him if he would help himself. He was on the payroll and was told to stay in Springfield. They would call him when they needed him. "Nothing could be nicer," my father wrote Newman Jeffrey, "and it's a bit of a switch from the usual treatment doled out to the has-beens of the movement."

Later that winter my father wrote my brother that he was going to at least four AA meetings a week and leading a few of them. Consisting as they did of "drunkalogues without relief," the meetings tended to bore him. In the ones he led he was bringing in some historical and philosophical material. "Some of them don't like it but a lot of them do," he wrote. He was having an especially good time explicating his agnostic humanism for the many Bible Belters in the meetings. He even referred once to Karl Marx, eliciting a dead silence. "They think I'm a pretty far-out character," he crowed. "That's good for 'em."

Alcoholics Anonymous was founded in 1935—the birth year of the CIO, my father would have noticed—by a hard-drinking Wall Street finance man named Bill Wilson. Hospitalized in Manhattan for the fourth time, Wilson experienced a flash of spiritual light that led him to the understanding that only a power greater than himself could deliver him from his problem, and that the best way to stay sober was to help fellow alcoholics who also wanted to stay sober. Teaming with Robert Smith, an Ohio doctor—the two became enshrined in AA lore as Bill W. and Dr. Bob—Wilson evolved the twelve-step approach to recovery and launched, haltingly at first, a democratic, nonhierarchical support network one joins by attending regular local meetings of fellow alcoholics. The meetings are held in school gyms, church basements, and unassuming rented or donated storefronts in towns and cities everywhere. There are today an estimated two million AA participants worldwide, as well as an array of spin-off twelve-step programs addressing other addictions. It was largely the example of Alcoholics Anonymous that caused the American Medical Association to redefine alcoholism as a disease rather than a moral depravity or failure of willpower.

I don't know how my father settled to himself the third step of AA, which is to turn one's life over to the care of God as one understands him. "It's been many a year since I have done any serious thinking about God and my relationship to him," my father wrote my brother. "I am finding the going a bit rough. But this time I am determined to win through." He had not attended church or practiced a religious faith since leaving the seminary in 1930. Publicly, to the end of his life, he called himself an agnostic or sometimes an atheist. His eldest sister, Berthe, a believing Presbyterian, considered this a pose. I don't think it was, but it's perfectly possible that hitting bottom as an alcoholic may have stirred the old embers of his Christianity.

Or not. Bill Wilson's spirituality had a strong Christian tinge, but he and Dr. Bob crafted the twelve steps as deliberately noncoercive and nonsectarian. Wilson was reading C. G. Jung and William James when he received his hospital enlightenment, and in the 1950s he would become friends with Aldous Huxley and experiment with LSD to assess its usefulness in treating alcoholism. (He found the experience liberating and the therapeutic prospects bright.) His aim was never to save souls but to help earnest people get and stay sober. My father may have decided, as I believe many nonreligious AA members do, that a higher power was manifest in the group itself. This would have been natural for a man who all his life had invested his faith in the power of people pulling together. The first verse of "Solidarity Forever," the anthem of American labor, could with some minor rewording be a theme song for Alcoholics Anonymous. The tune is "The Battle Hymn of the Republic":

When the union's inspiration through the workers' blood shall run,
There can be no power greater anywhere beneath the sun.
What force on earth is weaker than the feeble strength of one?
But the Union makes us strong . . .

In the late summer of 1967 I stopped in Springfield on my way to Portland to begin my sophomore year, and my father took me to an open meeting. The first words from his mouth were a shock, a good shock: "My name is Franz, and I'm an alcoholic." I had never heard him speak the word. And the response! "Hi, Franz," from the group in unison, coffee cups in hand. My father leaned forward in his chair with the anticipatory light in his eyes that meant he was going to tell a story.

"Did you hear the town drunk died?" I think he began. "Nobody liked him much, but they couldn't just leave him in the ditch, so the fellows took up a collection. They bought a casket and dressed him in a new suit of clothes, a nice shirt and tie. The preacher stood by the open casket and said, 'Well, boys, I want you to notice something as you pass by and pay your respects. You knew Harry just like I did, and you never saw him sober either. See how much better old Harry looks since he's quit drinkin.'"

My father laughed his overflowing, tickled-at-existence laugh, and the group laughed with him. He had picked up the joke at another AA meeting. Most of the crowd had probably heard it before, but it didn't matter. It was my father's gift to make a story funny no matter how many times you had heard it.

Toward the end of the meeting the leader asked me if I would like to say something. I panicked, as if a teacher had caught me daydreaming in class. I forced out a few banalities about what a good thing these meetings were, how honest everyone was. I didn't look at my father. I had told him in letters that I was proud of him, but I couldn't say it. I don't know why. Maybe I didn't quite believe in his sobriety yet. Maybe, by what I didn't say, I was taking a swing at him, paying him back for what he had been, the drunk slumped in his rocking chair with the Jim Beam almost gone.

I don't remember ever feeling anger toward my father for drinking—drinking was drinking, my parents did it and their friends did too—but I do remember being ashamed of him. The ball game in Bannockburn was one time, the "ballistic" remark another. There was also the morning when my best friend and I brought him some kind of toy to fix. Sitting on the side of his bed, hung over, my father fumbled at the toy for a while with his bathrobe loose and his balls hanging out, then handed it back unfixed. And there were many occasions in public when he lurched or stumbled, slurred his words, or laughed loosely in his throat too obliviously long.

Maybe he angered me more than I let myself think. I recall one morning at the Virginia cabin, when I was maybe fourteen. My father and I were sitting on the porch, him out toward the front edge, reading in the sun, me behind him and to one side, in the shade. I was handling his double-barreled 16-gauge shotgun—this was during my hunting phase—with a boy's obsessive fascination, breaking it open to expose the chambers, slipping in shells and slipping them out, seeing how fast I could click the safety off, how hard I could feather the trigger with my finger without firing the gun. I was bored, lonely, daydreaming. The shotgun fired. My father spun in his chair, the Chesterfield falling from his mouth. He stared at me, his face white, the gun smoking.

"What the *hell?*" he said. "Did you mean to do that?"

"Sure," I said.

"Don't you ever do that, Johnny. Don't ever fire a gun behind my back when I don't know what you're doing."

"Okay, okay," I said sullenly, leaning the gun against the wall.

"But I'm glad you meant to shoot," my father went on. "You weren't just foolin' around and the gun went off."

I sure was. I'd been fooling around and sent a wad of birdshot whistling past my father's left shoulder. Purpose is hard to identify, and probably always complicated.

January 24

Today my purpose wavered.

My beets, my Lutz Greenleaf Winterkeeper beets, their robust greens rising tall enough to wave in the breezes, are the pride and joy of my garden; and, steamed with the greens and tossed with butter, salt, pepper, and a splash of vinegar, they are the delight of my red-blanket dining table. To eat these beets is a sacrament. It is to take in the very sweetness of the soil, the good dense essential substance of Earth itself.

But there are vandals in my Holy Land. For weeks now, the dirt rats—euphemistically called ground squirrels by some—have been gnawing away from below, consuming altogether too many of the dark sweet globes, so that when I grasp the verdant greens of a beet and pull, I am rewarded with nothing but the greens and the skullcap of a former beet. The vermin never show themselves. I would willingly tithe them a few, but they have consumed close to half my beet patch.

I acknowledge that I don't have to eat beets. I have other crops, and plenty of canned food, and Welch's grape juice to ward off scurvy. But I love beets, and I grew these lovely, state fair–quality beets from seed. I will be here another two months at least, maybe three, and I want to eat beets. My beets.

And so, this afternoon I stood at the garden gate, wracked with a dilemma. I prefer to garden organically. I prefer to encourage my vegetable protégés to be happy, prospering, responsible members of the Great Family of Nature, sharing sun, rain, and sustenance with all their many relations, freedom and nutrition to one and all.

But the dirt rats of the Family have turned their nasty little teeth upon my innocent beets, which I have raised well and righteously, and which desire only to be large, swelling tankards of garnet-sweet goodness—for *me*, damn it, for the guy who has sown them and raised them into such fullness of being. And so, though I have grown my garden on purely organic fertilizer, and have tainted it with no chemical, I stood today at the garden gate holding in my hands, ambivalently, the same contract the Brothers annually renew with the mice: *Just One Bite.*

Outdoor rodents who accept the contract usually have the decorum to die underground in their squalid, flea-infested warrens. This thought comforts me, because I don't want their miserable corpses to poison the bodies of animals I like better, such as great horned owls and coyotes. This favoritism is morally bankrupt, of course. I acknowledge, as I must, that underground or aboveground, the toxic carcasses of poisoned dirt rats are bound to enter the food chain, and are unlikely to nurture the good health of any organisms, great or small, that consume them.

And so, and so, I stood at the garden gate and wavered. I stood in a pouring rain and struggled mightily with myself.

No I didn't. Reader, I did what you and I knew I'd do. I entered the garden, broke the bars of *Just One Bite* into pieces, and stuffed the pieces into every dirt rat hole I could find in the near vicinity of the beet patch. I faced the test that millions of American householders face every day, in the course of myriad small actions around our homes: whether to live responsibly, minimizing the destruction we visit upon the natural order, or to live conveniently, killing whatever little fuckers are messing with our purposes of the moment. And I failed.

By God, though, I will have beets.

January 25

Back at Reed, I quickly made a decision. I had intended to see my sophomore year through, but now I didn't want to wait. I wanted off the
escalator. I was falling off anyway. Not academically—I was getting a B
average or so—but college just felt all wrong. In October I warmed up
with a letter to my brother, declaring my intent to take a leave of
absence at the end of the fall term. I see now, with a wince, that I used
a lower-case personal pronoun and little punctuation other than an all-
purpose dash, and the rhetoric is pure overblown-adolescent, but for all
that it's sincere: "i am not here because i *want* to be here, i am here
because i took it for granted that i *should* go to college—my life through
nineteen years has been a simple deduction from certain premises of
family and social reality—i feel that getting out of school will be the first
positive act of my life . . ." From there I waxed into rock music criticism
and grandiose social commentary. The Doors and the Velvet Underground, I opined, were too negative—strung out speedfreaks and self-
satisfied smackheads, respectively—while Country Joe and the Fish
were a different kettle altogether: "in the Fish there is joy and hope, a
vision of beauty in life, a sense of the fullness there can be—that is what
i seek, Jim—life as its own end, not as a means to money, security, power
and all that junk—and it *is* junk—look around you and you see that
everyone is a junkie, a slave to dope, wealth, possessions, reputation,
power, alcohol, cigarettes, television, *academic learning*—anything and
everything—America is lost but i refuse to be sucked down with it, i
seek my own salvation . . ."

Later in the fall I wrote my father the same news, but with capital
I's, standard punctuation, less passion, and a more essayistic rigor. He
had made my job easier by sending me a copy of a talk he had given to
the Unitarian-Universalist fellowship in Springfield, in which he
expressed a pretty accurate understanding of youth disaffection in the
sixties and declared his solidarity with us, sounding almost Thoreau-
vian in his affirmation of the young. In the course of trying to define
what the Unitarians were about, he wrote:

We are active, sincere, dedicated traitors to our age group. We, as a group, are well over thirty—and those rebelling and raising particular hell all over the place don't trust us. They are probably right. We set up the triple-headed god—Money, Muscle, and Success—and bowed our head and bent our knee. . . . Since we can't join their ranks, we are doing everything we can to support them and to encourage them. We swear to them that our minds are not closed, that our judgments will not automatically be negative. We are interested in the values they discover, and we are sincerely appreciative of their efforts to enrich and to enlarge life.

Some of the ways we were enriching and enlarging life—by taking LSD, for instance—my father wouldn't have appreciated at all, at least as far as his own sons were concerned. He was a man more comfortable with rhetorical generalities than he was with particular acts, just as love of mankind in the abstract came far easier to him than the love of any particular human being. Still, his words were welcome, and they helped me see him as the young man I hadn't known.

My father had joined the Unitarian fellowship shortly after coming to Springfield, showing up the first time with his hat on his head and keeping it there throughout the service, to put the group on notice of his skeptical independence. He was familiar with Unitarianism—he had had a mutually respectful relationship with my mother's father, a Unitarian minister—and no doubt appreciated its theological openness. But more than any matter of creed, I suspect, it was probably the company of like spirits that attracted him. In the conservative small city of Springfield, Unitarians comprised a significant portion of the freethinking progressive community.

Before long he was attending regularly and giving occasional talks. He helped a divided, struggling fellowship through a difficult period to its unification in 1969 as the First Unitarian-Universalist Church of Springfield, and the following year was elected president of the board. There is a Franz Emil Daniel Memorial Library in the church today, with a stained-glass window bearing the words, "Write me as one who loved his fellowman." The fellowship served my father, though, every bit as well as he served it. In the last year of his life he would write to a friend that Unitarian members had been crucially helpful to him in the early stages of his alcoholic recovery.

❧❧

I knew, I told my father in my letter, that the military draft would be a problem. When I left college I would leave the shelter of my 2-S deferment and could be called for induction into the Army any time. The Vietnam War was heating up. I told him the truth—I didn't have a plan.

My brother had faced this pressure two years earlier. In the fall of 1965, having drifted between colleges for a couple of years, he enlisted in the Air Force and was assigned to a supply squadron at George Air Force Base in the Mojave Desert of California. U.S. troops were being shipped to South Vietnam in droves by then, including some from his unit. My brother would spend the next four years knowing he could be traveling trans-Pacific any time, even as he and many of his cohorts, along with the rest of the country, grew more and more skeptical of the war effort. He would later learn that tactical nuclear weapons had been stored at his base as the Johnson administration considered its options.

I spent the winter and part of the spring of 1968 living in D.C. with my mother and working a dull job in a downtown bookstore. I took classical guitar lessons and poured myself into practice, playing relentless scales and arpeggios, working at simple pieces. A friend in high school had played, played beautifully, and under his influence I had dabbled. Now I concentrated. I wanted to get one piece down, to play just one with fluency. I practiced until my left hand cramped from fretting. I watched my awkward fingers, willing them to move swiftly and true.

They didn't, but the government did. In February I was reclassified 1-A, then in March I received an order to report for a pre-induction physical on April 24th. I still had no plan. Periodically I stewed about it, arrived at nothing, and picked up the guitar or went out with friends and forgot about it.

Some were answering their call to arms with flair and boldness. One Reedie dropout reported to his physical wearing hip boots and stood in the undressing room with a look of bemusement.

"Take your boots off, son," he was ordered.

"It'll make a mess," said the Reedie. "There's red paint in my left boot and green paint in my right."

"Take your *boots* off, son."

He did, and proved himself a man of his word. He did six months at Lompoc for defacing government property. As a felon, of course, he was disqualified from military service.

My friend Ken Hyams handled his crisis with a more subtle theatricality. At his physical he checked yes to homosexual thoughts and suicidal thoughts, hoping he'd be diverted to a psychiatrist. But first he had to endure the physical exams, following colored lines through the Oakland Induction Center's gloomy hallways, part of a herd of nervous young men in their undershorts. The climax, he told me, occurred in a room where the examinees lined up facing the walls. "Okay," hollered the medic. "Drop your shorts and spread those cheeks!"

"Picture it," Ken later mused. "This guy in the middle of a room with eighty assholes trained right on him."

In his interview with the military shrink, he responded to questions haltingly, a complete damper on affect. The shrink asked how he felt about possibly going to Vietnam.

"Uhhhh . . ." said Ken. "I don't know . . . I've got a dog, you know . . ."

At some point, during a silence, the pressured absurdity of the whole experience welled up in him—the painted lines, the piece-of-meat process, the war, his performance, what was at stake—and a loud laugh burst from his throat.

Shit, thought Ken. I've blown it.

He received a 4-F deferment on psychological grounds. The report noted: "Blunted affect. Cognitive confusion. Laughs inappropriately."

(Ken will retire this year, in his early fifties, from a very successful career as a software engineer.)

I admired these exploits, but I didn't want to go to jail and wasn't sure I had the nerve to pull off a bluff such as Ken's. I was uncomfortable, too, with the prospect of misrepresenting myself, and so I considered seeking exemption as a conscientious objector. The criteria were strict. You had to demonstrate belief in a Supreme Being, and, as I understood it, you had to be a thoroughgoing pacifist. "Supreme Being" called to mind an emperor, a juridical god who peered into people's lives and issued edicts directing the course of history. I didn't believe in any such god, but I could scarcely begin to formulate what I did believe. Sacredness to me was a feeling, an intuition, an experience. How could I convince a roomful of old military men that I didn't want to join the Army and fight in Vietnam because I knew from taking LSD that everything was more sacred and beautiful than I could explain? I couldn't even convince myself.

But why, I also asked, did *they* get to decide? What qualified Selective Service to assess the legitimacy of my conscience?

Pacifism, of course, was an especially touchy subject in my self-debates. I suspected I wasn't a pacifist. I thought it ridiculous and grotesque to kill or be killed under the banner of stopping Communism several thousand miles across the Pacific Ocean. The North Vietnamese and Vietcong had done no harm to America, and no utterance by he-of-the-big-ears had come close to convincing me that we needed to harm them. *But*—if there was a real threat to the United States, or if the western world was in danger as it had been in World War II, I would fight. I thought I would fight. I hoped I would. How could I know what I would do unless I was there, in a foxhole, on patrol or ambush? I hoped I wouldn't turn and run, like the protagonist in *The Red Badge of Courage*, but maybe I would. I did have a less-than-brave record. Did my objections to the war conceal a simple lack of courage?

January 29

Yesterday was gray and cold and still, the atmosphere thickening palpably toward rain, which began in mid-afternoon and continued with a few intermissions through the evening. I love the tap of it on the roof, strengthening in surges and tailing away. It's company, in its way, very hospitable company. Last night it steadily approved my choice to sit in the easy chair reading poetry by the light of two candles. *This is well, this is well*, it said. *You're in the right place, my friend.*

The rain quieted toward midnight and seemed to have stopped, but when I went to the deck for air I found it had only shifted to a more subtle tongue. Snow was falling thickly in large flakes. There was little on the ground, none that would last through today, but to watch falling snow was a pleasure of this place I had not yet had. It made the quiet of midnight quieter.

Today, mist and low clouds till late afternoon, breaking up then to reveal the higher ridges well whitened. They've shown scant snow before, but now they look properly like winter. Rattlesnake Ridge, which dominates my view, is frosted halfway down. On Jenny Creek Ridge, across the river to the southwest, the needle trees are thickly laden, as they are to the northeast in the Meadow Creek headwater country, where the road between Dutch Henry and the world tops out at the pass. For several weeks I've assumed I've been snowbound. Now I'm sure I am.

This gives me a glad warmth as I go to the garden to cut a cabbage, as I lug in armloads of firewood. I'm in the right place, and I will stay until spring thaws me out. Oddly enough, this pleasure reminds me of hitchhiking from Portland to San Francisco eight years ago, when I was forty-five. I hadn't hitchhiked in twenty years. I was trying to write about the sixties and wanted to know again, directly, what it felt like to travel by thumb. The journey went fine, the usual stimulating lineup of rides— a longhaul trucker, a private detective, a racist farmhand, a gay Indian named Rainbow, a young rancher and horse trader from Pendleton whose wife had left him for another young rancher and horse trader from

Pendleton. There were two or three long waits between rides, but they didn't daunt me. I realized, standing for hours in balmy spring weather at an I-5 onramp in Red Bluff, California, that I was so relaxed and happy because my fate was out of my hands. All I could do was smile engagingly, work on the perfect arm-thumb extension, and show off to full advantage my harmless head of short graying hair. The rest was up to the drivers of America, to chance or providence or the merciful god of voyagers.

So it is here. The only plans I have to make are short-range and unweighty—what to fix for dinner, what book to pick up next, when to go fishing—and even those don't amount to real decisions. My doings just develop. I wake up when I wake up, usually between ten and noon. I meditate in the loft, make coffee or tea, read in the La-Z-Boy, and shift eventually to the Route 66 Distinguished Chair and my work on the French Provincial Formica table. Eat when I feel like it. Oatmeal at 1 P.M.? Why not? When fresh air and exertion appeal, I go "grouse hunting" or split and stack some green madrone or work at some other job—improve the water dips in the drive, prune a few more suckers from the apple trees. Lunch when I'm hungry. Another session, maybe, at the French Provincial.

When it's getting on toward twilight, I'll sometimes saunter up the drive to the Brothers' house with its longer view to the south, the blue ridges of the Big Windy drainage now whitened with snow. Their austere distant beauty stirs me with a vast loneliness I love, the loneliness of their perfection, regardless of me or of anything human. And that remote beauty heightens my pleasure in the more various and congenial beauty close around me here—the greens of needle and leaf, of moss on trunks and limbs, the gray bark of the leafless fruit and nut trees, the sleepy beige of last year's meadow grass, and the good moist earthen smells of the wet winter land.

Darkness comes as it comes, often with me in the easy chair with a drink, the council of trees taking on their nighted mystery, a screech owl giving its ghostly tremolo somewhere beyond my seeing. And then the lighting of the lamps, and my usual several-hour night shift at the French Provincial, with dinner in its time and briefer recesses to take in stars and moon, or mist and rain.

It's like the way I sometimes walked as a child, before objects and ambitions had totally gathered me in. Just walking along, maybe vaguely home from school or over to a friend's, but mostly just walking, picking up a stone or stick, wondering about something, walking along. It would be fine to lead my life in the world that way, or let my life lead me that way. Fine but unlikely. I'm set in my ways, conditioned, hooked on too many desires. But it's valuable to live it here, for a time, on those days when it happens. It'll be good to remember this when I'm back home, to open a window in my soul and admit this breeze.

Not every day flows so easy and true, but by and large I'm feeling a part of the place. Even with my little noises—the screen door banging, the clatter of pots and pans, the percussive shout of the splitting maul and the rattle of split pieces—I don't seem to break the brimful silence of the land. I seem to carry it inside me as I go about my living. One of Thoreau's sentences in *Walden* recurs to me: "I go and come with a strange liberty in Nature, a part of herself."

I feel so at home that I've presumed to perform a few low-level ministrations on behalf of the Brothers and their Oregon faith. I have held colloquy with the Global Warming Frog, trying to discern the import of his prophecy. I have made several errands to the pond on the upper property to learn the feeling there about Brother Frank's momentous Epistle to the Rough-skinned Newts, issued some years ago. The newts, hanging in the margins of the pond, stirring occasionally with a slow wave of the tail, a few of them languidly coupling, appear to have received the Brother's message with dreamish rapture. The pond brims with their good faith.

Today there appeared the first band of robins I've seen since fall. I felt called to stand on the deck and issue a welcome and blessing, the robins hopping about the greensward, picking at bugs and worms, absorbing my address in silence. Now, in the cold of early evening, they are less active. On the ground or in the apple trees, they keep still for long periods, their rufous breasts portly, white-ringed eyes pensive. I hope I didn't misspeak to them.

They're probably just thinking, "Hmm. We came a bit early this year. And who's the loudmouth on the deck?"

February

There is in God (some say)
A deep, but dazling darkness; As men here
Say it is late and dusky, because they
    See not all clear . . .
—HENRY VAUGHN, "THE NIGHT"

Myself is what I wear:
I keep the spirit spare.
—THEODORE ROETHKE, "OPEN HOUSE"

God, may our youth, in rebellion against complacency
and hypocrisy, not be hampered by good manners.
May they not sell out to affluence and possessions.
May they not tire and compromise in their search
for the good, the beautiful, the true.
—FRANZ DANIEL, UNITARIAN SERMON, 1969

February 1

Oh me. Just now I heard a vehicle coming down the drive and went hollow with horror. Who got through the locked gate? Some paranoid dope grower in a monster truck who thinks I'm a narc? Or, if a friend—the Brothers or a BLM ranger—bearing what awful news, that caused them to deliver it in person? Then I realized the sound was coming from behind me, a slight sustained flare-up in the damped-down stove.

God I was scared—but elated, too. Arrival! A visitor!

There's a subtle switch in me that flips back and forth and makes all the difference. The good, settled, flowing days, like the day of the snowy ridges, with an unfelt flip of the switch become too settled, too flowing, too even in texture one to the next. No two are the same, exactly, but when the switch is thrown all variety seems swallowed in the oppressive sameness of this beautiful small cosmos I inhabit.

In my ordinary life I stay home a lot, working on whatever's in progress, cooking, tending to the place, but there's also the meal in town with Marilyn, the occasional movie or concert, a ball game, conversation with a friend over pints in a pub, the now-and-again expedition to Portland or Seattle or San Francisco. Good doings, not distraction, or not merely distraction. I miss those.

Yesterday was my lowest day. The switch was irrevocably thrown. I dragged out of bed, meditated, but had nothing to give to it. Coffee tasted grim. I picked up one book then another, put them down. Rummaged through the fire-starting newspapers for crosswords, found two, but one was too easy and the other too hard. Read the funnies but they weren't funny, and I'd read them back home in October. Thought about walking, splitting wood. Didn't think long. Couldn't. As soon as my mind lit somewhere it flapped off again in irritated flight.

Said to myself: "A guy *could* sit down at the French Provincial and he might get something done."

Replied to myself: "Go to hell. I'm sick of you too."

Not surprisingly, my Muzak was acting up. It's been pretty sedate since I realized that it varies inversely to my degree of mindfulness and that I can knock it out, or at least change the station, by singing "Amazing Grace" at the top of my lungs. But yesterday mindfulness had flown the coop, and "Amazing Grace," in my foul mood, would have been a sacrilege.

And so, courtesy of the Radio Theater of my Left Ear, I was treated to the repeated chorus of "The Battle Hymn of the Republic"—*Glory, glory Hallelujah,* etc.—sung at an upbeat tempo by a cheery chorus of young Caucasian men and women. I could just about see the sweaters they were wearing and their white teeth smiling as they sang, full of bouncy ebullience and not one scintilla of soul. It was the final chorus they were singing, their voices soaring at the end—*His truth goes marching ONNNN!!!*—but it wasn't the end, out of every *ONNNN!!!* there marched brightly forth a new round of *Glory, glory Hallelujah . . .*

"Goddamnit, *shut up!*" I yelled, but like the fateful lightning of His terrible swift sword, the glory was unstoppable.

Gruesome crimes have been committed in the Rogue River Canyon. Just three miles downriver at Battle Bar, in 1947, a miner named Mahoney lost it and drilled his neighbor, and later himself, with a .30-.30. A decade earlier, another miner shot two young men who were coming up his stairs for a drink of water. He fled to California, was hauled back for trial, and was acquitted. Acquittal of murder seems to be a canyon tradition. I'm thinking of our own Dutch Henry, of course . . . Is it possible? Could Muzak Madness be endemic in the canyon, a local scurvy of the mind that drives men to murder? Could it even be the *same* Muzak? The Battle Hymn, if I'm not mistaken, dates from well back into the nineteenth century . . .

In any case, I was desperate. I had hit the wall, as the marathoners say, and the wall was singing at me. I went back to bed but couldn't sleep. Got up, vaguely hungry, and reached for a cookbook, *The Joy of Cooking.* Joy? I reached for another, *Farm Journal's Homemade Breads.* I leafed through it until I came to "Sticky Cinnamon Rolls," and there I decided to make my stand.

Having baked nothing more than biscuits and a few loaves of bread, I was dispirited and faithless as I opened cupboards and rounded up the ingredients. Almost quit when I came to "1 egg," which I didn't have, but pushed on. Melted butter in a bowl on the woodstove, warmed milk. Perked up when I caught the first whiff of yeast, dissolving with sugar in warm water in the mixing bowl. Then the warm milk (three table-spoons extra, I decided, to replace egg moisture), Crisco, and flour enough to form a kneadable dough.

It's kind of a miracle. It's easy to imagine the mix of wet and dry yielding a formless glop, but somehow the elements meld in a *dough*, a smooth and shapely organism, a ball of resilient glutenous power. I enjoyed the kneading, sprinkling flour till the dough no longer was sticky. I wanted more than the five minutes the cookbook allowed me. I thought of my aunts in their kitchens, flour on their aprons, their arthritic fingers mixing and kneading. "Never knead bread with a heavy heart," they used to say. I thought of my father when he occasionally baked, working the dough for Beef Wellington or rolling out pie crust, smiling, humming along to *Aida* or *Tosca* on the hi-fi.

It didn't double its volume in the bowl. The missing egg? Did I kill the yeast? Probably a disaster in the making, but what the hell. I rolled out the dough as instructed to a 10 x 15 inch rectangle, buttered it, sprinkled it with cinnamon and sugar and raisins, rolled it up jelly roll style and sealed the seam, and sliced the roll into one-inch cuts, just as the book called for. It almost looked like I knew what I was doing. For forty-five minutes the rolls rose and filled out in the pan, set in a fine rich goo of melted butter, brown sugar, and authentic maple syrup from Mother Margery (replacing the recipe's corn syrup, and much better).

I still wasn't quite a believer when I put the pan into the oven, but shortly the good smell came forth. When the smell of baking breadstuff is abroad in the house, all shall be well, all manner of thing shall be well. Give me your Gore, bring me your Bush, the Dow Jones and the balance of trade be damned. Here at Dutch Henry Homestead, rolls are swelling to golden perfection. Psalms might now be written, philoso-phies grown to wholeness.

I ate half the sweet, sticky, lusciously rich rolls for dessert. Gave me heartburn, but it didn't matter. I was already cured. Ate the rest for breakfast this morning, and I've been going all day on their fine spiced warmth within me.

⪻⪼

They weren't homemade, but it happened I was eating sweet rolls in the early evening of April 5, 1968. It was a far worse day than my worst day here. I sat with my sweet rolls on the roof of my mother's apartment building watching smoke rise from Northeast and Northwest Washington, D.C. It hung in a dark pall, the blend of several different columns. One seemed to be coming from the downtown shopping district. The radio news had reported that stores were being looted; some had been fire-bombed or torched by other means. The department stores were mounting large posters of Dr. King in their windows; smaller businesses were taping up newspaper photos. Later I'd learn that the first places hit in the ghettoes had been the loan agencies that preyed on the Negro poor. Then the small, high-price grocery stores, the liquor stores, and any businesses operated by whites, all of it feeding an indiscriminate wave of window breaking and grabbing of goods. Thousands of Army troops were in town, more on the way. A big contingent had been deployed at the White House, which they had surrounded with a cable barricade. Washington was besieged from within.

But calm, as always, where we lived, in the very white and comfortable environs of Connecticut Avenue Northwest, not far from the Sheraton Park Hotel. A curfew had been declared at four o'clock. When I heard of it on the radio I went out, slipped across Connecticut Avenue, and ghosted around Rock Creek Park for a while to see what I could see, which wasn't much—a few cars on the parkway, several cops cruising slow. I don't know what I expected. The action was far away, in neighborhoods that made me nervous even in normal times. I think it just felt better to do something, anything. Back home, I grabbed the sweet rolls from the kitchen and brought them up the iron fire escape to the roof, where I chewed and slowly swallowed them into my anger.

The rage of the burners and looters I imagined as something consuming, a fire that had smoldered all their lives from the insults and thwarted hopes they lived with daily, and now the assassination like gas on the coals. "Burn it," I said in the direction of the smoke. "You've got cause."

My own anger was something different, something colder. I didn't know who or what to direct it toward. Not the White House or the cops, not Congress, not the Pentagon or the troops in the streets—or maybe all of them, because, just as in Dallas five years before, who knew? They were after a suspect, the radio had said, but my anger told me we would never know the truth. Oswald had pulled the trigger in Dallas, but who had hired him and set him up and hired another gunman to kill the killer? We didn't know and we weren't going to know. Something had changed in America. Something had changed behind the scenes, behind the headlines, behind Walter Cronkite's earnest face on the six o'clock news.

I kept thinking of baseball. You play hard, the hardest you can. To win is everything you want. You might not like the other team, you might despise them. You might yell at them, you might fight if their pitcher throws at your teammate's head. But you don't hire someone to sit in the stands with a high-powered rifle and gun down their star player, their manager. You don't do that.

But now we did.

February 3

My own crisis was looming, my physical less than three weeks away, and I was thinking about Canada. It would hardly even feel like leaving the country, I told myself. I wanted to live in the West, and Canada had its own West, its own mountains and plains and wild coast, wilder than ours. It had all that America had and fewer people, a more civilized government, a saner foreign policy. My friends could visit and I could make new friends. I could go to college. I could make a life.

And yet, and yet . . . I never quite believed the pitch I was making to myself. An American president, placed in office through an election I had not been allowed to vote in, was prosecuting an undeclared war in a little mixed-up nation across the Pacific Ocean, and I had to fight in that war or else leave my country? I hated the war, I hated the government for waging it, for sending good men to die in it, but I didn't hate America. In fact, I liked to irritate my friends from time to time by telling them how much I loved America.

I did, and do. I had been to every state but Alaska, Hawaii, and North Dakota. I loved the Outer Banks and Great Smoky Mountains of North Carolina, where our family had made many visits, and the coast of Maine near Acadia National Park, where we usually stayed for a couple of weeks every year at my grandfather's summer home. I loved the Blue Ridge of northern Virginia, where our cabin was, the Shenandoah River and Allegheny Mountains to the west, and the slow and muddy Osage River with its limestone bluffs in my father's country in southwest Missouri. I loved the Rocky Mountains, though I didn't quite believe in them yet—we had lived in Denver only a year, when I was five. I didn't yet love the Southwest, too bleak and glary to my eastern eyes, but I loved the California coast, Big Sur and San Francisco, the dripping redwood country, and the rivers and snowy volcanoes of Oregon I was just beginning to know.

It was more than landscape. I loved the history and spirit and speech of America—Huck Finn's talk, Woody Guthrie's ballads, the folk songs of Lightnin' Hopkins and Elizabeth Cotton and Ramblin' Jack Elliott.

I loved the New York jazz clubs where my brother's ID had gotten me in with friends to hear Charles Mingus and Thelonius Monk. I loved New Orleans, with its beignets and jambalaya and wrought iron balustrades in the French Quarter. I loved the Kansas City and Omaha steak houses where my father had taken us. I loved the drama of the westward expansion as Bernard DeVoto's histories had brought it to life for me, the splendid tragedy of the Civil War, and, of course, the rise of men and women who worked with their hands and backs through the American labor movement. I loved Mark Twain's Mississippi River, Jack London's Alaska, John Steinbeck's California, Thomas Wolfe's yearning for an America lost and not yet found. I loved Hemingway and whatever of Faulkner I could pull into focus. I loved *On the Road* and *The Dharma Bums*—I'd read Kerouac outside of class in high school, read him again as I hitched across the country in 1967. I was reading Ken Kesey, Gary Snyder's packed and glinting poems, Kenneth Rexroth, the oracular verses of Robinson Jeffers—literature written and being written in my own time, in an American West I had tasted and wanted to belong to.

My love was more romance than reality, more passionate than informed or thoughtful. It was a teenager's love, an unstable blend of infatuation and wild yearning. But real. It drove me crazy that I'd have to leave my country for good to avoid shooting or getting shot in Vietnam. Stopping the spread of Communism? What in the world did it matter if Vietnam was half Communist or all Communist? The domino theory I found completely uncompelling.

I didn't discount the idea that I owed service to America. If I could have joined VISTA or the Peace Corps instead of the military, I would have signed up. To be approved for alternative service at that time, though, you first had to be approved for conscientious objector status, and there I ran up against my stubbornness again. To stay out of the Army you had to seek and obtain the Army's approval. They set the terms and they made the choices.

I liked none of my alternatives, but more and more, as the days ticked off toward the 24th, it looked like I'd have to swallow my resentment and slip north to a new life. I went to an American Friends draft counselor and learned that there were contacts in Canada who would help me find a job and a place to live and guide me through the legal red tape required for permanent residency. I asked what would happen if I didn't show up at my physical. I would be declared a draft delinquent, they told me, subject to induction at any time. I could expect the notice to arrive quickly.

They also mentioned another choice. A small but growing number of draftees were refusing induction, standing trial, and going to jail. Muhammad Ali, a convert to Islam, had resisted in this way in 1967 after his petition for conscientious objector status had been denied. The heavyweight champion said, "Man, I ain't got no quarrel with them Vietcong." Stripped of his title and barred from the ring, he would manage to stay out of prison but would lose three prime years of his boxing career as his appeal made its way through the federal courts. The Supreme Court would ultimately uphold his case on religious grounds in 1971.

Refusing induction was a felony punishable by up to five years in federal prison. The non-notorious and white of skin, the counselor told me, were getting two or three years, sometimes less, and conditions in federal lockup were better than in state pens and local jails. But spending two or three years of my life behind bars of any kind was not something I wanted to imagine. The other alternatives angered me. This one scared the hell out of me.

My mother was ready to support me whatever I chose. Other adults, men particularly, were more partial. The owner of the bookstore where I worked knew of my quandary and asked about it from time to time. He was genuinely concerned. "The choice you make will affect your entire life," he told me. "Think about your reputation, your good name. I'd hate to see you do something that will always haunt you."

That was one concern that didn't trouble me much. The rest of my life was a long way off, but the 24th was almost upon me. The subject came up after dinner when I was visiting old family friends in Bannockburn. Bob Bradley, the neighbor who used to bring along a pitcher of martinis to watch a ball game with my father, had been a military man and was a prickly character. He'd had plenty to drink this particular evening. He listened in silence as I explained my situation, no doubt with considerable self-pity and ranting at the government.

"Do you want to know what I think?" said Bob in his deliberate way. "The war isn't the problem, and neither is the draft. You are the problem. You've been asked to serve your country. The question is, are you a coward or are you not?"

What a jerk, I kept thinking as I drove home. But if he's so wrong, I also kept thinking, what am I so stung about? What *about* courage?

The 24th fell on a Wednesday. On the Friday before, I borrowed two books about Canada from the store and drove to the cabin for the weekend. I kept a fire going—it was chilly for April, patches of old snow on the ground—and practiced guitar until my fingers were stiff and sore. I tramped in the woods to relax. I opened the books but scarcely read in them. I came home Monday.

On Tuesday, after work, I went with my guitar-playing friend to hear Charlie Byrd at a jazz club.

On Wednesday I stayed home practicing guitar. After dinner I tried to write about what was going on but didn't know where to begin, *how* to begin. I didn't know if it was a letter, a note to myself, a story, or what. I fell asleep on my bed with guitar music playing all through me as I couldn't play it—the B Minor Etude by Fernando Sor, the notes struck perfectly, the piece unfolding with stately clarity and coherence, sounding exactly as it ought to sound.

February 4

Well, I needed a visitor, and a visitor came. Came sauntering from the northeast in short loping strides by the garden fence, more gray than brown with vague dark spots, sharp tufted ears, and a tail true to his name. Cougar's little brother, a bobcat. He went round the fence corner and sat, listening into the bramble below the garden. I had eased open the glass door to get a better look with binoculars. I made a slight squeaking noise, at which he turned his head, and when I did it again he came my way and sat smack in the middle of the barnyard facing the cabin. He couldn't see me. The broken black barring of his front and forelegs reminded me of our black-and-tan tabby at home. When I clucked my tongue, very softly, he looked up with a kind of indifferent interest, his barred, fat-furred cheeks smiling broadly, like a cartoon cat. As his attention faded after a cluck his eyes would partially close, as if he were content to fall asleep right there where he sat.

I've never had such a good long look at a bobcat. They're supposed to be nocturnal, but this one had not been reading the Audubon field guide. When I'd watched my fill of him I fetched the camera and crept onto the deck. Instantly wary, he took a few steps away, stopped to look back, and with the click of the camera he was bounding off in the loveliest high arcs, the solid black on his back legs reminding me yet again of his distant cousin who lives in my house.

He came, he stayed a while, he added himself to the history of this place. Wildness is a weave of stories I only glimpse. A raven lit one morning in the top of a pine and tried out his voices—quick whistles, crow caws, brief, deep, almost subsonic snorings. He went on for half an hour, the breeze scruffing his neck feathers, then lifted and soared into the canyon on black-sheened wings. At the river one day I watched a family of four otters, or four otter friends for all I know, two tussling on the far bank as the others slipped splashlessly in, then all four swimming upcurrent in a line, submerging and surfacing. Instead of rounding a rock peninsula in their path they glided over it, one, two, three, four, sleek and low to the rock, as if it were just another stage of their swimming, and they were gone upriver in the greeny slide and swirl.

Late one clear cold night in January, a spotted owl called in the canyon, enunciating its crisp notes as if trying terribly hard to be precise:

Whup   whup ^{whup} *wahhhhh . . .*

Such a simple statement, to have set off such a long and bitter squabble. Another evening, as I was eating, I heard from the near woods a meal in the making—a rasping, screeching, growling, thirty-second ruckus punctuated with yelps. Cat? Fox? Who knows? Something was fighting to take a life, something fighting to keep it. The climax of a story, characters and denouement unknown.

As wild, though soundless, was the rising of the near-full moon a week ago behind Rattlesnake Ridge. It was a night of low thin clouds and drifting mist. First came an intense suffusion of light overtopping the ridge, then—I watched through binoculars—the top of the giant orb itself, silhouetting a pair of tall, battered ridgetop trees with more broken-off limbs than whole ones. Vapors hung and swirled in a dusky, almost colorless light as the pocked and proud-fleshed moonface climbed, quickly, as if it had chanced to light a scene from hell and now hastened to leave it in darkness again. It was a terrific spectacle. Anyone with any sense should have been scared witless. *I* was scared.

Wild nights, wild nights . . . These seeings and hearings remind me, though, that the night I felt wildness most intensely came not here, not backpacking or climbing, not in a wilderness area, but in the near vicinity of human beings. In 1980 I was camped by my truck on a high, pine-forested ridge in the Mexican Sierra Madre, the country around the Barranca del Cobre, the six-thousand-foot-deep Copper Canyon. Shortly after dark, from the small canyon below me where no road went, I heard drums. One was low, brassy, almost like the sound of a tuba, the other sharper, less resonant, more like a snare drum. I could see two fires, no humans. The two drums called and answered in quick riffs, then the deep one set a heartbeat rhythm—ta-*dum*, ta-*dum*, ta-*dum*—while the other tapped flourishes around it. Now and then a dog barked.

The drums went silent for an hour, then a few more short cadences, and they were done.

I was hearing Tarahumara Indians playing their *tambouras*. The music of their domesticity, to me, was the sheerest wildness. The ones I heard lived not far from gravel roads, a rural mining town. They probably spoke some Spanish, made *tambouras* to sell. Beyond, deeper in the *barrancas*, I knew that thousands more lived in huts and caves, making music, eating peyote, playing a traditional game with a wooden ball in which they run the canyons continuously for hours, sometimes days, at a time. They may be the greatest distance runners in the world. They are unlikely, though, to outrun the incursion of roads and contemporary civilization that even then was taking aim at their mountain homeland. If I camped now in that same place I doubt I'd hear *tambouras*, but I bet I'd find plenty for sale in tourist shops.

These Klamath Mountains, before the miners and homesteaders, before the first Euro-American trappers and explorers, supported a human domesticity of their own. Athabaskan peoples lived in several bands in the coastal Rogue country and inland along the river, probably not as far as here. A Penutian-speaking people, the Takelma, lived inland from here in the broad and hospitable Rogue Valley, where Medford and Grants Pass now lie, and up into the Cascades. The Takelma came here to the canyon to fish and hunt. Together these peoples were given a name by the trappers, traders, and settlers who passed through in the 1840s on their way between the Willamette Valley to the north and the Sacramento River valley to the south, where gold was discovered in 1848. The Indians didn't much care for the growing flow of strangers through their homeland. They harassed immigrant parties and horse packers, stole horses and other valuables, and so earned, along with their river, the name "Rogue."

In 1852 gold was discovered in the Takelma country, and the Rogue River Indians were caught up in a small surging current of American history. Stephen Dow Beckham tells the miserable story in *Requiem for a People*. Entire streams were claimed out, displacing Indians from traditional fishing sites and leaving the waters unfishably muddy. Meadows of camas and seed grasses—Indian staples—were plowed up, acorn-bearing oaks were felled and burned, deer and elk populations diminished as miners hunted them. Before long some bands of Indians were going hungry, and all bands were ridden with tuberculosis, measles, and smallpox. Indians attacked homesteaders and prospectors; posses of volunteer miners retaliated against the first Indians they could find, which usually were not the offenders. Twenty warriors called to a peace parley by the federal Indian agent were massacred by volunteers, to whom they had surrendered their weapons, as they tried to swim the river to safety. Along the streets of Jacksonville, the main mining town, lynched Indians hung from oak trees. "The Cry was extermination of all the Indians," wrote one of the volunteers. They rode under a flag blazoned with that word: "Extermination."

About half the Indians accepted a treaty with the Oregon territorial government and went to live under federal supervision on a reservation in the Rogue Valley. The others withdrew, in the manner of occupied peoples everywhere, to the remoter parts of the watershed. Hostilities continued. In 1855, after civilian exterminators shot eight Indian men and fifteen women and children as they slept in their brush huts, the reservation Indians who still had the will to fight seized arms, joined up with the unreconstructed remnants of several bands, and followed the river downstream, killing every white they came upon. They holed up in the heart of the Rogue River Canyon at Black Bar, three miles from this cabin. There they fought off a vastly superior expeditionary force of federal regulars and miner volunteers, some five hundred strong, that camped in the Corral Meadows, just a mile down trail from here, and possibly in this very meadow. The troops withdrew for the winter, returned in April even greater in numbers, and finished off the Indians a few miles downstream at what is now called Battle Bar.

Survivors were shipped to two reservations two hundred miles to the north, where they mingled in a kind of living landfill with strangers, members of twenty other tribes and bands from around the Oregon country and northern California. Diseases killed most of the Rogue survivors within a few decades. Children were sent to boarding schools where they were force-fed English and Christianity. A land allotment act, intended to make farmers out of people with no farming tradition, resulted in much reservation land falling into non-Indian ownership. The two confederated tribes lost their reservations and tribal status altogether in the 1950s as part of a federal policy of forced assimilation into the mainstream culture. Each has since won back its legal tribal identity and some of its land. Each now operates a casino, the two most successful casinos in Oregon, as it happens. Soaking dollars from locals and motorists on vacation may be as close to justice as the Rogue River Indian descendants are likely to get.

Here, in the realm of my winter solitude, and down the river to the sea and up the river to its headwaters high in the Cascades, there is no sign, except to archaeologists, that the Rogue River Indians ever were. This canyon is now a federally designated wilderness where humans are barred by law from living. The silence I find so full and nourishing contains this absence, which is a greater unnaturalness than any change wrought by dam builders, logging companies, or river guides with dynamite. I feel no personal responsibility for the extermination of the Indians, and I don't feel I'm an intruder where I shouldn't be. History has handed me the chance to be here, and I've come with respect. But I do think it's the minimal responsibility of all Euro-Americans to know the stories of those who lived before us in our places, to know how it happened that they are no longer where they were.

To my knowledge, there is no living speaker of the Takelma language. The language itself exists on life support in the form of a few disks at U.C. Berkeley. There are descendants, but their allegiances, a century and a half from their ancestors' forced removal, are to other places. It is a blessing, maybe, that the anguish expressed in 1857 by a man known as headman George, on one of the northern reservations, is now buried along with his bones: "I would ask, am I and my people the only ones who have fought against the whites that we should be removed so far from our native country? It is not so great a hardship to those who have always lived near here. But to us it is a great evil. If we could be even on the borders of our native land, where we could sometimes see it, we would be satisfied."

February 7

My induction notice arrived in early May, a form letter from the president of the United States. "Greetings," it began. "You will report for induction into the Armed Forces on June 17, 1968 . . ." Wow, I thought. Two years ago you hand me a medal on the White House lawn, now you ship me off to the Asian swamps. And all I did was quit school.

I went back to the draft counselor and learned that I could transfer the site of my induction—the army didn't care where you reported, they'd take you anywhere—and so I requested and received a transfer to the Oakland Induction Center, the date delayed to July 10th. In the Bay Area I'd be in position to head north to Vancouver, where there was a strong network of support for Americans fleeing the draft. I'd be in the West, where I wanted to be. San Francisco was the West Coast center of the developing draft resistance movement, too. The previous fall had seen a Stop the Draft week, with protests and human blockades at the induction center. Whatever I decided to do, the Bay Area looked like the place to be.

At the end of May I took a Greyhound to Missouri to spend a week with my father and aunts before heading on west. My father smiled and scowled when he met me. I had quit shaving over the winter. My beard was still a patchy achievement, but I was getting to like it. My father didn't.

"You know what a beard means in California?" he asked, after we shook hands. "It means you're homosexual."

I rolled my eyes, didn't bother to reply. My father knew more than me about many things, but the culture of contemporary California was not one of them.

I had written him little about my draft situation, but my mother had kept him informed. He was concerned, and I knew we'd have to talk about it. It always took us a long time to get to the hard things, if we got to them at all.

His own hard thing, the enterprise of sobriety, was going strong. He was going to AA meetings and hadn't had a drink in a year and a half.

I have a self-evaluation he wrote around New Year's 1968, five months before the visit I'm remembering now. It ended up among his papers in the Reuther Library. "A year ago," he wrote then, "I was arrogant, self-centered, sarcastic, intolerant. I was two months sober, not whole physically, suspicious, withdrawn—but determined to give AA a chance." He was, in a word, "Selfish"—he capitalized the "S." A year later, he reports, "I'm still selfish—and all the other things, but I now have: Self-respect; friendships; understanding; sympathy; ability to help others." He credits for this change "a year of AA discipline," and his "discovery of decent, self-respecting people." "Decent" is a word my father commonly used in conversation and in union oratory. He saw the labor movement as a way to help working men and women lead decent, self-respecting lives. It's nice to know that at sixty-four he was beginning to see his own life that way.

In the course of calling on "wandering brethren" in the city jail, he had struck up a relationship with a municipal court judge. The judge told my father he might as well preach to the whole congregation, and so every Thursday afternoon the entire population of the drunk tank was herded over to City Hall for a class with Franz Daniel. He held another class at the Olive Street mission. Most of the men were lost causes, but a few came to AA meetings when they got out of the hoosegow.

The AA story about Harry the town drunk may have glanced through my father's mind a few days into my visit as we drove north out of Springfield into the grassy Missouri countryside. Someone in the Unitarian Fellowship had called to tell him that an acquaintance, a troubled woman in town, had killed herself. She had three small kids and no other family, few friends, no money. A mortuary had donated its services, cemetery space had been obtained. A ceremony was needed for the burial.

We were a small group at graveside—the children and the woman who was looking after them, my father and me, two or three others. It was a gusty day, the light shifting as clouds blew over, the wind whirling and pausing, buffeting our clothes. My father, in a dark suit, said a few words of welcome, smiling at the children, then opened a Bible and read from Ecclesiastes. The wind whipped his gray hair and tried to lift the thin pages he held firmly in place with his fingers. He spoke the verses clearly in his deep voice, making sure that all could hear in spite of the wind. Making sure that three children had, if nothing else, a measure of dignity on their awful day. He ended the service with a moment of silence.

On our way home my father punched in the lighter, lit a cigarette, and untied the large package we'd been carrying between us. He said, as I remember it, "Johnny, what are you going to do?"

"I don't know," I answered. "I'll decide when I'm out there, I guess."

"You've got an induction order staring you in the face. You don't have a lot of time."

I watched the green pastureland glide by, brick farmhouses, too many billboards. "I'm thinking I might have to go to Canada," I said. Now it was wide open. "I don't want to, but it's better than fighting in some screwed-up war that shouldn't even be."

My father smoked in silence, his eyes on the mild dips and rises of highway. He had supported the war at first, believing that all of Southeast Asia and India too were at risk if South Vietnam fell. But as Johnson had stepped up the troops, as the casualties had mounted and it had become less and less clear what they were dying for, more and more clear that we had entered not a war of Communist aggression but a civil war, he had cooled on it. He had even cooled on vice president and now presidential candidate Hubert Humphrey, an old acquaintance and stalwart labor ally who had once honored my father by calling him "the most dangerous man in America." My father was supporting Robert Kennedy in the primaries, and I favored Kennedy myself. I respected Eugene McCarthy but he seemed cold, colorless. Lyndon Johnson had dramatically, and quite selflessly, withdrawn from the race in March, defeated by a war he dared not lose and could not win.

"You need to think very, very carefully about that," my father finally said. "It's one thing to disagree with your country's policy. It's another to duck and run."

Right, I thought. Just like I've always ducked and run? We were almost home. I started counting blocks.

"You want to spend your whole life up there, on the run?" he went on. "They won't let you come back, you know."

"I know," I said.

"Johnny, please think this through. I just—"

"I've *been* thinking, damn it. What choice do I have? Some guys are just refusing, which is great, but they're going to jail for three years, too."

"That's a long time," my father said, and we let the silence hang.

The evening of my last day in Springfield we talked again. We were sitting in the dimly lit front room, in antique family chairs, well fed on a ham dinner. My father had smoked the ham himself in an apparatus he had built in the backyard that looked, he liked to point out, like a still. My aunts were cleaning up the kitchen, their talk floating out to us with the clatter of dishes and pans.

My father tried to express himself carefully, sympathetically. "It's a hell of a rough deal you're facing. It's a rough one. But I'm concerned you're letting yourself drift into it, and Johnny, I just don't think you ought to do that."

Suddenly I saw myself from his side of the room. What felt to me like taking hold of my life—leaving school because I didn't belong there, feeling my way against the draft, trying to play guitar—looked to him like just the opposite, like a young man—his *son*—letting go of his life, shrugging off responsibility, wasting his talents, refusing to make necessary decisions. For nineteen years I'd been an achiever. Now I was a bearded dropout with no plans except maybe to amble off to Canada for the rest of my life.

"I think I know what I *should* do," I said. "I just don't know what I *will* do."

My father sat forward in his chair, elbows on knees. He stared at the floor, thumb hooked under his right cheekbone, a cigarette between his first two fingers. The tip of the cigarette glowed as he inhaled, faded as he breathed out. I had seen him in that posture all my life.

After a while he asked, "Did you see the public letter Martin Luther King wrote from Birmingham, during the marches there?"

I shook my head.

"I'll see if I can find it for you. He wrote it from jail, and he wrote about why it was absolutely necessary that he should be in jail. He could have stood on any street corner and criticized the way Negroes are treated. But when he's given up his freedom to say it, look at the author-ity it gives him. Look at the integrity."

I looked and saw it—in King, in my father, in Walter Reuther, in all the heroes who had stood for what was right. I saw it just where I'd always seen it, not in me.

I went to bed uneasy. The draft mess had been *my* mess, my own knot to untie. Now the legend-man was trying to coach me into his own image. Setting me up to do the right thing. Setting me up, I wor-ried, my doubts ringing louder than ever, to let him down once again.

My bed was in the attic. I woke in the morning to footsteps on the wooden stairs, then my father's voice, as grim and miserable as I'd ever heard it. "Wake up, Johnny. They shot Bobby Kennedy. They killed him too."

It's commonly said, and pretty much true, that we all remember where we were and what we were doing when we heard that John Kennedy had been assassinated. But I wonder if we remember so clearly what we *felt*—the unprecedented horror, that new kind of grief. I wonder if we even yet know how that killing, and the ones that followed, have injured us. What have they contributed, I wonder, to the present ram-pant apathy and cynicism toward government, and to our general retreat from public involvement into the safer solitudes of self, family, and material comfort? Parents who lose a young child may be afraid to love again. People who lose their young leaders may be afraid to believe again, or even to care.

In 1963, at my desk in tenth-grade World History class, I had sat stupefied, uncomprehending, as the vice-principal announced over the P.A. that "our president" had been shot and killed. *What* president, I kept thinking. The school doesn't have a president . . . As it sank in, my horror was still dulled by disbelief. I sat around with friends all evening, hardly talking. All the next night I stood in a line along Constitution

Avenue that would extend three miles at its longest, dodging ahead when I could through the knots of mourners. It was bitter cold. At first light I just made it into the Capitol rotunda before they cut off the line. The only sounds as I passed the flag-wrapped coffin were the shuffling of feet and a few quiet sobs. *He's in there,* I heard myself think. The young president, the first politician who had excited me, lay in his coffin twenty feet away, the back of his head blown off. I believed it then, and felt it.

When Martin Luther King was gunned down I was less disbelieving—his murder was perfectly in keeping with the violence of Southern racism—but more angry, and now, on the Greyhound heading west out of Springfield, anger took me over. Another coffin, soon to be wrapped in another flag. Another dark-veiled widow, another round of eulogies. Whoever had done it this time, for whatever reason, all guns were looking the same to me now. The assassins' guns, policemen's guns, the guns in Southeast Asia, the same shadow was behind them all, and that shadow was wrapped in the same gaudy flag that wrapped the coffins, the flag we pledged to at school and faced at the ballpark when the anthem was played, the flag waving brightly on a million poles. If I ever owed it one damn thing, I said to myself, I owe it nothing anymore.

February 10

A confession.

Occasionally a small plane drones high above, or blaps and rumbles not so high above. If I were backpacking in the Cascades or the Utah canyon country, the plane would annoy me. I would take it as a violation of the all-too-brief wilderness sojourn I had hiked hard to realize.

But here I smile, glad for the company, and I think of Bill Graiff. He would have known any plane he saw, whether Deak Miller's or another bush pilot's, or wouldn't have known, and would have wondered who the new guy was. Lonely old grubber that he was, Graiff was not removed from community here; he had merely stretched his community thin enough that he could stand it. I left my world to spend a winter here. This was Graiff's world.

They were an interesting, oddball bunch, those last inhabitants of the canyon. I wish I'd known them. They came in with the Depression, many of them, built pole-and-shake cabins along the river or moved into cabins already built, packed in supplies on the Rogue River Trail, fished and hunted, passed the time working the crevices with pan or placer box for sparse flakes of gold, enough to buy their groceries and not much more. They found little wealth, did little harm. The occasional murders notwithstanding, they seem largely to have been gentle sorts, natural philosophers drawn to the charms and challenges of solitude. Reading their words in Kay Atwood's *Illahe*, I feel a certain spiritual kinship. Red Keller, who spent most of his adult life living alone in various canyon cabins, summed up the attraction this way: "You're free. If you want to go fishing, you go fishing. If you want to read, you can read. There's always something to look for, all the different animals . . . If a person is happy in the hills, well, they're foolish to stay out of them." For the most part, Keller lived away from the canyon only in summer, when the annually growing hordes of recreationists spoiled his solitude.

The Doctor and Mother Margery befriended Red Keller early on in their hunting and fishing vacations at Horseshoe Bend, and he became a valued companion, a caretaker of their cabin, and a mentor to young

Brothers Frank and Bradley, instrumental in helping the entire family absorb and practice the Oregon faith. Keller, with his genial expertise, taught the Brothers small sacraments that fathers don't know—how to fashion beautiful, rasty-tasting cigarettes from curls of red madrone bark, how to catch lizards with a long grass stem fashioned into a noose. A drinking alcoholic, Red Keller could handle a fly rod, build a cabin, cook sourdough biscuits and hotcakes, snipe a crevice for gold, read a book all day, shoot a deer and know what to do with it, and manufacture practically any part or tool he needed for his various purposes from detritus washed up by the river. And he could teach. He was the warm and able uncle that every boy needs.

Lou Martin, an old-timer who came into the canyon in the 1920s and lived for many years on Whisky Creek, spoke of the etiquette of interpersonal relations among the canyon dwellers: "If we heard something was wrong, we'd go right now; night or day, if he was sick or hurt and you knew it. Otherwise, maybe once a month you'd poke your nose around. That's enough for a short time. An hour and a half. You never stayed too long or you'd wear your welcome out. You soon learned that in the hills." A highly civilized culture, to my mind. Hospitality was extended *in absentia* as well. At Whisky Creek, Martin told Kay Atwood, "I never put a lock on the cabin; didn't have to. Anybody come around and wanted something to eat, they'd start a fire and they'd leave a note on the table. Perfectly all right."

He did different work, but Lou Martin could have been speaking of my sojourn here when he said: "Sometimes it would be three or four months that I wouldn't see another human being. As long as you're working, it don't make any difference. As long as your mind's occupied. When you mine for yourself you don't put eight hours in. It's twelve, fourteen hours a day . . . It never bothered me." I wonder how I'd be faring, twelve weeks into this retreat, if I didn't have these daily eight or however-many-I-want hours of writing to occupy myself. How would I do without this ongoing involvement that sustains me as I sustain it? Would I like just living here, just being? I'd get outdoors more, I suppose, maybe meditate more, and I'd probably read even more than I am, which is twice as much as I read at home. And how about no books? No paper, no pencil, no books. No clocks either, per my original plan. Just disappear into this place, having told Marilyn to come fetch me in five months.

I probably wouldn't do any better than Lou Martin would have done without his daily mining, though we came here for opposite purposes. Martin arrived from Maine with an awful burden he wanted to forget—his wife and baby, dead in the flu pandemic of 1918. He left their ghosts as far behind him as he could, and lived alone, and busy, the rest of his life. I came not to forget my ghosts but to remember them, and they're keeping me plenty busy. My father is more present to me here, in a way, than he was when he was alive and I was a boy. That father I took for granted. Drunk or sober, laughing or brooding or shouting, with his 225 pounds and his aura of legend and cigarette smoke, he was my father and that was that. But *this* father, the one who accompanies me now, swims in mystery—boy, son, student, idealist, fighter, carouser, brooder, ecstatic, thinker, drinker, seeker . . . Perfectly alone, many miles from another human being, I find myself tearing up at times, lumped in the throat with the living presence of a man whose ashes have rested in a Missouri graveyard for twenty-five years.

And of course there's another ghost here. As I lived my youth a mystery lay before me, the mystery of everything possible and yet undone, withdrawing into the future at the exact pace of my advancing age. Now, as my middle years roll by and wane, mystery remains before me but not in the same way. I have a trajectory, and though much is still possible and much is unknowable, I see, vaguely or surely, the general way I'm likely to tend. This knowing comes with a pang—not because I'm unhappy, but because I feel the unshuckable weight of my limits.

When I swung a bat as a kid I wanted to hit one pitch, just one, the way I'd seen Ted Williams hit one at old Griffith Stadium, the ball cracking off his bat impossibly fast and far, still rising, it seemed, as it passed over the tall green wall in centerfield and left the stadium altogether to bounce and carom somewhere in the dirty streets of Northeast Washington. I did hit a few long balls over the years as I played in recess games at school and summer-league games, but I never made the perfect swing and buried the ball in the sky as I longed to do, never hit it so far that it came down somewhere else entirely, beyond the confines of my life. And neither have I written a transcendent book, or done anything else on that order. And neither am I likely to.

And so the mystery before me in youth has resolved, as any life must, from pure potential to the actual successes and failures of my fifty-two years. But age can arouse a different mystery, as tantalizing as the first. In my mid-forties I began to turn and look back at the way I had come, and I saw that the life I had lived had not clarified behind me into a known topography—it was now mysterious in a different way. I'm the same guy who has opened his eyes from sleep some 18,000 mornings (or afternoons), and yet I'm not. I look back thirty and forty years and realize that I don't know the young man I see. I'm aware of some of the holdings of his head and heart, but what do I really know of what he wanted, why he did this and didn't do that? I know the places he's lived, the ones he has loved, the jobs he has had, his happiest and saddest moments, and I know where he will fetch up in the winter of the year 2001, but I can't honestly say, aside from such facts of personal history, how he came to be me, *why* he came to be me. Purpose, if any, is hard to discern, and more complicated than I can know.

And so, I'm hardly alone here. I invited two ghosts and came here to meet them. I want their company, but as company will do, they're usurping my time and thoughts. They've invaded my morning meditations, impossible to boot from that room once they've barged in. I'm sitting longer hours in their presence at this French Provincial table, day and night, never leaving the cabin at all some days except to piss from the deck or pack in a few armloads of firewood. I'm here in my chair, but I'm a long way from here. A troupe of cougars could be cavorting in the meadow, a band of cavalry passing down the drive—I'm staring at letters thirty years old and scratching at blank pages, following where the pencil leads. How long has it been since I went to the river?

For now, I guess, this is my river.

February 11

I hit San Francisco with little money and no friends to stay with, the O'Farrell Street flat now defunct. After one night in a fleabag hotel south of Market, I met a hippie in the Haight who told me about a communal house on Potrero Hill. I went, was immediately offered a sleeping pad on the floor, and within an hour was eating rice and curry with half a dozen housemates. Nobody pressed me about who I was and what I was up to. That evening we smoked dope in the living room, sitting crosslegged on the rug, listening to the quick riffs and long fluent tones of Ravi Shankar's sitar.

It was a year after the Summer of Love, and I would find that the dark side of the counterculture was clearly showing—speed and other hard drugs, predatory sex, ripoffs of various kinds, random vandalism. San Francisco in 1968 was no utopia. And yet, even as it was souring and falling apart, the hippie culture retained an authentic life. Friendly strangers, young and in motion, shared food, shelter, temporary fellowship. A twenty-year-old arriving near-broke in San Francisco today will look a long time to find a free and congenial inn such as I found overnight in the spring of 1968.

An informal coffeehouse at Howard Presbyterian Church, at the tip of Golden Gate Park's panhandle, was the local center of the draft Resistance. Someone there took me to a big upstairs flat on Waller Street, below the Haight, which several activists shared. One room was available, a side porch that had been walled and roofed in. The roof leaked but the room looked good to me, and looked even better once I'd painted it, according to my personal psychedelic aesthetic, in glossy, eye-jarring red and blue enamel. My furnishings were a twin mattress on the floor and a wooden chair, borrowed from the living room, in which I sat for hours practicing guitar. I found a now-and-again job working for a Greek contractor who renovated old Victorians and put in earthquake reinforcements.

Vince O'Connor was the unassuming head of the flat family. A few years older than me, he was tall and full-framed, had thinning black hair, wore thick glasses, and spoke softly with a shy smile. He put in long hours with the Bay Area office of the Catholic Peace Fellowship, which seemed to be an energetic force in the peace community—it put out a newsletter, organized rallies, put Catholic men struggling with the draft in touch with counselors and progressive clergy. Vince had qualified as a conscientious objector but then refused to perform the alternative service he'd been assigned, deciding that he couldn't in conscience cooperate in any way with Selective Service or the military. In a few months he would go to trial, and as a fairly prominent agitator he would probably face something close to the five-year maximum sentence. He approached his fate with equanimity and a lot of hard work on behalf of others.

Another flatmate, Loren, was a draft counselor with the Central Committee for Conscientious Objectors on Market Street. Loren took long baths in the evening accompanied by a jug of red wine. Rod Rose, a short friendly guy with an open-mouthed smile, had refused induction and was quietly awaiting indictment and trial. He played blues on a steel-string guitar. The one woman among us, whose name I remember as Karen, actually had a paying job. When I asked her what my share of the rent would be, she gave a short laugh. "Your share? Usually I pay it. Just give me what you can."

Often there were others in the flat as well—Resistance members and other activists, most of them there to confer with Vince, and AWOL soldiers or sailors who didn't want to go to Vietnam or didn't want to go back. Hippies, young drifters, guys like me dealing with the draft. Some stayed for weeks, sacking out in the living room and in bedrooms not in use.

As my induction date approached there was no particular moment of decision—more of a gradual settling, the way bare feet sink into sand as ebbing wave-wash flows over them. I drew resolve from the example of those around me, and from a certain document that the Selective Service System had released in an unguarded moment in 1965, and that the Resistance had distributed far and wide as a pamphlet titled "Channeling." It made clear that Selective Service had coercive designs far grander than the mere procurement of cannon fodder for the armed forces; the agency also aspired "to control effectively the service of individuals who are not in the armed forces." This it did by carrot and stick, offering deferments to those well schooled and well heeled enough to go to college and graduate school and pursue careers in fields "essential to the Nation." The document defined those essential vocations pretty specifically: "Dedicated service as a civilian in such fields as engineering, the sciences, and teaching constitute the ultimate in their expression of patriotism." Such fields, in other words, that might win the Space Race and the Cold War for the United States of America.

Those too poor or academically unequipped or unwilling to respond to the carrot suffered the stick, or rather the cudgel—"the club of induction," as the writers called it, one of a total of two metaphors in the pamphlet's seven abstract and dispassionate pages. The document ends with the confident spirit of an agency that has discovered its calling: "Delivery of manpower for induction . . . is not much of an administrative or financial challenge. It is in dealing with the other millions of registrants that the system is heavily occupied, developing more effective human beings in the national interest." This channeling, or "pressurized guidance," the writers frankly acknowledged, "is the American or indirect way of achieving what is done by direction in foreign countries where choice is not allowed."

It gave me grim pleasure to know that I had already jumped the tracks that Selective Service had set for me, that if I was going to be a "more effective human being," I wasn't going to be their kind. Someone in the flat had a ratty edition of Thoreau's "Civil Disobedience," which I hadn't read in school—not the kind of literature an orderly society teaches its children—and this time Henry David spoke right to my heart and my best hopes for myself. "Why has every man a conscience, then?" he asked rhetorically. "I think that we should be men first, and subjects afterward." Thoreau seemed to voice the very temper of the 1960s when he argued that if an unjust law "requires you to be the agent of injustice to another, then, I say, break the law. Let your life be a counter friction to stop the machine."

It bucked me up to hear this man of the nineteenth century, not a leftist or even a thoroughgoing pacifist—he fiercely advocated John

Brown's actions—speak his version of the American way, and it bucked me up to be around other young men who had refused or were going to. One night when Vince O'Connor came home late from the Catholic Peace Fellowship office I asked him what his job was, how many others he worked with.

"My job?" He smiled, peering through his thick lenses. "I'm the staff. The office is about half the size of this room."

"You're *it?*"

"I'm it."

Vince didn't act like a hero, but in his way he was one. If he could embrace five years in the pen, I could make it through two or three. And it did not escape me, of course, that to refuse induction would make *me* a hero, or at least a worthy, in the eyes of some. I was far from averse to that. I vaguely imagined giving speeches, being interviewed, imparting sage counsel to other young men. I even looked forward, in a way, to going to prison. It promised a kind of salvation from my chronic uncertainties. My life would be out of my hands, and I was ready to give it over. I saw myself having philosophical discussions with other inmates, and I assumed—I really did—that I'd have long quiet hours during which to practice guitar, and I'd get really good. Of course they would let me bring my guitar.

In the early morning of July 10th, somewhere in the gray streets of industrial Oakland, I joined a crowd of other inductees ordered to report that day. Most were arriving in buses from outside the Bay Area. A sergeant greeted us cheerily. I guess he was a sergeant—he wore one of those skinny caps. He seemed to smile especially hard at my scraggly beard and bushy hair, my army surplus jacket.

We were told to sit on benches on one side of a large room and complete our paperwork. I fumbled with the forms, my hands shaking. They wanted health history, names of kin, other information. I stopped reading and turned to the guy on my right. I asked him if he wanted to go to Vietnam. If he believed in the war. If he thought it was worth fighting. Some of us were refusing, I told him. He had a choice. He didn't have to sign the papers and he didn't have to go.

He was a slight kid with big ears, his blond hair already cropped for the army. He looked at me with a fear in his eyes I will always remember. At the time, I thought he was afraid of Vietnam, and he probably was. But mostly, I think now, he was afraid of what I had said, afraid of choice in that room where choice had been forsaken. And what could he have made of the bushy-haired, bespectacled, very agitated young man sitting next to him in an army jacket and jeans worn through at the knees, peppering him with rapid-fire, only semi-coherent questions?

He was probably eighteen, two years younger than me. I've wondered many times what became of him. If he went to the war. If he came back. If his name is on the wall in D.C. If I've seen him without knowing him in the paper or on TV, in a wheelchair, maybe, long-haired and bearded himself, declaiming a little too loudly at a hearing, telling a story that nobody wants to hear about how his buddy's face was blown off by a piece of shrapnel as he lay next to him, how he doesn't sleep so well, maybe drinks too much, how his life went irredeemably wrong somehow in what he thought had been service to his country.

But probably not. More likely he's married and working in Modesto or San Jose, his hair still short, graying like mine, his kids a little older now than he and I were in 1968. More likely he remembers me, if he thinks of me at all, with contempt. But when I think of him it's that disbelieving fear I see, and I see how young he was. Except for the sergeant, I may have been the oldest one in the room. None of us were old enough to vote. None of us were old enough to drink in a California bar. The blond kid was a boy, I was a boy, all of us hunched on those benches were boys, and whatever we felt about it, we were responding to a fate we'd had no say in forming, a fate brought down on us by older men safe in their coats and ties and crisp uniforms, secure in the shining stone fortresses of Washington, D.C.

The blond kid had no interest in talking to me, and neither did anyone else. They were glancing, snickering. I had come with big plans to move fluidly among them, speaking with poise and assurance to each. I was going to address them with a passionate Resistance speech until the powers that be dragged me out of the building. I was going to be an organizer, like my father, but I couldn't even organize my own feelings. To hell with them, I thought. They'll be on cots in some barracks tonight, some jerk officer yelling *Shut the fuck up* then yelling them awake at five in the morning. I'll be drinking wine and sleeping with my girlfriend in San Francisco.

Embarrassed, exhilarated, thoroughly scared, I got up with my papers and walked a few steps away. The sergeant gave me a long look from his desk across the room. Next to his desk was an open doorway into the rest of the building. A heavy black line had been painted across the linoleum in the doorway, the line where you left the civilian world. From that black line I saw the routings that Ken Hyams and others had told me about: a series of narrower colored lines, red, yellow, green, took off down a hallway, turning off variously into rooms and other hallways. The floor had been waxed to a brilliant polish.

Absurdly, I drifted around the room gazing at military posters on the walls. They showed earnest men, handsome in their uniforms, pursuing their jobs with capable smiles. One was working with radar equipment, another driving a Jeep. There were no weapons in the pictures. No blood or napalm, no fire. Just clean-shaven white faces, and one black, intent on their duties.

There was no reason to stay, but now that my moment of truth had arrived, I guess I wanted to draw it out. I had dropped out of college and now I was thumbing my nose at the United States government. I felt recklessly alert, as if calling a bet for more than I could afford to lose with nothing but a pair of sixes and a wild hunch.

"Son?" the sergeant called. "Do you intend to join the army today?"

I smirked at him. Any man who had risen to the level of sergeant, I figured, could deduce the answer without my help.

"Better think it over," he said. "Think it over real good."

"I have thought it over," I said, disappointed at the quavery reed that was my voice. "Have you thought about the innocent people you're bombing in Vietnam?"

"If you're not gone in ten seconds," the sergeant said, instantly on his feet, "I'll be givin' you a hand."

197

Everyone in the room had turned to look. I scrawled "STOP THE WAR" on my blank papers, tossed them clumsily onto the sergeant's desk, and walked out into the foggy morning, wired and free.

February 14

Any mobile phone user in the Rogue River country with his or her
monitor on, as well as the mobile operator and the answering machine
in a certain residence a hundred miles north, and possibly a certain
human being within that residence, heard the following from unit 7796,
assigned to Dutch Henry Homestead, at 10 P.M. this Valentine's night:

THE CANDLE

On the table in the pewter stick
You sent with me, it throws light
To write this by, my dinner done,
And I watch the flame standing
Not quite still on its melted pool,
Holding within it a bluish dark
Around the curved black wick
Whose tip glows red, the pale
Body of the greater flame
Pouring upward into shadows
Through a point that won't resolve,
Because the flame shifts
And wavers like a thing alive—
Like nothing but itself, but still
I saw the ears of those two does
This morning, how they twitched
And slightly turned, and the screech owl
Last week, who bobbed and tilted
In the flashlight's beam, needing
To know what had ruined his view—
Like nothing but itself, my love,
But I saw you as well,
An inclination of your face
That I've long known, and that lively
Stillness when you sleep, rapt

Within a dream. The flame flickered—
Did I speak?—and as it did, I heard
You laughing your delighted laugh,
As if whatever I'd just said
You'd found amusing, as if this flame
Were your conscious mind itself,
Hearkening across the table—
And then *I* laughed, remembering
That I'm the one who all this time
Has been hearkening to it, my love, to you.

One day early in that summer of 1968, I was walking east on Haight Street with a bag of laundry over my shoulder when I found myself face-to-face with Cathy Hendricks, who had been my girlfriend at Reed. We hadn't been in touch for many months. She too had left Reed, was living now in Mendocino, in the city only for a day or two. It's hard to argue with fate, and who wanted to? After a quick trip upcoast she was living with me in the Waller Street flat. We upgraded to a double mattress from Goodwill that turned out to have bedbugs, which found Cathy first, then me—I had scoffed—a few nights later. The bites felt exactly as my father had often described them when telling of his life with my mother in New Orleans in the early forties—"Like a goddamn poker straight out of the fire."

This made me feel properly bohemian, but Cathy was less charmed. She had lovely long dark hair, a flashing smile, and a restless spirit. Our time together was volatile. I was too laconic, too self-enclosed, too moody for her, and she was a bit too mercurial and tightly strung for me. But I liked being with her, sleeping with her, going out with her to hear Janis Joplin at Winterland or the Fillmore. Cathy was the main provider, once she landed an office job with the ACLU, but I did my part. When I wasn't working or had been too long between paydays, I got pretty adept at shoplifting blocks of cheese and packages of ground beef and other staples from Safeway, my army jacket with its big pockets providing the perfect vehicle. Safeway, in my considered judgment, deserved theft because it was Safeway—big, corporate, and very Establishment.

Once or twice a week I would forage more honestly. I went down to the municipal pier at the foot of Van Ness and spent the day working a couple of crab traps, baiting them with fish heads or meat scraps that storekeepers gave me. I would lounge in the sun, smoking cigarettes and putting on a hippie show for the tourists. One elderly couple stood and watched me as I raised a trap, dumped a couple of crabs into my bag, rebaited and lowered the trap and leaned against the railing.

"Do you catch many?" the woman asked.

"Yes, I do," I answered, "because I know how they think. I can hear them. Their conversations."

"Ah . . ." the woman said.

"I fill my bag, sell 'em to rich people, and give all the money to the army. That's why I'm in uniform," I said brightly.

The couple hurried off.

My hippie show would get my brother arrested later in the year. It was an edgy time in the military. The Tet offensive in February had destroyed any illusion that we were winning the war, despite half a million troops deployed. Weed and speed were rampant among GIs in Vietnam; officers were beginning to die in unaccountable explosions, no enemy in sight. Stateside, organized demonstrations were rising from within the ranks. My brother came up from George Air Force Base for one of them, a march in downtown San Francisco, and a night or two later he was walking with me on Market Street, in uniform, when a military paddy wagon screeched to the curb and two MPs popped out full of righteous bluster. "*Who you consortin' with, airman?*" yelled the more insolent of the two, cocking his head at the rowdy-haired guy in bad jeans and army surplus jacket who was watching in amazement. "My brother," said my brother. "*Get in the van,*" barked the MP, and with that my brother was gone. They stuck him in a cell somewhere and released him a few hours later. Technically he was farther from his base than his leave allowed, but they had nothing substantial to hold him on. The military command just wanted the rank and file to know they were being watched.

The crabs I brought home from the pier made for good eating and a smelly kitchen, which I don't remember ever cleaning up. Cathy did, I suppose. And Karen, who probably was happy to have another woman in the family. Resistance men tended to be smart and sensitive but not especially progressive on questions of gender roles. The primary role desired of women was expressed in a hopeful saying of the time: "Girls say yes to boys who say no." The phrase "gender roles" would have made no sense to me. I was my father's son. Men cooked once in a while, usually something major for company, but washed dishes only when camping.

I hadn't lived with a woman before. It made me feel more mature, more confident, more able—more, I guess, of a man. The previous fall, at Reed, Cathy had been my first sexual partner. *Right!* I remember thinking the first time we went that far, *of course!* I'd dated in high school, done some pretty vigorous making out in the car, but hadn't been assertive enough—or with a girl assertive enough—to get the deed done. Some of my friends were doing it. I felt retarded, playing catch-up, and so in my senior year I blew it with the first girl I felt something like love for, a shy, lovely blonde named Phyllis. I'd gone with her for several months when, under a tree on New Year's Eve, champagned and very warm with her, I asked if she loved me enough to have me physically. *No,* she said, a little fearfully, *not yet,* and a week later, stupidly, I dropped her cold.

I thought I was going to get it done at last one night that spring, when a more experienced friend and I left Benbow's Tavern and decided to look for hookers. He knew where to go: Swann Street. We didn't have to wait long. A black man smoking a cigarette beckoned us off the lamplit sidewalk, collected twelve dollars from each of us—ten for the woman, two for the room—and soon two youngish women in shorts were leading us, with giggles about what nice "boyfriends" we looked like, down an alleyway and into the back of a brick home. That's where it went all wrong for me. They took us through a living room lit only by the bluish radiance of a television, which an older woman was watching. She ignored us. The bedroom was adjacent, separated by a sheet hung in a broad doorway. There was one double bed, on one side of which my friend and his girl quickly got to business.

My girl was considerably older than his—this room was brightly lit—and looked vaguely like the cleaning woman who came once a week to the apartment I shared with my mother. We sat on the side of the bed. I could hear television commercials. The woman stroked my leg a little, but no part of me felt erotic. All I wanted was to leave. "What's the matter, honey?" she asked. "Your time gonna be up and you're not gonna have nothin'." She sounded genuinely sympathetic, like an aunt or a grade school teacher. "I'm sorry," I said, "I'm not feeling too good." My friend, fortunately, didn't take long.

My prospects seemed to brighten again that summer, which I spent waiting tables at A. V. Ristorante Italiano on New York Avenue, which was then the most authentic Italian restaurant in D.C. Congressmen, performers, and men who looked like Mafiosi ate there regularly. The jukebox was entirely Italian opera. Grace, a fierce-eyed waitress and a member of the owner's family, liked to flirt with me, and one night near closing time, when she and I were stowing cartons in a storage room, she unzipped me and had me in her mouth almost before I knew what was happening. We had to stop—too soon, too soon—when we heard footsteps and a waiter's voice. "After," Grace whispered. I finished my shift in a state of semi-exultation, fantasizing, and at closing time waited under the awning out front. Grace walked out and laughed when she saw me. "Silly boy," she said, "I go home to my husband," and she went to the curb to hail a cab.

So I was well ready when the big night finally arrived, with Cathy, at Reed in the fall of 1967. It was less and more than I had imagined. Less, in that it was so natural, so simple, so . . . normal. And more, for something like the same reasons. I felt myself washed through with a strangely clear vision that people everywhere were doing the same thing, this thing we called *making love*, and that all of them, all of us, were perfect beings exactly as we were—perfectly adequate to the lives we had been born to, perfectly eligible for human happiness.

And now, the next summer, in my leaky-roofed room in the shabby end of the Fillmore district in San Francisco, the feeling returned. It was the sex but not only the sex. Living and eating and sleeping with a partner, working my carpenter's helper job, I felt more authentic somehow, more legitimate. I was a hippie and a draft resister, I had half-dropped out of conventional society, but I was also feeling for the first time like a householder, an average Joe, a guy going about his life like men everywhere. Allen Ginsberg, in his poem "America," chants a long list of political and personal grievances, tells the country to go fuck itself with its atom bomb, but then, in the final lines, announces a certain qualified allegiance:

> I'd better get right down to the job.
> It's true I don't want to join the Army or turn lathes in precision
>   parts factories, I'm nearsighted and psychopathic anyway.
> America I'm putting my queer shoulder to the wheel.

My life felt like that, somehow.

February 15

On an August morning that summer, maybe September, someone rapped at the door to the flat. The door, accessed by a decrepit flight of outside stairs, was right by my porch-become-bedroom. Cathy and I heard Vince O'Connor open it and say hello, then a man's voice. He identified himself as an agent with the FBI and asked to see John Daniel. The red and blue woodwork flared brighter, I remember, when he spoke my name. Cathy urged me to lie low, but I recognized my moment. I gracefully resisted her pressure and pulled on a pair of jeans. At the doorway, Vince was stalling, unsure if I wanted to show myself. "I'm John Daniel," I said over his shoulder.

But Vince, in his worn plaid bathrobe, didn't move. He asked the man, politely, if he was carrying a gun. The agent replied that he wasn't obliged to say.

"Then I have to assume you are," Vince said, "and we have a rule against weapons in this home. Please leave it on the porch."

He actually said it. I remember clearly. I don't remember if the agent laughed or scowled or stared or what. I don't remember his face at all. He wore a dark blue suit and black shoes, a tie with subdued slanting stripes. His hair, I'm pretty sure, was dark and short.

I prevailed on Vince and the other flatmates to let him in as far as the kitchen. I appealed to their sense of hospitality, but my real concern was less noble. I feared that my moment might elude me, that Vince was stealing my show. While the others milled around fixing breakfast, the agent and I sat at the little kitchen table. He told me I had broken federal law and was facing imminent indictment. He asked if I knew what the penalties were. I told him I did. He told me that federal prison was not a place I wanted to be. He asked if I knew what it meant to be a convicted felon. He asked why a bright young man like me, a good kid, would ruin his future and good name. He told me it wasn't too late to change my mind. I could still submit to induction.

The agent spoke as if he cared about me, and I believe he did. In his voice I heard my boss at the D.C. bookstore who had been concerned about my future. I heard certain male teachers I'd had over the years. I heard my cousin who had been a cadet at West Point. I heard my father—not the picket line brawler and firebrand orator, not the drunk, but the Germanic figure who liked me to shave and get regular haircuts and wear nice clothes and behave with manners and do well in school.

I told the FBI man that I needed to follow my conscience, that the war was immoral and illegal, that the draft was unjust, but the phrases sounded pat and hollow to my own ears, lifted out of movement literature. I wasn't even sure it was me talking. He heard me out, attentively, then said: "You won't have another chance. Are you sure you know what you're doing?"

"No," I said, sounding at last like me. "Are you sure you know what you're doing?"

He smiled thinly and got up to go, but Vince—who must have been waiting for the moment—pressed a mug of coffee on him and asked how he felt about the war.

"I don't make foreign policy," the agent replied, or something to that effect.

"Of course you don't," said Vince, with his shy smile, peering through his thick lenses. "But surely you have an opinion."

"I didn't come here to tell you my opinions."

"You work for the American government," Vince pressed. "The government is napalming villages in Vietnam. You've seen the pictures—kids with their skin on fire. How do you feel about that?"

"I respect your view of that," said the agent. "My job is to enforce federal law."

"What about higher laws?" someone said. Cathy and everyone in the flat, except for two very nervous AWOL soldiers, had gathered in the kitchen. "Martin Luther King broke lots of laws. You recognize no higher authority than the U.S. government?"

"I recognize no higher civil authority. Do you?"

"Do you leave your conscience at home when you go to work?"

"My conscience tells me to do my job," the agent said, looking for a place to set his mug down. But our avid battalion hemmed him in. Somebody peppered him with Gandhi. Someone lobbed Thoreau at him. Someone reminded him of the Nuremberg trials. How could he say he was only doing his job?

The FBI man conceded us nothing. He stood his ground, he hewed to the discipline of his office, but by the time he escaped the peace-people's kitchen and made his way down the creaky outside stairs, his blue-suited figure laughably out of place in the derelict world of Waller Street, we had made him earn his morning's pay.

February 18

A week or two ago I walked down the Corral Trail for some fresh air. This trail angles southeasterly downslope from the cabin, crossing a little stream known—for its association with a particularly onerous work detail when the Brothers were young—as the River Kwai. The trail plunges into and then climbs out of the verdant ravine of Meadow Creek, then contours the lower slopes until it loses itself in a big meadow just above the river where packers and miners once corralled their livestock. Only a few fenceposts are left. Along the way to the meadow are the biggest trees in the area—undulant red madrones reaching their green crowns far out over the slopes, and Douglas firs as thick at the base as I am tall, over a hundred and fifty feet high, their lower bark charred by a long-ago fire.

I paused a moment by several of the trees. I usually do. I touch the bark, and sometimes I lean close and smell it. (I stop short of hugging, but not always far short.) It seems disrespectful not to acknowledge a life so long in its place.

And yet, I've felled big trees for firewood—not here, and not this big—and used to love to watch the timber cutters work when I was a logger in Washington State for a couple of years in my twenties. Let me confess it. There is a knee-wobbling, scrotum-shrinking, let-out-a-whoop thrill in watching a tall tree topple—the stressed fiber creaking and popping as the massive wood-weight leans, leans more, then gains momentum with a rush of wind and a snapping of limbs as it grazes other trees and at last sends shock waves through the ground and up your legs when it hits with a crunching of its crown, a waft of lichen and needles and bark flakes raining slowly down.

We've cut too much old-growth forest in the Northwest, but if I had lived a hundred years ago I might have been one of the cutters. Who would have worried about depleting such vast stores of vast trees? Red cedars twelve feet through at the base, Sitka spruces nearly as tall as a football field is long, an abundance of matriarch-patriarch hemlocks and Douglas firs, many of the biggest growing right by rivers where they could be felled and floated to the mills. I hope I would have found an easier way to make a living than working one end of a misery whip, but on the other hand, I might have welcomed a vigorous outdoors life providing material for the building of communities.

The trouble is, we never stopped building, never stopped cutting. With the construction boom after World War II we logged farther and faster every decade until the 1990s, on private lands and public. Stripping the old growth, installing orderly plantations, we gradually starved ourselves of sensory knowledge of big forests made of big trees. In the same way, we stripped our rivers of the salmon whose runs were once so seasonally thick that horses refused to ford streams, and farmers could pitchfork all the bright fish they wanted. Now we live among remnants—scatters of fish, patches of forest. No one alive knew the forests and rivers in their prime, but the land has a longer memory. In these remnants it remembers the epic abundance that was and could be again.

But there have been human losses, too. The decades when timber was king saw the flourishing of small communities across the Northwest, supported by the sweat of men doing hard and dangerous work in the woods and mills—work they liked, work that provided essential materials to the American people. They knew the land in the way that most had known it from the beginnings of our history: through their labor. Over the course of the twentieth century, they came to be outnumbered by a larger class of urban and suburban residents who did not work the land, whose engagement with it was largely recreational, and from whose numbers the conservation and environmental movements arose. Hence the timber wars of the 1990s, when environmentalists brought legal actions against the U.S. Forest Service and other land management agencies and forced major reductions in the timber cut on federal lands. This change was necessary—the annual harvest had been running unsustainably amok—and was welcomed by those, such as me, whose contributions had funded the legal actions and whose recreational interests were served by the reduced cut. To many timber communities, though, the new harvest regime—which came on the heels of earlier jolts from mill automation and exposure to the vagaries of a global market—spelled disaster. Mills closed, small businesses withered, social problems soared, and many proud, independent men who had lived three or four generations in place were forced to move their families in search of different and usually lower-paying work.

The luckiest and the most resourceful have managed to land on their feet in their own communities. I met three of them in the summer of 1994, when the Brothers brought in a crew to deal with some tipsy trees behind the writer's cabin, one of which had snapped in two over the winter and impaled the entry porch with its upper half. The trees stood on steeply sloping ground as close as ten feet from the cabin. While a wiry kid climbed and swung on a rope in the treetops, deftly lopping madrone limbs and dismantling their trunks from the top down, the faller, a man in his mid-thirties, was dropping the conifers. He studied each tree carefully before cranking up his long-barred saw and slicing out an undercut, taking his time, the saw as light in his hands as a carving knife. Then he deepened his backcut inch by inch, leaving the saw idling in the tree as he tapped in a wedge or pumped his hydraulic jack—looked up, tapped or pumped, sawed deeper, dab by dab, until the heartwood creaked and gave and the tree went down. He dropped them carefully along the hillside, nesting one behind the other in a stable deck braced by stumps and trees left standing. None came close to hitting the cabin. It was artistry. He could have driven a stake into the ground eighty feet away with every tree he felled, or come very close.

They were a friendly and talkative crew, much like the men I had met when I worked as a logger, but the mood suddenly changed when the faller, on a break, took a drink of water from one of the tin cups lying around the cabin and saw the words stamped on the cup's bottom.

"*Sierra Club*," he just about spat. "You belong to that?"

"No," I told him. My Wilderness Society coffee mug was safely shut up in the cupboard.

"The Sierra Club don't know a damn thing about these woods," he went on, eyeing the cup he had set on the counter. "They live in the city and love the wild animals. Hell, they don't *know* the animals. But they know all about how to manage these woods, don't they."

I wasn't looking for a fight. I told him about a prominent environmentalist, more at home talking with politicians than walking in the woods, whose colleagues had written him a mock remedial guide to birds with categories such as Little Brown Birds, Ducks 'n Stuff, Call 'em All Redtails, and the like. The faller and his crewmates smiled a little.

"But don't you think these forests have been logged a little hard?" I asked them.

"Look out there," said the third crew member, a hefty man who might have been thirty. "Does that look logged too hard to you?"

I found myself looking instead at the guy's t-shirt, which was blazoned with the image of a Campbell's soup label. The flavor was Cream of Spotted Owl.

"That's the wild Rogue corridor," I reminded him. "Can't be logged. But up out of the canyon, what about that?"

They'd have none of it, but I thought I detected an ounce less conviction in their denials. They hunted and fished and worked in the woods, or had worked. They knew the dusty roads where the men and machines went in and the timber came out. They'd seen the stripped mountainsides, some of them as steep as cliffs, streaked with puke-outs, patched over with brush and paltry planted seedlings. They knew that salmon and steelhead runs were a fraction of what they'd been, and that clear-cut logging was one big reason why.

"Look here," said the faller, as steadily as he handled his saw. "That's a working forest out there, or it used to be. You're a writer. Do you want paper to write on? Do you live in a house? If you do, and if other people do, *somebody's* got to go out there and harvest some trees."

"Sure," I said, "but we've been taking too many . . ."

"What's too many?" he shot back. "I don't notice any of them new houses standing empty very long. There's a market for all the lumber and plywood they make."

We talked on a while, agreeing on little, and they went back to work, taking down a few smaller oaks and madrones the Brothers wanted for firewood. By four o'clock they had their saws shut down and their ropes coiled. We joked a little about the small clearcut they'd made of my retreat. The kid who'd been swinging in the treetops gestured me over to their pickup and pointed, with a grin, to the bumper sticker:

EARTH FIRST! WE'LL LOG THE OTHER PLANETS LATER

And then, just before they left, the faller surprised me. He looked straight at me, and there was the hint of an appeal in his flat, declarative voice. "Look," he said. "There may be better ways to log. That's all right. Things change. But this is what I do." He gestured toward the big trees he'd laid neat as pins across the hillside behind the cabin. "This is what *we* do. We grew up in this country. We've got kids. We'd like them to grow up here too."

As their truck jounced up the drive, leaving me alone with silence and the sweet tangy odor of conifer sap, I wondered what my father would have made of our conversation. I could see him with his elbows on his knees, his lips pursed, his face downcast, nodding his head slightly, his characteristic manner when wrestling a tough problem. He would have seen justice on both sides, I'm sure. He would have pointed out that the timber workers themselves had not decided to overcut the national forests and cause mills to be built across the Northwest—their bosses had, some of them leaders of large corporations, with the help of politicians whose campaigns the corporate leaders had amply funded. He would have observed that injunctions—the legal tool environmentalists skillfully used to force change—always brought bitterness with them and left bitterness behind them. He would have said that no one, right or wrong, enjoys being run over by a majority, and no one likes to be condescended to. I don't think he would have claimed any special privilege for the timber workers, but I suspect he would have said of them what he said in a speech about factory workers laid off by automation in the 1960s: "These are not just statistics, not just 'people'—these are men and women who have homes. These are men and women who have obligations to society. These are men and women who are citizens, who want to measure up. Are they to be treated just as casualties?"

Not far below the homestead, I left the Corral Trail and scuttled down to explore an area of mossy crags and boulders. As I made my way among the rocks I began to see bones—scraps at first, then a big leg bone—elk?—and still lower, a long intact skull with teeth. Horse. One of Dutch Henry's, maybe, but more likely one of Bill Graiff's three, dead half a century at least. An odd place to find horse remains, in a confusion of boulders well below the trail where a horse would have had a hard time getting if it had wanted to, and it wouldn't have wanted to. But water and gravity have had fifty years to do their work.

My first impulse was to pick up the skull and lug it home to the cabin, but an eeriness made me leave it alone. However it had got there, it belonged in its mystery, half-embedded in gravel among verdantly mossed rocks in silent woods. At the cabin it would only be one more thing.

Something interesting happens when you write your way back inside your remembered past, as I'm doing here. A remarkable number of ordinary events from your present life—decades later, many miles removed—connect, willy-nilly, with the story you're spinning from memory. Finding bones in the fastness of the Rogue River Canyon in the winter of 2001, I was instantly reminded of bones I found and did take home, or tried to, in the summer of 1968 as I waited to be indicted for refusing induction into the army.

It was the one time in my life when I've put gathered bones to practical use. I took mescaline one day with two AWOL soldiers who had been crashing at the Waller Street flat while they figured out what to do. I'll call them Kenny and Howard. We hitched across the Golden Gate Bridge and walked the heights of the Marin Headlands, exulting in the brilliantly clear day. It was us and the wind and sky, a soaring hawk or two, the spangled sea far below us and not far at all. Kenny and Howard broke up laughing when we happened on one of the empty cannon bunkers built to defend the bay from invasion during World War II. When he caught his breath between convulsions, Kenny said, "Let's serve here, Howard. Let's protect the San Francisco fucking *Bay*. We've got to do our part, man."

A little later I found the bones, deer bones, most of a skeleton. Some of the bones had dry gristle and shreds of hide attached. I started putting them into a black plastic garbage bag, which I can't remember if I'd found or brought from home. Ribs, leg bones, vertebrae, I placed bone after bone into the bag. I had no idea what I would do with them, but once I was filling the bag I saw no reason to stop. "These are good bones," I remember saying to my companions, who derided my obsession.

In late afternoon we hiked back, me with the bag slung over my shoulder. We arrived at the bridge too low on the slope. Trekking uphill along the west side of the bridge, traffic rushing overhead, we came to two dangling fire hoses and decided to save ourselves some hiking by climbing them. "This will be your boot camp," Howard told me, a gleam in his eyes. It was maybe a twenty-five-foot climb up the hoses, which were a little stretchy and very grippable, to the bridge railing. Kenny and Howard went first, me following with the bone bag tied around my belt and halfway pulling my pants off.

It was a bad mistake. There is now a bikeway on the west side of the Golden Gate Bridge, but in 1968 there was no bikeway, no sidewalk, nothing. Pedestrians walked, as they do now, on the east side only.

We stood three abreast, backsides crammed against the railing, our spaced-out minds at a loss as rubbernecking drivers surged by in a continuous rush at the tips of our boots. With timing so perfect it gave me a paranoid panic, a highway patrol car slowed in the right lane, its cherry top flashing, and stopped in front of us. "*Get in the car,*" the trooper barked through his loudspeaker.

We did, solving the immediate problem but posing another. Kenny and Howard were wanted by the military, and, for all they knew, by civilian authorities as well. I think they had been AWOL for more than thirty days, which made them deserters, facing serious time in the stockade with none of the legal rights of civilians. I'd given my driver's license to Kenny, who was about my height and weight, but we didn't match in hair color or eye color. (Licenses then had no photo.) I don't know what Howard was carrying. I had no ID. Why keep any cards at all, I'd been telling myself.

The trooper pulled over just past the toll booths and told us to get out. He had us line up against the car, facing him. "What were you doing on that side of the bridge?" he wanted to know.

We told him about hiking the headlands and climbing the fire hoses. Above his mirror sunglasses, his forehead scrunched. "Let's see some identification," he said. Then he looked at the bag in my hands. "What you got in there?"

"It's some bones," I said.

"Bones?"

"Yes sir, it's just some bones I found."

"Let's see," he said.

I handed over the bag, Kenny and Howard watching intently. The trooper set it down and fumbled at the wadded plastic. He took off his sunglasses, went down on one knee. He reached in, said "Jesus, what —" and all in a motion the three of us were running south on the downsloping freeway. The cop shouted. I heard his car starting. We ran until we could jump off to the right into cypresses and eucalyptus trees and lose ourselves in the parkland of the Presidio. Kenny, bringing up the rear, grinned at the trooper in his car and flashed him the peace sign.

We took the long way home, meandering through the Richmond district and Golden Gate Park, and we couldn't stop laughing. Kenny kept saying, "Bones, man. Boo-koo bones. You gave that officer of the law a bag of stinkin' *bones*."

"I told you," I said. "Those were good bones."

Kenny and Howard moved out a week later. I have no idea what happened to them.

February 19

My father had a problem with the military, too, but his problem was getting in. By 1942, when he and my mother were living in New Orleans, several of his labor movement friends had been drafted or had volunteered. My father's Selective Service classification was 3-A—no imminent draft. At thirty-eight, he was probably too old for immediate conscription, and he wrote Margaret that he wanted to finish his work in New Orleans before he volunteered. A later letter seems to suggest that he did volunteer, and was deemed too old or physically unfit. He had hammer toes, and possibly fallen arches, but no other physical irregularities that I know of.

Whatever happened, in January 1944, he was taking Coast Guard training in Philadelphia and wishing in a letter to Margaret "that I was doing more of what I should be doing to win the war." As his friends ship out to Europe, he confesses "a personal feeling of inadequacy." In March he writes, "If the FBI passes me I'll be sworn in"—to the Coast Guard—"next week." I can find no further mention of the Coast Guard or of the war in my father's correspondence. The FBI might not have passed him. As a very visible labor agitator and a former Socialist organizer, he must have warranted a substantial bureau file. Or maybe he was approved—his younger friends had also been Socialists—and was too chagrined at the nature of his service to write about it. The duty he had been expecting, if admitted, was one eight-hour shift every five days guarding the highly vulnerable waterfront of Philadelphia.

But my father was fighting, of course, all along. The story at the heart of his legendry comes from this same period of his life. I never heard it from his lips. I don't know how it first came to me. It seemed always a part of his aura, the rich clothing of his past. In recent years I've filled it out with details from letters and newspaper clippings.

In March 1943, after moving to Philadelphia and learning that his wife was pregnant with the child they would name George, my father traveled to LaFollette, Tennessee, on a mission for the Amalgamated

Clothing Workers. The union represented eight hundred workers at two shirt factories there, which at the time were turning out uniforms for American troops in Europe. Since voting in the union, the workers had won several wage increases. Now the union locals were threatened—not by the mill owners, but by a rival union.

This was the part of the story I never understood as a kid. In the songs we played on scratched-up records in our living room, songs I still sing when I'm driving or showering, labor seemed a thoroughly united movement. It was *Solidarity forever, for the Union makes us strong.* Joe Hill, the Christ of the labor gospel, had been executed—framed on a murder charge by the Utah copper bosses, according to our text—and had risen again in song on behalf of all workers, all unions. *Where working men will organize, Joe Hill is at their side.* It was all for one, one for all. As it's written in a great song out of the east Kentucky coal fields, there was really only one question:

They say in Harlan County
There are no neutrals there—
You'll either be a union man
Or a thug for J. H. Blair.

Which side are you on, boy,
Which side are you on?

I didn't know that the union side had been bitterly fractious from its beginnings. The more workers a union could sign up, the more locals it could organize and hold, the greater its economic and political clout. Some union chiefs set about building major fiefdoms, and none more successfully than John L. Lewis, the charismatic and poundingly eloquent president of the United Mine Workers of America. The son of a Welsh immigrant coal miner, Lewis rejected the American Federation of Labor, cofounding and becoming first president of the Congress of Industrial Organizations. But he soon chafed even in that harness, and by the early forties he had pulled his mine workers from the CIO and was staging a major power display, defying President Roosevelt and the war effort with a series of coal strikes and raiding other unions to enlarge his base.

The United Mine Workers controlled the East Tennessee coal fields. The shirt workers in LaFollette, as elsewhere in the Appalachian region, were largely wives and daughters of miners. Lewis saw a natural opportunity. He announced the UMW's intent to take over the shirt industry, and the Amalgamated—a loyal CIO union—sent my father to LaFollette to see what he could do to hold the locals there. He wasn't optimistic. "The situation looks very gloomy and for the life of me I don't know how we can stop them," he wrote sister Margaret from his room in the Russell Hotel. He must have known, and shared with my mother, that the situation was dangerous as well as gloomy. Three months pregnant, daring to believe that she wouldn't miscarry this time, she wrote to him: "Only one thing, lunkhead. Accidents caused by stupidity are unforgivable. When you want a beer in LaFollette, go to Knoxville. You have no right to be stupid and why should I have to worry?"

My father was working one day in the Amalgamated office with Ed Blair, the union's business agent, when eight men clattered up the stairs and barged in, at least one with a drawn revolver. Nothing was said, but Blair and my father had no doubts about the source and purpose of the visit. The thugs cut the telephone lines and went to work pistol whipping the two Amalgamated men. Both were quickly bloodied and overpowered. As my father momentarily pushed off one of the goons, a shot was fired. The bullet caught my father full in the chest and knocked him to the floor, where the knuckle boys pounded and kicked him some more.

The Amalgamated secretary was on her way up the stairs as the visitors left. "As the eighth man came out of the office he brandished a gun and mumbled something," she would tell a Knoxville newspaper. "I found Franz on the floor in one part of the office. Ed was lying in another corner. Both men were lying in pools of blood. Hair and blood covered the walls where Ed and Franz's heads apparently had been beaten against the wall."

According to a newspaper account, Blair's face was swollen beyond recognition—both eyes blackened, several teeth knocked loose, his lower lip smashed open by a pistol butt. My father was less disfigured but more confused. He had a gashed cheek, a badly wrenched hand, cuts all over his head and welts and bruises all over his body, but he felt no pain where he'd been shot. He worried that Ed Blair, not he, had taken the bullet. As his wits returned, he reached for the inside breast pocket of his jacket and pulled out his wallet, which was stuffed with a little money and a lot of papers. There was a ragged hole in the wallet. When he opened it, a flattened slug fell out and clunked on the floor. The wallet had been directly in front of his heart.

My father kept the wallet and slug to show to friends, though both had disappeared by the time I was growing up. I'd like to have touched the shield that made my life and my brother Jim's life possible. The Knoxville newspaper account, and a story in a labor newspaper, specify a .44 caliber bullet. It's a little hard to believe that any wallet could have stopped a shot of that heft, but my father when I knew him in later years did indeed carry a long folding wallet—he called it his pocketbook—usually crammed with papers. At the time of the shooting, he told a friend, it contained many notes for speeches. Yet again his oratory served him well.

It annoys me that I never once asked my father to talk about the incident. I'd like to know if he really was as cavalier about the scrape as his letters suggest, or if that was just the fighter in him needing to sound tough. Recuperating in a Knoxville hospital, he wrote his friend Newman Jeffrey that his only real worry was that his kidneys might have been kicked loose, but that they seemed to be okay. His cuts were healing. The stitches would come out of his cheek in a day or two. His hand was out of its splint but he couldn't write so well—the letter shows it—so the full story, he told his friend, would have to wait for later.

A man could be forgiven for reassessing a few things after such an experience, but there's no evidence that the beating my father took and the death shot he could have taken ever caused him to rethink his line of work. From Tennessee he went to Missouri for a few weeks to visit his mother, do some fishing, and heal up. Osceola, and his mother's attentions, were always his refuge. In a letter he wrote there to Margaret, he disposes of the incident in two sentences: "John L.'s boys gave me a rough deal down in LaFollette March 22nd and I came out to Osceola to heal up. I'm all right now and I'm in good shape." If my father harbored any bitterness toward Lewis, I can find no sign of it. He had several chance encounters with the man in the late forties and early fifties, he would tell a labor historian years later, and they spoke casually. My father gathered the impression that the great lion of the labor movement was "a lonely man, not completely living in the past, but spending a lot of time with it." He characterized Lewis as a leader of greatness.

February 21

I thought I might become a morning writer here. Alone in the rhythms of light and dark, I imagined I'd get up with the birds and have my workday finished by noon, as the writers I most admire have done, the afternoon and evening mine to nibble like a well-earned apple. No dice. I do more daylight writing here than I do at home, but that's because I do more writing here, period. Evening into the wee hours is still my prime work time. I've always felt a tinge of embarrassment about that, as if being a night writer were a little sleazy, but evidently it's how I'm wired. At last I embrace my true nature. I am *Scrivener nocturnus*. Perhaps I need the company of darkness to stimulate the darkness of my own unconscious—to excite its interest, or maybe just to make it feel at home. You won't spot a mole in the light of sun, but in the quiet of midnight he just might poke his nose aboveground and take a ramble.

During the shortest days here, the sun sank behind the woods to the west as early as 3:30, and it sets not much later now. As the high, west-facing slope of Rattlesnake Ridge turns a deepening green-gold with the last sunlight, a tinge of ghostliness comes over my home meadow and woods. It's as though the crisp shadows of afternoon suddenly dissolve, and in a progression without increments, their constituent darkness interfuses the remaining light. Silence gathers with the dark, even as the river whispers a little louder from the bottom of the canyon. Apple trees, fence posts, deer in the meadow, all singular things withdraw into background, less and less present, insubstantial as fading memories. And then, with dusk, the pointed silhouettes of the trees, monuments of a mystery precisely stated against the glowing sky.

By day I can walk among those trees and note characteristics of bark and foliage and habit that distinguish one species from another, and features that distinguish individuals within a species. I can call them by their common names and some of them by their Latin names. I see them clearly, but there is a blindness in that seeing. As I watch the trees in darkness it's not distinctions but the trees' commonality I see, not their names I know them by but their essential namelessness. With an evening planet and the first few stars above them, they announce their membership in a wilderness vaster than daylight eyes can apprehend. I feel closer to them. They seem to have crept nearer.

Thoreau, a morning person and a prodigious walker, took some of his rambles at night because he found it "necessary to see objects by moonlight as well as sunlight, to get a complete notion of them." Outside at dusk, he wrote in his journal, "I begin to distinguish myself, who I am and where; as my walls contract, I become more collected and composed, and sensible of my own existence . . . I recover some sanity . . . The intense light of the sun unfits me for meditation, makes me wander in my thoughts." In the dewy mist of a low-lying field, he reports, "I seem to be nearer to the origin of things." And later, in open moonlight: "Our spiritual side takes a more distinct form, like our shadow which we see accompanying us."

I know what he means. I love the lit particularities of things, their jags and curves and rough or silky textures, the *exactly this* that they present. But my vision catches on those surfaces, is snagged and tugged about by their multiplicity. At night, when I see nothing clear, I seem to see farther, deeper. I love that too, that dark in which all things blend and which itself is no mere absence, no shroud obscuring the real, but a boundless presence. It frees me from the tyranny of appearances.

It's because of darkness, of a kind, that I prefer novels and memoirs to movies. Even when a character is closely described in print, when a place is shown in tightly focused detail, the image still is the reader's to complete—or not to complete, to hold sketched and open in the psyche's eye. On the screen, the character's face and body and clothing are precisely what they are, the house and garden just so. These may closely replicate the novel's representations, but still, for me, scenes and characters almost always lose something for being incarnated as *exactly this*. In film, an actor portrays a character that is itself a kind of actor, a visual reduction of the imaginal character conjured in words. Story, read silently or aloud, needs no actors.

In Thoreau's time it was common for inexpensive portraits to be drawn as silhouettes, the subject's head shown in profile as a sharply defined solid shadow. This practice waned with the advent of photographic techniques, but not everyone saw the change as an improvement. A photo, the critics argued, shows merely a particular moment; a silhouette is a timeless outline. The photograph's lit and focused specificity was felt to obscure the greater truth of spirit, which, though not directly observable, could be suggested by the silhouette.

Such a view seems laughable today. We believe in what we can clearly see and rap with our knuckles and measure with our keen and keener instruments. Spirit, after all, is unlikely to show up at a mall or under a microscope. The word means *breath,* the life that breathes in all things, and though it breathes in us, we are strangers to it. We have routed it out of ourselves and our earthen world into some bodiless realm of light where we don't live. Or it's ourselves we've routed. We've turned away, blinded by obsessive attention to our careers and constructions and possessions. Spirit is here where it's always been, nothing different from visible things but not confined to things. It lives in shadows, in the opaque green depths of the river, in mist as it drifts the canyon in subdued daylight or the light of moon, and in the silent majesty of dusk, when a man alone in a darkening house can sense it gathering around him and feel glad.

February 24

The story I thought I was living in 1968 didn't take the turns I expected. All through the fall I waited to be indicted by the United States Attorney and brought to trial for refusing induction. Selective Service had acted almost instantly when I'd left school; now that my fate was in the hands of the federal legal system, nothing. At least one acquaintance who had refused in July had been indicted by Thanksgiving. For a while I considered calling the U.S. Attorney's office to ask what they were waiting for. "Listen," I imagined myself telling them, "I need to make plans."

Other than going to jail, though, I had no plans. I worked when the Greek contractor had work for me. Cathy and I were restless together and then restless apart. She made trips to Santa Cruz, Santa Monica, and after a while she was back in Mendocino and we were getting together only occasionally. I was dimly aware that I wasn't ready to live with a partner, and she may not have been ready either. (We are good friends to this day, and the letters she has shared have helped me remember the young man I was.) I took classes at a music school and studied guitar, but I was losing patience. Long hours of practice yielded the same cramped fingers, the same flubbed notes, the same halting renditions of pieces I wanted to play beautifully, that *had* to be played beautifully. I wanted to be good, right now, and I was a long way from that.

Some days I manned the Resistance card table here or there on downtown sidewalks, handing out leaflets and dispensing stop-the-draft, stop-the-war patter to passersby. I didn't have my heart in it, and the few Resistance meetings I attended bored me. Somebody dragged me to a Students for a Democratic Society meeting, and that bored me even more—droning monologues, critiques, critiques of critiques. By that point in the sixties, some in the New Left were scorning the Resistance for its one-issue focus and absence of serious ideology, dismissing it as little more than a cult of personal heroism indulged in by middle-class whites. They weren't entirely wrong, but the New Lefters themselves, of course, were middle-class whites. Their belief that the Marxist-Lenin-ist doctrine they espoused united them with workers and minorities was at least half delusional, and ideological stiffening, in later years, would take some of them to grim extremes—those who shifted from wanting to stop the war to wanting North Vietnam to win the war, whatever the cost in American lives, and those who felt moved to turn airy doctrine into very tangible and lethal bombs.

Against that record, the Resistance commitment to nonviolent action, whatever its limits, holds up well. But in 1968 there were earnest, idealistic, and energetic people in both camps, and in other progressive camps. I just wasn't one of them. I thought of my father. As a Socialist in the early thirties he had taken meetings by force with his bravura speechmaking. I sat in silence, burning to leave.

The demonstrations and police depredations at the Democratic Convention in Chicago hadn't particularly inflamed me. I never watched television, looked at a newspaper only rarely, and violence, by then, had settled in as the regular weather of the times. Across the Bay in Oakland, Black Panthers were walking the streets with shotguns—unconcealed weapons were legal then—and copies of the California Penal Code, monitoring the police (or pigs, in the Panthers' lexicon). I wanted no part of that fight or any other. I remember watching a street skirmish while riding a Muni bus on Market Street. Half a dozen long-haired protesters, one of them swinging his stick-mounted sign, were tangling with four or five cops equipped with batons and shields. One of the cops wrestled away the sign and was swinging it himself as the bus moved on and I lost sight. I don't remember even wondering what the demonstration had been about.

As the presidential election approached, my father was supporting Hubert Humphrey—of course—against Richard Nixon. He speculated in a letter that Humphrey, freed from his vice-presidential vassaldom under LBJ, would reassert the progressive views he seemed to have aban-doned. I didn't answer his letter. Robert Kennedy's assassination had gutted me of caring. I was six months short of voting age, but I wouldn't have voted anyway. Humphrey, the weak fool, had sold out on the war and thus was no better than Nixon, that shameless redbaiter and pan-

derer my parents and their circle had cursed and derided from as early
as I could remember. A race between the Hump and the Dick, as a
friend and I dubbed the esteemed candidates, was no race at all. It was
the Establishment against itself.

I know now that I was wrong and my father was right. Youth has an
absolutist cast of mind. It wants uncompromising heroes, noble knights.
It craves home runs, scorns the sacrifice bunt, takes little interest in
small distinctions. Henry Thoreau, even in his thirties, remained under
the sway of such absolutism—"Age is no better, hardly as well, qualified
for an instructor as youth, for it has not profited so much as it has lost,"
he pronounces in *Walden,* and elsewhere in the book he testifies: "I
have yet to hear the first syllable of valuable or even earnest advice
from my seniors." An odd claim from a man whose Harvard cultivation—though he belittled the college and his professors—shows in
every page of his writing, and little more thoughtful than the imperative that I and my ilk would voice a century later, to trust no one over
the age of thirty.

Some as they age do indeed betray their values, get lost in the status quo, lose their passion, and youth has every cause to disregard their
advice. But the best become wholest and wisest in their elder years, and
their advice tends to be measured and nuanced—not because they have
copped out, but because they have learned what Henry James called
the great tragedy of human life: that everyone has a case. Only what is
Right has a case, youth proclaims—what is Right *is* the case. It was this
temperamental extremism that caused Thoreau to see a hero in John
Brown, who, in the service of noble values, became a terrorist and murderer. (Though, as Robert Richardson points out, it isn't clear that
Henry David knew of the Pottawatomie massacres when he wrote so
praisefully of Brown.)

In the presidential election that's surely been settled by now for
every American except me, neither candidate was appealing—but I
found Al Gore, wooden and schoolmarmish and blundering as he was,
clearly the better choice. Ralph Nader was no choice at all, unelectable
and poorly qualified for the job. I've been thinking that Gore won, but
now I'm doubting it. I had a dream some nights ago in which Marilyn

asked if I knew who was president. Neither Bush nor Gore, I said (per-haps hopefully). Wrong, she said, it's Bush.

In any case, if Hubert Humphrey had been elected in 1968, I think there's a better than even chance he would have ended the Vietnam War far sooner than Nixon did, without secret bombing campaigns, without thousands more Vietnamese and Cambodians dying, without thousands more American men and boys coming home in body bags. Fifty-eight thousand Americans died in Vietnam. More than six out of ten were twenty-one years of age or younger.

My father, concerned about my legal situation, and worried that I still might be tempted to run to Canada, wrote often. I had no inten-tion of running, but despite his entreaties to stay in touch, I wrote him rarely and never called him. After the FBI visit, I had no hard news. I had nothing of substance to say to him about what I was doing, what I wanted. I didn't think of myself as drifting, but I knew he did, and in fact I had put my life on hold.

The Haight-Ashbury scene was souring fast—broken windows, boarded-up storefronts, hard drugs, occasional Molotov cocktails light-ing the streets as somebody's protest against something. The neigh-borhood of our flat, the Fillmore just below the Haight, was poor and black, filled with kids who didn't like long-haired, peace-loving whites any better than they liked whites in suits and ties. I was hassled on buses, bumped and baited on the sidewalks, raising my old fears about having to fight. One night in December a young black man in a white suit pulled a gun on me and pushed me into a building entryway on Divisadero.

"I want your money," he said.

"All I've got is some change," I said.

"I'm gonna reach into your pockets, motherfucker, and if I find some cash I'm gonna shoot you."

He found my change, less than a dollar's worth, and a crumpled bus transfer. I did the generous hippie thing and told him to please take the change. A stupid move—it angered him.

"Don't want your fuckin' change," he said, and tossed the coins hard at my feet.

I walked home quickly, giddy as a speed freak, reflecting that a stick-up man who wears a white suit and chooses a scruffy hippie to hold up might lack the judgment to succeed in his chosen vocation—not that I was qualified to make any judgments about vocations.

The quality of boarders at the flat was deteriorating too. On Christmas Eve I had to take a kitchen knife away from a teenager who'd been sniffing glue, or sniffing something. I borrowed a flatmate's car and drove the kid to a hospital to get him sedated, then drove back to pick him up when he called at six o'clock Christmas morning, calm and claiming to remember nothing.

Just after New Year's I made a decision. The FBI man had told me to stay in the Bay Area, but if the prosecutors were going to loaf around with my case, why should I? I left Vince O'Connor a mailing address care of a friend at Reed, stuffed my clothes into my knapsack, and hitchhiked to Portland.

February 27

Some animal took a few light steps on the bedroom roof last night—maybe cat-weight, more than rat-weight. My headlamp revealed no shiny eyes peering down through the skylight, only treetops. A chill of loneliness hit me. Turkey, come back! I've got more cabbage than I could eat in five years, and it's tougher than all hell anyway. Better suited to your gut than mine, which is in revolt. Even the deer have been making themselves scarce of late.

And the Global Warming Frog has gone silent, perhaps because his prophecy has come to pass. After a cold spell—brisk days, nights in the twenties—it's fifty-eight degrees this afternoon. Not a wisp of cloud, sun pouring in the west window and climbing my right side as I write. It's a damn solarium in here. Stretching in the dooryard earlier, I noticed a scatter of low-lying *daisies* in bloom. They're only an inch or two tall—adapted to frequent mowings?—but daisies they are. And daffodils poking up by the mint bed.

Two or three times over the winter I've seen bear prints at the river. At least one *Ursus* has asked, sensibly, why interrupt this balmy idyll to hibernate? On my way down to fish a couple of days ago I happened onto one of his thrashing grounds, an area the size of a small living room pocked with fresh diggings and scrapings, shredded rotwood strewn all around. The good fellow had thrown himself an exuberant banquet of such grubs, mice, honey, or other delectables as he could scrounge up, then tromped away without even calling the table maid.

Though the bear was long gone—or at least shortly gone—it was a tad spooky to stand amidst his devastations. It also piqued my loneliness. Like any animal still wild enough to have retained its good sense, this bear wanted no part of my company or anything human. He was now following his nose with swaying steps somewhere up- or downcanyon, utterly unalone because he was apart from nothing. And there I stood, detached from everything around me. It occurred to me that in that moment I was the least confident, most confused, least perceptive, and most self-absorbed creature in the Rogue River Canyon. The only one who hears things that aren't here, who walks in the present with his attention decades in the past and hundreds of miles away, who berates himself and pats himself on the back and minds far more than his own business. Or minds too much his business. The lives of nature *do*—the osprey falls on the glint of fish, the ant travels its odiferous trail, the bear lumbers noisily through brush. Me? I dither, stop and start, ever distract myself, again and again turn glancingly from the moment.

There is plenty of awareness in the canyon. The bear, the osprey, even the ants evince their own degree of consciousness, which must, like physiological features, be a graded continuum across the gamut of living things. I'm lucky enough, I believe, to possess the most acute consciousness here—not the sharpest perception, which surely belongs to the osprey's eyes, to the noses of bear and deer, to owls who hear the footfalls of mice. Yet, given this miraculous endowment, I and my kind use it poorly. We fill our awareness with trivia and distractions, turn it to distrust and hatred, to violence against our own kind and the other lives of nature. Yes, we do make beauty and often act generously with this chance or intended spark that has lighted our minds, but around that beauty and generosity, look at the brutality and stupidness. Look at the ways we squander our gift, as no bear, grouse, osprey, bobcat, or even a single ant would waste theirs.

The very thought of bear gives me another sadness, because bears are the one darkness that clouds the Brothers' Oregon faith. The Brothers suffer the bane of bears. Often enough they or the writer-resident return to Dutch Henry to find that a restless *Ursus* has been at work. Once the Brothers discovered the deck side of their own cabin laid open by claws, the bear having stripped off many venerable sugar-pine shakes and raked through the ¾-inch plywood interior wall into the back of a cupboard, enticed, evidently, by a can of smoked oysters some years past its safe-to-consume date that had rusted and sprung a minuscule leak—to the bear's snout, an olfactory bonanza. The Brothers, cursing and muttering, beyond the help of sacred sayings, set to work in their avid way splitting new shakes with froe and mallet, and mounted fearsome panels of out-pointing six-inch spikes at the deck corners, as if fortifying a medieval castle.

They called in a government trapper to deal with that bear. The man's name was Merv Wolfer, and as he set up his trap—a steel-grate cage on a single-axle trailer, baited with twelve mini-marshmallows—he told a story about a fellow bear trapper. The man had gone to check a trap in some remote place like Dutch Henry and found it sprung with a bear inside. He did the usual routine—put the bear to sleep with a tranquilizing dart, entered the cage to determine the animal's sex, age, and condition, and had about finished this data gathering when he heard a terrible sound. The hinged trap door, which he had left propped open, had unaccountably slammed shut, and when the door of a bear trap shuts, no animal, bear or human, can open it from within. The man was working alone, no partner, no radio he could get to, but at the moment he wished himself a lot more alone than he was. The bear would soon be waking, hung over and grumpy, possibly hungry, cer-tainly displeased to find himself sharing close quarters with a human being. The trapper fumbled through his pockets for something useful and found his only chance: a set of fingernail clippers. He swiveled out the tiny nail file, punctured the hide at the bear's neck, enlarged the puncture into a rough incision, found the jugular vein and opened it up. He had a twenty-four hour wait in the presence of bear and a lot of bear blood—brooding, no doubt, on the gloomy metaphoric implications of a trapper trapping himself in his own trap—before his work fellows found him and let him out. He was hungry, the bear having eaten all the marshmallows.

To the Brothers, this story was only the umpteenth corroboration of what they have known from their youth: that no good can come of relations between men and bears. Merv Wolfer trapped and removed a bear that almost certainly wasn't the vandal that had torn into their cabin—too small and emaciated—but it really didn't matter what bear he caught. At Dutch Henry there is never a dearth of bears for long. Usually they visit their boisterous attentions on the garden here at the lower house, which contains several apple, cherry, and plum trees. As the tree fruit matures in summer, the bears come around—as of course why wouldn't they?—and discover this year's method of piercing the Brothers' fence. In early years they went over or through it. One writer-resident remembers watching from the deck as a fine black bear momentarily poised himself, all four feet on the top of a fence post, before entering the garden of his bearish delight to thoroughly harvest and half-wreck the plum tree. The Brothers hardened the perimeter. They installed a solar-powered electrified strand to repel the cocky beasts, who were not repelled. Chortling to themselves, the Brothers hung little metal trays full of peanut butter from the electrified strand, aiming to deliver the full effect of fifteen volts to any and all bear tongues, but the bears swiped them aside, plowed through the fence, and continued to ravage the garden.

Irked mightily, the Brothers designed and fabricated a new fence at their legendary coastal armory, a *pièce de résistance* of a fence with seven-foot posts of four-inch steel pipe sunk into concrete footings, closely spaced strands of heavy-gauge wire, tightenable with built-in ratchets, and additional electrified wires. This seemed to work for two rather peaceful years, restoring serenity to the Brothers' rites and meditations, but those turned out to be years in which the bears, as it happened, had merely been attending to other sectors of their canyon portfolio. When the older fruit trees had healed themselves and new ones had started to bear—well, bears burrowed under the fence in a trifle and gorged themselves on green midsummer apples, breaking down limbs, adding small mountains of droppings to the garden's topography, and suffering no bellyaches, because bears do not get bellyaches.

Nothing else in nature so afflicts the Brothers. With other dangerous creatures they have established cordial relations, or at least *détente*. Rattlesnakes long ago accepted a treaty whereby they keep off the homestead property; scorpions have consented to remain in their secret catacombs; skunks pass through under letters of transit that bind them to strict continence; and the rough-skinned newts, those hedonists whose skin secretions—never lick one—contain a fatal neurotoxin related to that of the deadly blowfish, agreeably confine themselves to their pond and occasional overland rambles. It is bears, and bears alone, that leave the Brothers ill-tempered and brooding, muttering oaths and *fatwas* under their breath—and over their breath—as they conceive yet newer shields, torments, and battlements against . . . themselves?

Every faith, like every person, has a shadow side, some part of its own being it is unable or unwilling to recognize and accept. Banished by the conscious mind to outer darkness, this portion of being returns to haunt the banisher in roundabout and guileful ways—a disturbing dream, an encounter with a humpbacked beggar he once mocked, an embarrassing, inexplicable misstatement from his own lips, the dust bunnies he ignores in the corners of his rooms, the spider that descends toward his sleeping face. Or, signaled by the crack of a dead limb in the forest, by a careless crunching of brush, a dark, lumbering hunger approaches to snuffle and claw for its due at the fences of all that we believe to be ours, the heavily armed borders of the conscious mind . . .

Whence cometh this bane, this single blot upon the faith? Perhaps there lingers an odor in this meadow, detectable only to the snouts of bears, of the stores and stores of their own muscle that Bill Graiff kept in his cellar, of the countless bruins he killed and dressed here, their bear blood seeping into the soil and rising every spring with the grass, encouraging vague campaigns of retribution among their living ilk. Or, the Brothers may have earned the curse in their early Rogue River days at the gold claim at Horseshoe Bend. More than once a troublesome bear would bust into that cabin in the family's absence and bedevil its entire contents, including the flour bin—in a fit of ecstasy, it seemed, the bear would turn himself into a mighty brush and thoroughly whiten the interior walls, leaving nose prints to punctuate his work. On one occasion when Mother Margery and Brother Bradley boated in and found the cabin in such a state, Red Keller—friend, caretaker, mentor—offered to trap the transgressor. He hung a slab of bacon in a tree and set the great toothed jaws of the trap under leaves on the ground, chained to the tree. They woke in the cabin that night to awful bawling moans and a terrific thrashing. Red Keller decided that Brother Bradley, a stripling of fourteen, would take a large step toward manhood that night. The young brother, as directed, leveled the .25-.35 he'd been handed at the great dark animal churning and bellowing in darkness and pulled the trigger. His shot, somehow, found the bear's heart. The lad was feted as a hero as he, Red, and another man dragged the bear down to the cabin, gutted him, hoisted him on a block and tackle, and skinned him out. The next day they ate of his meat.

It was a giddy experience for Brother Bradley, but not one he sought, an initiation too early and too severe for a lad of fourteen. Over the years the memory of executing that bear has not rested easily with him. It troubles his dreams, and I know it must loom close in his mind when he and his brother drive into the homestead for spiritual renewal and discover, with grimaces and loud imprecations, the latest improvements made by the true owners of their estate.

February 28

Time went slowly here at first, dauntingly so. Then the year turned, January shot by, and now it's almost March. On misty or rainy days like today I feel settled, but the springish days rattle me. My mind roves and buzzes. As light as this winter's been, in another month or sooner I'll probably be able to drive out of here. I want to and I don't. I want to see Marilyn and our place, to eat oranges and fresh lettuce. (I ate the last of my Romaine in January.) I *don't* want the noises, the distractions, the various obligations old and new, and whatever dispiriting news I've missed. I know for sure that I don't want to leave until I actually leave, but already I'm feeling the pull of the world, with desire and dread all jumbled.

I've realized that life out there, ordinary life, is a weather for me. It can be pleasing, like a mild breeze, or exhilarating, like a windstorm in the treetops, but often it's a dry, shifting wind that irritates and wearies me. Most people seem to thrive in it. They seek it out, move easily about in it, call it happiness. Somehow I'm not quite suited to it, can't keep my bearings or equanimity. I'm too stiff, too rubbable the wrong way. Here, though I miss the fair breezes, I'm secured from the weather that tries and tires me. It's a safe harbor, this sojourn.

And, in truth, I've found the company here agreeable. Whoever that guy is, the one who shuffles around in down booties and sweat pants, glancing out the windows, rattling in the kitchen, he's pretty benign. I do wish he'd take better care of himself—shave more often, clean his fingernails, subdue his unkempt hair, tuck the tie string of his sweat pants behind the waistband. And I wish he'd deal with the greasy skillets he leaves on the stove, the deplorable condition of the toilet bowl, and this entire general disarray of books, papers, fishing tackle, wine bottles, cobwebs, and clumps of dust. And—since I've begun this bill of particulars—though the man is for the most part blessedly quiet, he does have the most startling habit of unexpectedly letting loose now and then with a whoop or howl or fragment of speech—"Hummmm *baby!*" or "Achtung!" or "*Alllllll* my *ex*-es live in *Tex*-as . . ."

But these are mere annoyances. In the main, we get on fine. I'll even miss the fellow when I've pulled out in a month or so and left him to make his way with the ghosts of Graiff and Keller and Martin and Henry Rosenbrook. But I will leave, and I know exactly why. I will leave because I have much in the world to return to. I have a wife whom I love and who loves me. I have a house on an acre in the country, which, though nothing as wild as this, is a fine place to live and work and wake up in the morning. I have two stepsons, a brother and a niece, many friends and acquaintances. I have an active, ongoing interest in the affairs of my locality, state, region, and nation. I have a vocation and a modest career.

Despite the rubbings of the world's weather, I have a *life*, a life I've never considered before from the perspective of three and a half months removed. A life I like. This may seem yet another underwhelming realization to have derived from this experiment in solitude, but at the moment, as I lean back in the Route 66 Distinguished Chair and look out on the wettened meadow, rain tapping gently on the roof, it feels substantial, almost like a breakthrough. I've enjoyed leaving my life, and I'll enjoy returning.

I'll return to precisely what I did not have and was yearning for (though I didn't know it) when I was twenty, on the loose and at loose ends, waiting for indictment and prison, waiting for something to happen, waiting for life to track me down in my lonely freedom and give me my due. Hitchhiking, my chief mode of transport back then, is the perfect metaphor for what I was—a brief visitor in the lives of others, my progress and sometimes my direction dependent, randomly, on theirs.

In Portland I hung around the Reed campus and fell in with several other dropouts looking for work. We heard that the Weyerhaeuser Timber Company was hiring choker-setters—the entry-level logging position—in Longview, Washington, and the morning after visiting the hiring office we were eating very large pancakes served by very large women in a boarding house on Oregon Way called the Baltimore Hotel, then bouncing up into the Cascades in school buses called crummies to put in our first day of work, dispersed in various crews, in Weyerhaeuser's devastated empire—mountainsides where every tree had been felled and bucked into thirty- and forty-foot logs that lay jumbled like so many giant pickup sticks.

The choker-setter's job is to clamber through that wreckage of a forest with a thirty-foot braided-wire cable and noose it around one end of the log he's been assigned, then bail out of the way as fast as he can and watch as his log and one or two others are dragged pitching and flailing up the hill by the main rigging, to which the chokers attach like leaders on a fishing line. The logs are unnoosed at the base of the diesel-powered, hundred-foot steel tower that works the rigging, on a landing by a road, and then the chokers come back, and in this way the pickup sticks are slowly picked up, piecemeal, and piled ready to load onto trucks. You set your choker many more times in the course of a day than you want to count. In winter you do it usually in cold rain or wet snow, with stinging fingers and a fair bit of shivering, foot-stamping, and falling on your butt. You w ork in the company of men who are not themselves choker-setters but once were, rural men who take a certain delight in their knowledge that a college kid with long hair, wire-rimmed glasses, and a bright yellow plastic hardhat—the kind that wordlessly flashes GREENHORN—is in fact a choker-setter and is in fact working for them. The veterans wear hats of battered tin.

On one of my first mornings, as I tried unsuccessfully to claw an opening through freezing mud beneath a Douglas fir log about six feet through, the hooker—short for hook-tender, the crew chief—shoved me aside, rammed the choker under the log with a couple of brisk thrusts, deftly danced around the log to slip the choker's knobbed end into its sliding socket bell, and bounded log to log into the clear with me clambering awkwardly behind him. He punched his whistle, and as the chokers cinched tight and the turn of logs started up the hill, he looked away shaking his head and said, loudly enough for the rest of the crew to hear, "Shit . . . oh . . . *dear*. Never send a boy to do a man's work." His name was Ron Downing, he was probably thirty-five, and he was a champion tree-topper in the timber carnivals.

Never send a boy to do a man's work. It stung me when he said it. It seemed gratuitous, cruel. Of course I wasn't as fast as him or the others—I'd only been working a few days. And of course there was more to my reaction than that. I wasn't doing *anything* very well. I was hungry for approval, for affirmation, so hungry that I felt thoroughly shamed by a man who hadn't gone to college, didn't read books, had never listened to a symphony, had voted for Richard Nixon, and believed in the Vietnam War. I cussed him and disdained him behind my burning face, but in that moment his approval meant more to me than anything in the world. That's how much a boy wants to become a man.

And the only way he can do it, of course, is to get sent or send himself to do a man's work, and when he fails at it to keep trying. I put a little more into my job from that morning on. I fought off my weariness and moved a little quicker, got a feel for sticking to bark and slick bare wood with my spiked boots. When the empty chokers came down the hill, I'd grab mine and make a race of it, trying to get my log belled up and ready to go before the other choker-setter got his. In the afternoons, I waited and waited and waited before asking what time it was. I started chewing tobacco, though it made me a little woozy. The work was still cold and wet and exhausting, but as the weeks went by there were stretches when I enjoyed it, when I felt fit—clambering eight hours a day, uphill and down, through a bedlam of fallen forest will definitely shape you up—and pretty good at what I was doing. I felt superior to any new choker-setter who joined the crew. That was novel—to feel better at something, outside of school, than somebody else.

Ron Downing scarcely said a word to me—he didn't speak a lot to anyone—but one morning in the spring as I waited in camp in the idling crummie I heard him talk with another hooker out in the rain. The other man said he was short a choker-setter that morning and needed to move a lot of timber. "You can borrow one of mine," Downing said. "He's green yet, but he gets after it pretty good." And he shouted for me to come out of the crummie. I did, my insides warm and smiling.

I worked on the other crew for most of a week. The rigging slinger— the one who assigns the logs and signals commands to the tower—was a tall, bearded man named Darryl DeWitt, who loped through the workday at something close to a sustained run and was disliked by most of the men because he was religious and anti-union. I was happy to belong to my first union, the International Woodworkers of America, but DeWitt's labor views didn't bother me, and neither did his Christianity. What nettled me was his boundless appetite for the work of logging, which seemed as fresh at four o'clock as it had been at eight in the morning, and which left me—even the new, motivated me—muttering in his wake. There wasn't an inch of slack in the man. He worked weekends too, running his own one-man gardening and landscaping business in Portland.

"I charge top dollar," he told me one day, "and I give 'em their money's worth."

"Doesn't all that work wear you down?" I asked him.

"Work don't wear a man down," Darryl DeWitt answered. "I like to work. It's fightin' it that wears you down."

I didn't think of Ron Downing and Darryl Dewitt as teachers at the time, but teachers they were. If a boy is lucky he has several fathers, and some of them have to be very unlike himself. Some he may know only for days or hours; some are much older, some—like Vince O'Connor, in my case—closer to his own age. He needs those who treat him kindly, who entice and nurture him, and he needs those who treat him roughly, who force him. Back in February, when Ron Downing had grabbed my choker and shoved me out of the way, I thought he'd done it out of dislike for a college kid playing at being a logger. And he probably had, but he also wanted to see if I could become a better worker, and I did. A boy wants to become a man, and needs to become a man, even as he fights it as hard as he can every step of the way.

March

You know, he's young and still unproven,
And to himself unspoken . . .
—AL STREHLI, "SALLY"

Every man is a warrior when he aspires.
—H. D. THOREAU, *Journal* (1840)

Let me seek, then, the gift of silence, and poverty,
and solitude, where everything I touch is turned into
prayer: where the sky is my prayer, the birds are my prayer,
the wind in the trees is my prayer, for God is all in all.
—THOMAS MERTON, *Thoughts in Solitude*

March 3

Today, in a fine rain, as mist moved through the canyon in slow, diaphanous drifts, I went fishing and caught no fish. And I felt accompanied, as I always do at the river. I saw no animals, but the mist and rain were company, and the river, as always, seemed more alive than I was. I listened to the shifting fricative chant of its rapids, the sloshing pour of slower water over rocks, and the smaller, singular sounds, the licks and lilts and gurgles, the sudden splashes that surprise. Once, the river almost formed a syllable, and I was so sure I'd heard my first name spoken that I whipped my head around—and saw mist, fine rain, a wealth of green-mossed boulders, the river running on. It's been a long time since I've heard my name called.

On only one visit, back in mid-December, have I found the river considerably changed in character. That day, after heavy rains, it was several feet up and running muddy, sweeping over many of the midstream rocks that usually are exposed, and quieter on that account. It was an intent streaming power, absorbed in its own enactment, its murky body showing nothing of its depths—Eliot's strong brown god. I could almost imagine it at full flood, dozens of feet wider and deeper, rafting tree trunks and human flotsam, leaving clumps of leaf debris in the tough twigs of scrub oak trees now high and dry, up the bank and many vertical feet above my head.

Aside from then, I've found the river up a foot, down a foot, but much the same. Yet more beautiful, somehow, every time I trek down to its edge. Its green translucence slides and sidles around gray boulders, rippling slightly, riffling, gliding almost glassy smooth. At the tail of a pool its fluent body narrows, quickens, vees into a rapid where it breaks over stones in a rushing white pour, then gathers itself, roiling, and settles into the easy drift of the next pool, its surface stirring with upwellings, slow swirls, a variegated sheen of living light. This easeful liveliness is my favorite of the river's passages. Like the slow movement of a symphony, it is where soul comes closest to the surface.

Today I put down my pole and just listened for a while, and watched.

What is it about the river that refreshes me? Many things, of course—
its sounds, the cool waft of its odors, the way it admits the eye but only
so far, holding back its secret life. But most of all, it's the lively ease of
its flow, its concerted complications, its sure continuous motion which
is also a sure stillness. The river goes and goes, and here it is.

And something more. I have been to the mouth of the Rogue, and
I have seen the river at various points along its length, and I have hiked
to the springs in the high Cascades that are considered its source, but
all that hardly matters. Here in this short reach that is my winter park,
where I have visited the river two or three times a week for better than
three months now, here the river appears from around one bend and dis-
appears around another. Here it is a creature of mystery, voicing rumors
of distant places known to it and not to me. Baptisms, I've read, were
performed originally only in flowing water, which was also called living
water. No one knew where rivers came from, and yet they did know.
Rivers came from the unseen, the beyond, and to touch a river's body
was to touch the beginnings of things and to be made new.

But if rivers connect us to the beyond, they have also long symbol-
ized the boundary that separates us *from* the beyond, just as surely as this
swift and rocky Rogue River bars me from its far shore that stares me in
the face only fifty feet away. *River of Jordan is chilly and cold, chills the body
but not the soul . . .* That particular crossing I'd like to put off as long as
possible. I'm afraid, of course, but it's also that I'm so much in love with
this shore, this Nature I was born to. The trouble I have with Buddhism
is that I resist the notion of detachment. Why would I want to detach
myself from these verdant boulders, this flowing river, this mild rain?
From my wife and friends, my work? What good could be greater than
this? I'm with Robert Frost when he writes, "Earth's the right place for
love: I don't know where it's likely to go better." Earth's the right place,
and I would just as soon never leave.

But I will have to leave, and I am some years closer to my leaving
than I am to my arriving. The shooting star on Christmas Night was a
long and bright one, but all shooting stars are brief. The years slip by like
an afternoon's sun. My skin is drying, my hair gone gray; I wear glasses
for reading and a hundred other things. My body is enacting my non-

negotiable detachment from life. So the lesson, or goal, or purpose, it seems, must be double—we're here to learn love, and we're here to give up what we love. Now and then, in a very quiet state that sometimes comes in my morning meditations, I can see that truth and watch it without fear. Now and then. Mostly, I seem to be making little progress as a meditator. I sit, aware of the discomfort in my legs, my mind buzzing here and there like a restless fly, my body hankering for coffee. I'm a meditating impostor, just putting in the time.

I watched the river for a long while with such thoughts, then turned my head at a slight noise—a quick *ffft*—and saw a great blue heron, freshly lit on a rock not twenty feet away. He turned his head, giving me one yellow eye, then the other. He'd been wading deep somewhere, his breast a draggled iridescence. I asked how his luck had been. He gave me a yellow eye. "Same here," I said, and the heron flexed his dark stick legs and pushed off low above the water, lighting far downstream on the other side.

With the river still running in me as I hiked up the trail, I tried to remember something I'd read in *Zen Mind, Beginner's Mind* about crossing a river. When I got to the cabin I thumbed through the pages and found it. Suzuki-roshi says: "Our life can be seen as a crossing of a river. The goal of our life's effort is to reach the other shore, Nirvana. 'Prajna paramita,' the true wisdom of life, is that in each step of the way, the other shore is actually reached. To reach the other shore with each step of the crossing is the way of true living."

It won't quite focus for me. The crossing is the end of life, and the crossing is life itself. The crossing is the whole of living and dying, and that means, it has to mean, that I'm already in the river. I waded in a long time ago, back when I was a toddler splashing in a Carolina creek, and still before that. All my life I've been stepping my way through the current with its cold insistence, my feet groping on sand and riverbed stones toward whatever depth awaits me. If nothing else, I don't want to sleepwalk. Slip or stand, I want to be aware of the crossing. To reach the other shore with each step, I must realize each step I am taking. And somehow, to truly have known this familiar shore, to truly have loved it, to truly have been here at all, with every step I must let it go.

March 4

In the spring of 1969, soon after his sixty-fifth birthday, my father officially retired from the AFL-CIO. He had done little work since the New Mexico debacle in 1966, called upon only occasionally to make a speech or consult on an organizing drive. He ended his forty-year career in the labor movement grateful for the generous treatment he had received from Walter Reuther's Industrial Union Department, still bitter at George Meany for so unceremoniously dumping him, and profoundly disappointed by the stultification of the American labor movement. The fire that he had fed and that had fed him since the late 1920s had burned down to embers and ash.

Most of his labor cohorts felt the same. Phil Van Gelder, a friend and comrade from the 1930s on, wrote my father in 1967: "The labor movement staggers on. We are all just going through the motions now, which I suppose is better than not going through the motions." When I interviewed Van Gelder shortly before he died, he told me this about the thirties: "It looked as though the world was going either socialist or fascist, one way or the other, and we knew which side *we* were on." He meant not that he and my father and their kindred had considered themselves revolutionaries in the strict sense, but that they had felt part of a work that had the power to transform American society and perhaps the world. It's probably impossible for any of us not then alive to appreciate how it felt to be a committed progressive in that decade, to be young in a nation and world in flux—to share the giddy belief that the stakes were all on the table, that history was somehow coming to a head in their very day. In their own country, burgeoning unions were taking on powerful corporations and winning. An American president was saying, "If I were a worker in a factory, the first thing I would do would be to join a union," and was instituting some of the reforms that the American Socialist Party had been campaigning for since its birth. And then the war, in which all the stakes in fact were on the table, the nation pulling together as something like one—accepting sacrifices, workers doing their parts along with tycoons, the economy beginning to hum again.

But the postwar reaction was hard and swift. The Taft-Hartley Act revoked or limited many of the organizing rights granted only twelve years earlier in the National Labor Relations Act, and enhancements of Taft-Hartley in the decades that followed have further hamstrung the right of workers to organize and have effectively secured the power of management to stamp out unionization before it can begin. Employers routinely flout, without serious penalty, those protections that workers who wish to unionize do enjoy. Tens of thousands of workers are fired every year for joining or trying to organize a union, and if a union is voted in, employers can stall off negotiations for years. I think my father would probably agree that this tilted field of labor law and workplace practice was and remains the main cause of the decline in organized labor's power that began in the 1960s.

But Taft-Hartley came from without. My father was more embittered by what he saw as the betrayal of the American labor movement by its own national leadership. In 1968, the year before my father retired, Walter Reuther had yanked his million-strong auto workers union from the AFL-CIO, disgusted by the federation's disinclination to organize the workers who needed it most and its jingoistic embrace of the Vietnam War and Cold War anticommunism in general. Reuther's brother Victor, a major labor leader in his own right, told me in a 1997 interview that the merger, in retrospect, had been a mistake. Without the stifling stewardship of Meany and his executive council, he thought, the CIO might have had a chance to find out just how far industrial unionism could have advanced in the United States.

Maybe not much farther than it did, because the economic history of the second half of the twentieth century was working against it. The industrial private sector of the workforce has shrunk drastically, due first to automation and later to our wholesale export of industrial work beyond our borders, and union membership in that sector has fallen to less than ten percent today. Meanwhile the public-sector workforce has burgeoned, and it is there that the modern labor movement has achieved most of its limited successes. Government workers, including many white collars, have come to appreciate the power of collective bargaining, and public employers have been less able or less willing than their private counterparts to exploit the tilted playing field. This trend was evident in the outcome of the Los Angeles–Orange County mass organizing drive from which my father was fired in 1963. The drive fizzled—and would have had he not been fired—garnering not the hoped-for half-million new union members but only a few thousand. Yet it did have one notable success—it doubled the southern California membership of the American Federation of State, County, and Municipal Employees.

But it's fair to say, too, that labor's own successes have contributed to its decline. Though there was, and remains, a considerable underclass that didn't share in the general trend, the standard of living of American workers rose dramatically between the first decades of the century and the 1970s, and unionism deserves a major share of the credit. The gains were not given but won, and they were won because workers, at some expense of blood and money, had the courage to organize and strike. Nonunion workers too have shared in the general improvement in pay scale, benefits, and working conditions. Capitalism, so prodigious at producing wealth and so poor at distributing it, proved itself capable —under pressure from government and organized labor—of providing enough of the good things of life to enough working people to ease, though hardly to eliminate, the explosive economic tensions of the first half of the twentieth century.

Due both to its failures and its successes, unionism hardly registers in the American public's awareness as we enter a new century. One of my favorite bumper stickers whimsically responds to this ignorance: "UNIONS: THE FOLKS WHO BROUGHT YOU THE WEEKEND." And who brought us, in addition, the eight-hour day, the minimum wage, employer-sponsored health insurance, paid vacations, pensions, and several other advantages now totally taken for granted. But the labor movement is likely to reassert itself. The economic gap between rich and poor has doubled since the 1960s, and real wages today are lower than they were in 1973. Those who benefited scantly or not at all from the prosperous economy of the 1990s—agricultural workers, commercial and domestic service employees, home health care workers, office support staff—put in hard hours and in some cases jeopardize their health for wages so meager that the workers qualify for food stamps. Many are forced to hold two or more jobs, neither of which qualifies them for health insurance. Even white-collar high-tech workers are finding themselves unemployed due to "global sourcing," a bloodless way of saying that workers in India will do the same job for far less pay. If American capitalism has proven more supple and generous than my father and others in the 1930s believed it could be, its bottom line has moved not an inch: employers, even enlightened ones, will spend as little on their workers as they can. Tensions are mounting that may revitalize the American labor movement.

My father, though disillusioned by organized labor's faltering career, never gave up his belief that its goals could be achieved. If he were alive today he would be brooding on the sad state of the labor movement, but he also would be cheering its small successes, keeping an eye out for opportunities. My father was an American optimist. He looked for the infield single, the sacrifice bunt, a walk here and a stolen base there. "Democracy," wrote E. B. White during the Second World War, "is the score at the beginning of the ninth." The ninth was beginning in the thirties and forties, and the ninth is beginning today. For those like my father with the courage to take the field, the courage to care and to act, it is and always will be the beginning of the ninth.

My father had a second, shorter career, one that was already thriving when his labor career came to its end in 1969. It began on November 5, 1966—his sobriety date—and lasted until his death nearly ten years later. You could call it a career as a sober civic and cultural activist in Springfield, Missouri. Its basis, its *sine qua non*, was his ongoing involvement in Alcoholics Anonymous. He continued to attend meetings, two or more per week, and continued to work with "AA brothers" who had fallen off the wagon and landed in the drunk tank. "I have an excellent relationship with the judge here," he wrote Newman Jeffrey, "and I have an even better one with the girls in his office. If he would ever try to cross me—he'd have trouble. They keep my picture up on the bulletin board and it makes the Republican office holders mad as hell."

And he was doing much more. He stepped down that spring as chairman of the Unitarian-Universalist Fellowship he had helped to grow and stabilize, but remained as secretary, in charge of organizing Sunday programs. He was a member of an American Civil Liberties Union committee investigating police brutality in Springfield. (The brothers he pulled from the drunk tank had sometimes been well worked over.) He belonged to a Civil War roundtable discussion group, in which he pursued his keen interest in the Kansas-Missouri border war. He made occasional speeches to Rotary and Kiwanis groups on the labor movement as it had been. He corresponded with a UCLA professor who was writing a biography of John L. Lewis. He was active in Democratic Party politics at the local and statewide levels. And he regularly wrote book reviews for the Springfield *News & Leader*, specializing, it seems, in nonfiction—American histories, American biographies, and muckraking journalism.

With his sisters, my father kept up an active social life, hosting bridge parties, teas, and dinners at which he often served hams or turkeys he had smoked himself. He also received and very much enjoyed the attentions of women. One female admirer, as he was recovering from an appendectomy in the summer of sixty-nine, brought him a sumptuous purple robe straight from the department store. I don't know that he actually dated women, but he saw them socially, and I'm told by one of his Unitarian friends that he set the terms early in these acquaintances by divulging that he was impotent. This could have been a ruse to avoid entanglements, but given his age and heavy smoking it might well have been a fact.

Depression is a risk factor for impotence, and, though there's no sign of it in his letters, my father would later tell a friend that he had been seriously depressed throughout 1969. I know that he was seeing a psychiatrist—something he never would have done pre-Menninger's—and that he had new physical troubles. A bad shoulder wouldn't let him raise his right arm above his waist, his prostate was giving him fits, and in July he had the appendectomy, which left him with a lingering low-grade infection. Except for his temporary debilitations from alcohol, my father had always been physically hale. At sixty-five he may have been taking, for the first time, a long sober look at his mortality.

It must have been shortly after his appendectomy, in mid-July, when my father received in the mail a bill from Buck Ambulance Service, in Portland, Oregon, for the transport of John Daniel to a Portland hospital earlier that month. Baffled and very alarmed, he managed to reach me by phone—I had quit logging and was living in a Reedie house in Portland—and I sketched what was probably a very disjointed outline of what had happened. The next day I wrote him a six-page letter with the full account of a three-day fast I'd conducted, going without sleep as well, as an experiment in meditation. I'd taken it a bit too far, I told my father, and collapsed of exhaustion, but I'd suffered no harm and now was fine. The ambulance service—called by a concerned friend—had asked for a parent's address as well as my own, but I assumed, of course, as a twenty-one-year-old, that the bill would be sent to me. I was outraged, I told my father, that they had needlessly caused him such anxiety.

He would have been far more alarmed, and would have responded I don't know how, if I had told him the truth. I had indeed been awake three days and nights, and I had been awake those days and nights because I had been injecting myself with methamphetamine. I'd been injecting myself with methamphetamine because my friend John Sterne had introduced me to its pleasures, and its pleasures were intense—a tingling of scalp and spine, a euphoric rush of feeling GOOD, a great-day-in-the-morning aliveness of perception and thought that made everything interesting, anything at all, from the structural anthropology of Claude Levi-Strauss to a bottle cap on the sidewalk.

Over those particular three days and nights, I probably did much of the following: drank many Coca-Colas, practiced rock climbing moves at Rocky Butte, read Zap Comix and Hermann Hesse's *Magister Ludi*, ate doughnuts, took money from my savings account and bought more meth, slouched in an overstuffed chair listening to John Sterne rap incessantly with great conviction though I often had no idea what he was talking about and surely he didn't either, smoked countless packs of cigarettes, shot more meth, watched others shoot meth, fantasized for hours about climbing Annapurna, roared around on my BSA Lightning motorcycle with Sterne on his Triumph Bonneville, drank beer to settle my head, shot more meth, wrote twelve- and fifteen-page letters to friends, considered hitchhiking to California but realized I would run out of meth and would have no connection, drank old-fashioneds in the Temple Lounge at Hung Far Low, walked downtown across the Burnside Bridge and back across the Morrison Bridge, and started to crash in the middle of the third night while Sterne was still rapping and walked home at dawn to my house on Gladstone Street.

No one was up. I cut a piece off a watermelon in the kitchen and ate it in the living room easy chair. I found half a joint in an ashtray and lit up. I noticed a shimmering around the upper edges of my vision. Suddenly my heart was pounding so fast and hard I knew it was about to explode. It didn't occur to me to wake my roommates—too embarrassing, I didn't know them well. It did occur to me to run outside and down the block and pound on a front door. When no one answered I ran to another house. My heart was hammering in my chest. It couldn't last much longer. A man yelled "Go away" through his door. I ran to another house, and another, and a young man opened the door. I explained that I was having a heart attack and needed help right now, *please*. With poise that I now find astonishing, he invited me to sit on the couch while he called an ambulance. He and his wife waited with me.

The medics had me lie down in the ambulance and gave me a small paper bag and told me to hold it to my mouth and breathe into it. "You're hyperventilating," one said. "No, it's my *heart*," I said. The two of them talked casually to each other, resuming an interrupted conversation. I breathed into the bag, convinced they didn't understand, they were going to let me die. When I dropped the bag, one of them picked it up and handed it to me as he went on talking to his friend.

I remember nothing at the hospital except giving personal information, getting an injection, and falling asleep. Sometime that afternoon I woke feeling fine, as I would later tell my father. They made me stay until a doctor had time to talk to me. He asked how much speed I had taken. I answered vaguely, worried he might get me busted. I'd been psychotic, he said. Meth does that. You're fine physically, he said, but you're lucky. That stuff can kill you. I nodded attentively, told him I'd learned my lesson. I was done with speed.

I wish I could say how I felt and what I thought about as I left the hospital and took a bus home. I was relieved that only strangers knew about my paranoid crash and burn, but aside from that I don't remember thinking about what had happened that morning or the previous three days. I don't remember feeling scared or worried or anything at all. It was as though it had all happened to someone else. If I thought about anything it was probably the hike and climb in Olympic National Park I'd been planning for weeks.

March 6

We're fattening into spring. The buds on the apple trees look ready to pop, daffodils are opening in the dooryard. Robins hop about in droves, mute, while other birds limber up their spring patter. Flickers, and the occasional pileated woodpecker, give their fussy serial cries, as if terribly wronged with only a vanishing hope of redress. Jaybirds emit incessant bursts of ack-ack. Wrens issue raspy scoldings.

I thought I heard the honk of a Canada goose yesterday evening. Saw no goose, but fishing today at Horseshoe Bend I heard honking for sure, and a pair of them glided in and landed in the still water on the far side, where the river slows and widens out of the Bend. They climbed a small beach there. Handsome couple. Their honking was bold and brassy, most American. More saxy than brassy. And sexy, no doubt, if you're a goose.

The lower meadows down the Corral Trail and the river terraces below are greening and growing. Wildflowers are up—I picked and pressed four to identify at home, which is of course where I left the field guide. It must have been in the high sixties when I got to the Bend. No cap, no gloves all afternoon. And wild fishing! I hooked ten, maybe more. Kept one, a stout sixteen-incher. Lost a bigger one that jumped three times and won its freedom on the third, practically onshore. My right shoulder is sore from casting; my left elbow sore from something; my still-healing right pinkie sore from gripping the rod. I'm hooked, totally hooked, on fishing this river.

I observed one species of mammal, first sighting since I left the world. Two fishermen in a boat. I was well up and away from the river, eating cheese and bread, when they drifted by. I tried to ignore them but couldn't stop looking. One of them spotted me, hollered a greeting and what sounded like a question. They were no doubt surprised to encounter a boatless human this far into the canyon. I sat mute and raised my stout walking stick in what I hoped was an eloquently ambiguous gesture. Their boat drifted on. I noticed my heart beating fast.

I tried to feel outraged, but the two fishermen were not a repugnant sight. Two creatures going about their business, like the geese and fish and otters. If only our human presence in nature were just that—a seemly number adventuring in good humor, taking a modest portion of meat for our sustenance. How did we ever get to be so *many?* Because a more-than-modest portion is available, if a species knows how to get it, and we know how. And because there's nothing in nature to stop us, other than the dynamic equilibrium of ecology. Many lynxes plus not enough hares yields fewer lynxes. We think we're the exception, the fair-haired child of creation, the lynx for whom there will always be plenty of hares, and we may be right. We've accomplished remarkable things. We are technological geniuses. We may pull off the upset and transcend nature altogether, which seems to be our goal. But I hear my father saying of Jim Lemon, "There's no percentage in *that* goddamn swing." And I've been listening all this warm winter to the Global Warming Frog, and he too tells me the odds are long and getting longer. As the bumper sticker says, Nature Bats Last.

But the two fishermen were pleasant to see. Men often have an ease about them, a settled stillness, while fishing. I remember my father, the one time I recall fishing with him. We were at a pond somewhere in the East, some friend's farm we were visiting, a summer noon. He was wearing the baggy denim jacket he often wore at the Virginia cabin, sitting on a lawn chair he had carried down from the house. He fished the old-fashioned way with a very long bamboo pole, the line tied to its tip. He baited with a piece of worm, lifted the pole tip high, and let the line with its red and white bobber swing out over the water and splash lightly down. The bobber floated, drifted slowly. I can see the water turn opaque and shiver with a breeze. My father lifts his line and swings it out to another spot. The bobber skids sideways—once, twice—and goes under. My father raises his pole almost vertical, and the fat bluegill jiggling on the hook swings straight to his hand where he sits in his chair, sober and smiling the smile of a child.

In a version of the Grail myth that Jungian analyst Robert Johnson tells, an adolescent prince pursuing his knight errantry happens on a deserted camp in the forest where a salmon is roasting over coals. Hungry, the prince reaches to pull off a piece of the fish and burns himself.

He pops his fingers into his mouth and tastes a morsel of salmon, and with that taste he sustains a crippling wound he will carry almost to the end of his life. He is unable to love, to be warm with others, to experience joy. During his reign as king he lies on a litter in his castle as every night the Grail is borne in sacred procession, healing all present except him. Every night he is offered a restoring beauty that he cannot receive. Only one thing helps. When he goes fishing in the moat around his castle, his pain temporarily eases. He is known as the Fisher King.

Fishing balms him, Johnson suggests, because it puts him in indirect contact with the wholeness of being his wound deprives him of. He touches unconsciously what he cannot realize in his conscious mind. My father wouldn't have seen it in those terms, but as he sits fishing in my memory's eye he looks very much like a Fisher King salving his pain. Burned in his youth by his little brother's death and then his father's, burned as a man by the death of his firstborn son and by the personal and professional betrayals that he unconsciously did so much to earn, he never came into the kingly wholeness that his gifts might have won for him.

Few men do. Most of us are Fisher Kings, and fishing is a way to touch our unknown depths. For me it usually brings quiet happiness— unless it's been too long since I've hooked a fish—and an alertness much like meditation. I can't see far into the sliding green current where I cast my line. As the lure bounces along the rocky and sandy bottom I'm feeling in the dark, trying to read braille, sometimes sensing a strike just before it occurs—the rod in an instant arched and thrumming with an unseen power of which I see only glints and shadowed surges as I work it closer, and finally, if I'm lucky, raise it to the light of day, a sleek iridescence flailing in my hands. I've eaten a lot of steelhead this winter, but it's the strike and play I fish for, that sudden calling of a wild purpose awakening a wild purpose in me. Most of the fish I give back to the river, where they hover briefly in the shallows then dart away, dark backs vanishing into the deep.

Writing, like any art, is a kind of fishing. Poems and essays and stories arise from unconscious depths where the writer must feel for them in the dark. They rarely arise fully formed, but they never arise unformed at all. Like a fish on a line (many of them tenuously hooked), they approach in resistant glimpses—associations, snatches of narrative, darts of feeling or idea—and the glimpses carry intimations of an unseen wholeness of which they are part. To realize the wholeness takes luck, patience, and usually a long interplay between consciousness, which connects and enlarges the glimpses in provisional wordings, and the darkness beneath the surface—the deep river of the human psyche, fed by weathers of experience and springs of innate knowing, stirring with dreams, intuitive promptings, and the murmured, insistent, half-heard urgings of spirit and soul.

I'm luckier than my father in having this writing way of seeking my own wholeness. I'm not sure what I'd do without it, but I know that writing distorts me, too. Cowboys get bowed legs, football players get bad knees, timber fallers go deaf, tennis pros get a lopsided pair of arms, and writers get calluses on their butts and various crampings of the psyche and personality. I think my own stiffness and brittleness are at least reinforced if not caused by what I do. Like Thoreau, I am used to sharing myself exclusively with the page in front of me, working out my views and feelings there—not in dialogue with others, thank you very much. This makes me not the easiest-going husband, friend, or associate in the world. I'm not, as they say, a people person. And I don't suppose I'm likely to become more of a people person after spending the winter in this unpeopled world of my own.

❧

It's hard to convey to those who have never shared the obsession just how normal it feels to use hard drugs. From the inside, it doesn't seem extreme or self-destructive or even obsessive. Speed enlivens body and mind, turns simple awareness aglow—of *course* you take it, why would you not? Of course you hang out with others who take it, and of course you are vastly attentive to the ritualistic procedure by which you give it to yourself.

You tap your meth crystals from their paper packet or tiny plastic bag into a soup spoon. Add one syringe-full of water. Heat the spoon with a match or candle to dissolve the crystals and purify the solution. Drop a little wad of cotton—sterile, please, though of course your fingers aren't—into the spoon, draw the solution into your syringe through the cotton filter. Check the needle for cotton fibers. Your belt, which you've previously removed from your pants and re-buckled, is ready to serve, looped in a figure-eight around your legs at the knees and your left upper arm. Spread your legs, tightening the loop around your arm, which bulges the veins of your inner elbow. Pick a vein—mine are obligingly prominent—and slip the needle in, look for a bloom of blood in the glass barrel of the syringe, relax the belt, and squeeze the good stuff into your bloodstream, taking care to squeeze in no air. Withdraw the needle, hold cotton over the puncture if necessary. Enjoy the rush. It's right away.

Speed sets you in motion, within and without, and thus puts you in some degree of harmony with the general busyness of society. You do things. You walk, drive, play cards, polish the motorcycle, you even—as I demonstrated that unfortunate early morning in June—meet the neighbors. Heroin and morphine, on the other hand, slow you to a languorous crawl. Two hours, three hours after shooting up—who's keeping track?—you're still lying on the same mattress on the floor, idly scratching at a mild itch somewhere on your body, perhaps your right flank. You may have exchanged not a single word with your companion, if you have one, but you're far from bored. Boredom implies a need to do things, and that need has been obliterated. Your mind drifts along in a semi-dream state that is quite amply absorbing. Eventually a disagreeable restlessness comes over you, which focuses after a while as an irritated realization that you're not as loaded as you were before, that it's time to take another hit. Or, if there isn't another hit, to eat, drink, and grudgingly, irritably, resume your life.

John Sterne and I had grown up together in the D.C. suburbs. We were both ace students and social misfits, Sterne a tad smarter and a tad more misfitted than me. As teenagers we regularly stole beer from the back stoop of one of his ham radio acquaintances and got ourselves blasted. At Reed, which Sterne chose over Princeton, he did fine academically but not so well socially and personally. The first girl he had sex with gave him gonorrhea. By the time I drifted back to Portland in 1969, he was very withdrawn and very depressed and hard drugs were very much his thing.

It still surprises me, and embarrasses me, that they became my thing. Unlike Sterne, I wasn't depressed. I had some money, I had a working-life high from my logging job. I had an ambition—to re-enroll at Reed in the fall, as an anthropology major. I had a brief, lovely, roll-in-the-grass relationship with a sophomore Reedie. And I had no news from Vince O'Connor or Selective Service or the United States Attorney for Northern California. I had told my draft board and Vince that I could be reached care of John Sterne at Reed College, but I dared to hope, a year after refusing induction, that my file had slipped into one of the thin spaces between cabinets. At the same time I felt frustrated, even wronged. They were supposed to indict me, try me, and lock me up like a martyr. They were robbing me of the only good story line I had.

It makes me squirm to write about shooting meth and heroin, but it disturbs me even more that I evidently felt so empty that I *wanted* to take hard drugs. And what the drugs do, of course, is make you still emptier and needier. I don't know if I was ever addicted in the clinical sense, but all I wanted, coming off a meth high or an opiate drift, was more meth or more opiates. I'd heard my Aunt Margaret, and maybe my father, speak passingly of depression. I had no inkling what the word meant until I'd crashed from speed a few times. I remember sitting for hours one night in my room in the Gladstone house, wrecked and sleep-less, watching a patch of street light on the floor beneath the window. *It's right there*, I kept thinking. *If I could just go over there, just that far, I'd be happy again.*

I didn't think about my father in such moments—I never thought about his drinking in connection with my drugging—but I think about him now. I think of those many mornings in the fifties and early sixties, and afternoons too, when he lay in his bedroom or sat in his bathrobe in his living room rocker, sallow-faced, stubble-cheeked, smoking auto-matically, his eyes dull and elsewhere. Who in that condition would have wanted to deal with a child? A wife? A career? Who *could* have? And I think about him in the summer of 1969 in Springfield, too—not yet three years sober, depressed, waking up earlier than he wanted to each morning in his small downstairs bedroom, every day wanting a drink, wanting that old estranged reliable friend, the only one that knew how to put him at ease—and turning instead to the events of his day, his twelve-step work, his AA brothers and sisters, his many concerns for his household, his family, his community, his country. What I saw dimly then I see clearly now. My father, a brave man all his life, summoned his greatest courage in his last years, when he flat refused to summon it from a bottle.

March 8

Slow drifts and roils of mist have been moving all day in the canyons of the Rogue and its tributaries, obscuring and revealing the green wooded ridges. I've been watching a great Douglas fir on a near ridge lapse repeatedly into mist and grow distinct again in soft gray light, the same tree but each time freshly born, dewy with its own creation. This is my favorite mood of Rogue River weather. The landscape seems most alive, most in its element on these days. It has *gravitas*. It seems to disclose a slow, secret life, invisible on clear days, that moves like mind. A line of Emily Dickinson's keeps coming back to me: "Nature spending with herself / Sequestered Afternoon . . ." The paradox of this particular country, it occurs to me, is that it most reveals itself when partially veiled.

I hardly think anymore about the breakthrough I hoped would happen here. The notion of it seems a mite silly now, the very word too abrupt and violent. Break through what, to where? The mist moves in the canyon, moves in my seeing, and my seeing moves with the mist. This is where I am, and glad I am to be here.

Memory has its own mists. They move on the landscape I look back on, obscuring this, revealing that, leaving many features vaguely formed. I see pockets, patches, now and then a larger view. The terrain is both familiar and strange. Yes, I was there. No, surely not, I couldn't have been. But yes, I was there, I did that . . . The part I've come to now, my life in 1969, is the piece of country I have visited least and would just as soon leave to the mists. I've never accepted this passage of my story, and so I know I've got to deal with it. I've got to go back, acknowledge it—acknowledge *myself*—and move on.

My lowest point, ethically speaking, came while I was scratching up some money doing odd jobs through Manpower. I worked most of one day in the modest home of an elderly couple I'd been sent to, scrubbing their floors, straightening up the back porch and garage, mowing the yard and weeding their flower beds. The man and woman were picky and rode close herd on me, which annoyed me, but for all that weren't terribly obnoxious. At the end of the day, I asked to use their bathroom. Coming out, in a small hallway, I passed a jar filled with silver change on a small table. I picked it up and filled my two front pockets.

As I walked home, my pants heavy with nickels and dimes and quarters, I told myself that the old couple didn't need the money. What could it be, fifteen dollars? They owned a house, for God's sake. But that was bullshit and I knew it. I'll pay it back, I told myself. When I have more cash I'll leave an envelope in their mailbox. But that was bullshit too. I never returned their money.

I used that cash, like most that came my way, to buy methamphetamine. But much as I'd like to blame my stealing on my drug habit, I really can't. At twenty-one I was a small-time thief of several years' experience. At the music school in San Francisco where I had studied guitar, angry at some small slight—or more likely, at my own desultory musical progress—I walked back to Waller Street one night with a portable stereo I'd noticed in a basement closet. No one was using it. What did they care? Why shouldn't I get to listen to music at home?

I thought nothing in those years of walking out of a supermarket with food items tucked into my clothing. I did it out of need and convenience both—I was hungry, I didn't have much money, I was between paychecks or not working. But I'm sure I would have stolen beer and wine, too, if I'd had a way of concealing them. Who was I harming? I stole only from big stores like Safeway, and what was Safeway but a bastion of the Establishment, a faceless corporation that profited from the need of human beings to feed themselves? My friends and I used to laugh scornfully at the very name—Safeway, the *Safe Way*—which surely had been chosen for its subliminal appeal to the herds of cautious shoppers who docilely did the bidding of corporate America.

It's that glib rationalizing, even more than the petty stealing, that bothers me now. My friends and I learned through the grapevine the pattern of telephone credit card numbers—ten numerals and one letter, appropriately deployed—and talked to each other coast-to-coast for hours, proud of our savviness in duping Bell Telephone. At the big discount drugstore where I worked while still in high school, I did favors for friends. One of them would come to my register with a couple of cartons of cigarettes, I'd ring up seventy-nine cents or so, make the change, and my friend would be on his way. Cigarettes were cheaper then, but not that cheap. I did such favors for myself, too.

One of my brother's friends had pulled off a bigger scam. I don't remember exactly how it worked, but the friend had convinced an airline that his suitcase had been lost, had filed a claim for its fictional contents, and had received a handsome check. During my first summer home from Reed I enthused about this exploit to a group of friends that included one of my high school English teachers, and I was stung when she berated me. It's just an airline, I said weakly. Just an insurance company, really. "You know better than that," she railed. "It's theft. It's simple theft."

If I did know better, I too often ignored what I knew. Some of us who came of age in the sixties had a slick spot in the conscience where what we wanted to do skidded all too easily into what we felt we were entitled to do and what we did. At a time when many were taking principled stands against the draft and the Vietnam War, for civil rights and social justice, when we were decrying the government for its deceit and corporate America for its greed, we weren't holding our own lives to rigorous standards. We romanticized ourselves as outsiders, fugitives from the American mill that stamped out uniform human blanks. And because we were the ones who saw the truth, the ones who belonged to the future, we considered as ours any useful item that the Establishment—that useful term—wasn't smart enough to keep bolted down or locked away.

There was one theft, though, that I have a hard time feeling guilty about. It occurred on Thanksgiving Day 1966, my first holiday away from home. I'd driven the Jeep, full of friends, to San Francisco and was staying at the O'Farrell Street flat. There were maybe ten of us there. Funds being short, it seemed necessary to steal a turkey, and a guy named David and I set out to do it. David had a plan I wished I'd thought of. First we went to the Mayfair supermarket, where we bought some potato chips and crackers, enough to half fill a grocery bag. Then we walked over to Safeway with our Mayfair bag and strolled past the turkeys, sizing them up. When the aisle cleared for a moment I grabbed our choice of birds and quickly slipped it into the Mayfair bag, David lifting out the chips and crackers and dropping them back on top.

We probably could have left the store then without incident, but I like the style of what we did. I picked up a few apples in the produce section and we went through the checkout line together, David holding the grocery bag with its Mayfair logo facing forward while I paid for the apples. We told the girl how lousy the apples had looked over at Mayfair, how glad we were to find these good ones. No, we didn't need a bag. There was room in the one we had.

That theft paid well. It paid David and me the tense edgy high of doing the job, the rush of relieved exhilaration when we knew we'd pulled it off, and the admiring plaudits of our peers. It paid us the turkey, which the bunch of us roasted and tore apart happily. And, unlike my other thieveries, it paid me a story I still like to tell.

It wasn't theft that tripped up Bill Clinton, the first president of my generation, but it was a similar self-indulgence. His erotic life was not the public's business, and impeachment was an absurd overreaction, but Clinton, a canny politician, knew very well that journalists no longer acknowledged a firewall around the private life of the president, and that his enemies were eager to capitalize on anything the media could turn up. Yet, figuring he would never get caught—forgetting the oldest law, that the gods hate hubris—he allowed himself an affair with a twenty-one-year-old intern and then compounded that mistake by lying about it and permitting others in his administration to unwittingly echo the same lie. And so the first president to have come of age in the 1960s, perhaps the greatest presidential intellect since Thomas Jefferson, stupidly corroborated the cultural conservatives' chief indictment of our generation—that we abandoned personal responsibility to follow our hedonistic desires. If it feels good, do it, and Clinton did it.

The affair itself was no vast or venal indiscretion, and human enough. It was morally less corrupt, in that it was consensual, than my theft of fifteen dollars from an elderly couple in Portland, Oregon, in

1969. But I was not president of the United States. Clinton was carrying the hopes of a great many liberals and moderates who had waited twelve years for a Democratic president. The effects of his dalliance and dishonorable lies can't be measured, but it's certain that more than Bill Clinton's reputation suffered damage. He hamstrung his administration's agenda for the last three years of his term. And considering how close the present election has turned out to be, I'm convinced it would have been all over on election night, in Al Gore's favor, if the president of the United States had mustered the self-control to keep his zipper zipped when Monica Lewinsky snapped her thong.

⚘

Tonight, late, the mist has cleared, the temperature has fallen, and great tall cumuli are streaming out of the northeast in silent splendor, from my left to my right, illumined by a near-full moon falling far in the west.

March 9

This would have been a braver expedition if I'd left the wine and whiskey at home. I considered it, but not for long. It's part of what I am, I rationalized. This is an experiment in solitude, not self-abnegation. But it would have been a worthy challenge. I had the last nip of Scotch—Springbank, fifteen years old and mighty tasty—on February 25th. Since then it's been two glasses of red wine each evening, and I'm on the last jug of that. Happily, this causes me no panic. I missed the whiskey only for an evening or two, and I expect the same when the wine runs dry. For me, drinking is part relaxation, part anesthesia for accumulated aches and ills of body, and habit, I'm realizing, as much as anything. It's early evening? Let's have a couple of drinks. Hell, let's have a third. This sojourn was an opportunity to break the habit, as I've done with TV and news, to resume or not to resume when I go back to the world. An opportunity missed.

Many writers drink, and many of that many drink a lot. Some, certainly, would be hard drinkers whatever they did for a living, but there seems to be something about the vocation that spurs the drinking, too. I think it's two things. Alcohol turns off the on-duty switch that tends to stick in the on position for most writers, probably most artists of all kinds. It frees us to socialize, enjoy a ball game, play like children, things we're not necessarily so good at doing. As Samuel Johnson replied to a friend who had asked why he drank: "To get rid of myself, to send myself away." The other thing it does, for some of us anyway, is what I believe it did for my father before it totally took him over. It feeds the creative fire. It puts us in closer touch, for intervals, with the essential passions that stir us to self-expression. This doesn't necessarily mean writing under the influence—though doing so, I've found, can sometimes break a log jam—but keeping ourselves open to the state of enthusiasm, in which all things are possible. The artist without enthusiasm is lost. And the artist who draws too much of his enthusiasm from the bottle is also lost, as the examples of too many twentieth-century American authors attest. We may need the loosening ebullience of Dionysus, but we need

him in balance with the light and clarity of Apollo and the warrior's discipline of Henry Thoreau.

Drink, for me at least, is not nearly as good at drowning sorrows as
it is at firing joys. When I was younger I tried to anesthetize painful
feelings with beer and whiskey, but it never worked. Being drunkenly
miserable was no better than being soberly miserable. Only time, if anything, can balm the worst pains. And making art. Creative work must
in the end amount to more than self-therapy, but it is, nonetheless, genuinely restorative to the writer—it permits him a way to make whole
some of the bruised or broken or undeveloped parts of his being, and to
make whole is to heal. It's likely that I carry the same genetic predis-
position toward alcoholism that my father surely had, and if I do, I think
I can justly say that I am handling it better than he did for most of his
life. That is not due, however, to superior strength of character or any
other virtue. Franz Daniel's sorrows were much larger than mine, he put
and left much more of himself on the battlefield, and, though a thinker
and a gifted man, he was not an artist. He didn't have a way to stop
pouring drinks and pour himself into the page instead.

Either way, though, with whiskey or without, wine or no wine, my
spirit comes and goes. When it's gone, as today, it's nothing as black
and empty as depression that I feel. It's a tinge of sadness that colors my
awareness like chamomile tea when hot water hits the bag. There's a
weight to it, but it's a weight I can usually stir into action—writing,
reading, doing chores—and it brings with it a sense of authenticity. It
seems to slow me down from skimming the surface of things and to open
me to the fullness of experience. In 1979 I was in eastern Oregon during a partial eclipse of the sun, and when the light changed, it cast the
landscape both darker and clearer. Ordinary daylight, when it returned,
for a while seemed to wash the land with too much light. For me,
melancholy casts that darker, clearer light.

I wouldn't be surprised if all night writers were melancholics, but
not all melancholics are night writers. Thoreau, that quintessential
morning person, wrote of melancholy as an indispensable condition:
"There is a certain fertile sadness which I would not avoid, but rather
earnestly seek. It is positively joyful to me. It saves my life from being

trivial. My life flows with a deeper current, no longer as a shallow and brawling stream . . ." I don't have to seek my own sadness, earnestly or otherwise—it finds me regularly enough, and I bet the same was true for Henry David. It goes, it comes, and it is indeed fertile. Depression is barren, denying as it does all feelings other than hopelessness. Joy is unitary, a single intense pitch with small modulations, and unsustainable in any case. Melancholy is a mix of feelings, a mélange shaded strongly with sadness but containing happiness too, even glints of joy. It accepts and reflects the wholeness of living, even as it laments one's errors and limitations.

My friend Simone Di Piero has written of Van Gogh that "his melancholy was the motor that ran hot and impelled the work; it was what he called 'an active melancholy, which hopes and aspires and seeks, not melancholy that despairs in stagnation and woe.'" Many artists of all kinds must be prone to such a state of being, and surely Beethoven was. His slow movements, especially in the Seventh and Ninth, build with a sad gladness that seems to acknowledge all woe— death, cruelty, illness, the failure of love—and to lift that burden into a transcendent beauty, a beauty not of joy but of earned happiness, a beauty the heart can call enough. Life, this beauty says, for all its suffering and evil, is no accident, no meaningless stirring of dust. Arguing the existence of God has always seemed oddly benighted to me, beside the point, like speculating about the weather while standing in a warm summer rain. The point is here and now. I look out on these trees, this landscape ridged and furrowed by time, and I see not intent but accomplishment, not disarray but order, not insensate matter but spirited meaning. I see such a fullness of being that my heart aches with it. This is the gift, the given world. To accept it, to bear the privilege of being, is to belong to a majesty we can't comprehend. In the end, we can only be grateful.

For all my father's failings, he was a teacher. He never spoke of what moved him in Beethoven's music. I don't know that he was capable of saying, but it was he, drunk in his rocking chair, raptured and stabbing the air—*The strings, Johnny, the strings!*—who caused me to recognize what it is that I love. As a child I couldn't put into words the sense of majesty I felt, even as inadequately as I've done here, but I know I felt it, and I understand now how important that awakening was. It saves my life from being trivial. It deepens with mystery the stream of my being. More than anything else, it moves me to write. I want to touch the majesty of existence all I can, learn its contours, sing it praise. Not to lay it open to reason, which there is no need to do and can't be done in any case, but to understand it in the old sense. To stand under it. To stand with it and in it, as long as it will have me.

This afternoon, looking out the window at the spacious glory of the Rogue River Canyon, that seems plenty.

⸙⸙⸙

Did I say that I marvel at my father's unwillingness to quit drinking after his New Year's collapse and his stint at Menninger's? Well, he's not the only Daniel I marvel at.

Within three weeks of my early morning psychosis in Portland I was shooting speed again. This seemed unremarkable to me. It was no problem that I'd had a manic-panic episode—I just wouldn't get that fried again. I would make an adjustment. I would let myself run for no more than one or two nights, not three. Thus committed to the path of moderation, I spent a lot of speed-time reading anthropology books with the fervor of a religious convert. Yes, I enthused, I had found myself. I would get my degree, travel the world doing fieldwork and climbing mountains, and write books about my adventures. I beamed into my future with a hyper-alert and overflowing optimism.

I did begin to climb rocks and mountains in 1969. Trekking up Mount Hood with two friends, watching stars give way to dawn, I almost sang for joy. The unbounded view from Hood's eleven-thousand-foot summit seemed to open me up from within. Climbing gave me the bodily satisfaction of hard physical work and the exhilaration of adventure with a whiff of danger. Only a few days after my morning meltdown I hitchhiked up to the Olympic Peninsula and packed in twenty miles to climb Mount Olympus, my first solo foray, and it went rapturously—across a glacier, up a steep snowy dome, and at last a rocky summit pinnacle where I spent two hours, snow peaks and jagged ridges ranging all around me. As I glissaded and plunge-stepped down the snowy shoulder of Olympus I felt godlike indeed. For the first time since early childhood, it seemed, I was completely happy and whole. I was doing what I'd been born to do.

In Portland I would sometimes practice rock climbing moves at Rocky Butte while revved on speed, enjoying the heightened concentration, reveling in sun and sweat. Every time I took speed, though, whatever I happened to be doing, I found myself noticing, then on later occasions nervously anticipating, the first slight sense of not being totally high anymore, of a distant dread sliding over me like wisps of overcast into a sunny sky.

In July, after a night spent cranked on meth, I drove with a carful of friends to climb Mount Washington in the central Oregon Cascades. All the way there, crashing off my high, I kept thinking *There's something wrong with the car* whenever we hit a rough patch of road. From Big Lake, in late afternoon, we hiked south on the Skyline Trail toward Washington's volcanic pinnacle. The lupine was in bloom, intensely blue. I was exhausted, hot and panting from the start, and soon fell behind the others. I hurried to catch up, stopped to take a few huge breaths, hurried on. Then suddenly I was watching myself collapse on the trail, my forearms seized in a spasm against my chest. My heart was booming, my breath coming in ragged surges. I must have managed to straighten my arms enough to get out of my backpack, because I remember lying free of it on the trail, my pulse roaring in my ears. I was about to die, I knew, yet I was self-possessed enough to administer a panicked self-aid that would have looked comical if anyone besides squirrels had been watching. I lay across the trail, my upper body against the uphill bank, to lessen the blood pressure in my head. *No,* I thought, *the other way,* and I shuffled around so that my head was down and my feet up, and then thought *No, this is wrong,* and shifted back, certain that my life depended on getting it right and that I was getting it wrong each time.

I don't know which way I was lying when my friends came back and found me. "Oh, shit," I remember one of them saying. I don't recall much of what followed. We camped right there by the trail. My friends were worried, but relieved that I seemed okay. I don't know if I ate or not. I lay in my sleeping bag most of the evening, fretful, feeling my blood pulse in my body. Long after dark I fell asleep, and this time I didn't wake up feeling fine. I felt sapped and leaden, in no shape to climb. My friends headed up to scale the mountain as I waited in Cold Spring Meadow, trying to sleep, harassed by flies, hot sun, and my obsessive thoughts.

I was sure I had hurt myself in some irreparable way, and I couldn't come to terms with it. Nothing within spoke for the whole me, for the presidential scholar/adult-pleaser/college dropout/draft resister/ hippie drifter/mountain climber/sneak thief/methamphetamine me, and I could not reason or wish or will the parts together. "I'm hopelessly divided from myself," I said aloud at one point, part whine, part pronouncement, part simple anguish. I, with my noble baloney about living an authentic life on my own terms, I was nothing. I was a ruined mess lying miserable in a beautiful wilderness that had no beauty for me, incapable of doing what I had come to do with my friends because I had wrecked myself while telling the world that I was finding myself.

We hiked out in the early evening. I kept an Otis Redding tune going repetitively in my head to keep my feet moving, my heart steady, my mind in one piece. (I wonder if this is how Muzak first implanted itself in my brain.) I slept in the car as we drove, then slept long on a bunk at the Reed ski cabin on Mount Hood where we stopped for the night. In the morning, feeling a little more together, I walked to a restaurant on the highway, looking forward to coffee and a doughnut. But the place was bleak, the people grim and ugly, the doughnut tasteless. Instead of a lift from the coffee, I felt myself draining away from within as I sat at the counter, smoking cigarettes and staring at my hands.

I did go back to school in the fall. Living with a roommate in an upstairs apartment in southeast Portland, I took Intro to Sociology and Anthropology, Linguistics, Twentieth-century European History, and something else I can't remember. The history course stirred me a little, but the others didn't. I was only going through the motions of being a student. I broke off time and again from reading or writing a paper to draw vague diagrams of my blown-out mind—flow charts that didn't flow, hierarchies with nothing at the top. I didn't know what I was draw-ing, but something was missing, something was wrong, and it was my own fault. I was too embarrassed about my meth habit to go to the Reed infirmary for counseling (if they even offered it). I did go once to a low-cost downtown clinic, but didn't tell them much. Someone informed me that the seizing up of my arms had probably been related to hyper-ventilation, nothing more serious, but my worries wore on. A clinic doctor gave me Valium, which mellowed me out while it lasted.

Friends and teachers probably noticed nothing wrong with me. I kept up my habitual air of self-sufficiency, climbed a little, played poker in the ongoing game in Reed's lower commons. I did a little morphine or heroin when John Sterne had some. Sterne, for his part, turned blue after taking three hits of heroin one night and might have died if fellow users hadn't revived him with mouth-to-mouth resuscitation. I wasn't with him that time. Somehow, through stubbornness and sheer will, he managed to continue his senior year at Reed and would graduate, along with my other classmates, in the spring of 1970.

I left Portland in December, pretty sure I wasn't coming back, and spent Christmas in Missouri with my father. He had let his graying hair grow out a little. It curled down close to his collar in back, in keeping with the times and with (I assume) his commitment to understand and affirm the youth culture. He even had a new, light blue suit with slightly bell-bottomed trousers. He was clearly unhappy, though, with my re-newed disenchantment with college and my general aimlessness. When I remarked one day that I might go logging again, or work part-time at something and develop my climbing skills, he snapped, "What the hell's the future in that?"

"What's the future in anything?" I said. "Isn't being alive enough?"

"Look here, Johnny. I see men in the jail over there who never got an education, never had a single advantage. You can't just throw away your opportunities."

"I'm not throwing anything away. I don't know what I want yet."

"You expect to find out by climbing mountains, or timberjacking?"

"Maybe climbing mountains is what I want. What the hell's the mat-ter with that?"

My father let out a dismissive snort. "It's kid stuff," he said. "It doesn't contribute."

Well, I thought to myself, *a guy could do a lot worse. If only you knew.* I felt as I had as a young teenager when my father had seen me reading a comic book and said sharply, "You're too damned old for that."

After Christmas I took the Greyhound to Washington. I'd been tired, sleeping a lot, since the end of the semester, and in D.C. I saw a doctor and found out I had mononucleosis. Long bed rest was the only treatment. It did away with any necessity to think about returning to college, climbing mountains, contributing to society, or really anything at all.

March 11

Today, between whacks of the maul on green madrone, I suddenly feel, *hear* with a bolt of concern, my heart thump fast—and I laugh out loud. I've just heard the first drumming grouse of the spring. It's one of those now-and-again moments here when I feel so happy I don't know what to do but holler. Sadness seeks quiet; happiness makes a joyful noise. In meditation sometimes the face of a young smiling chimp will arise out of nowhere, and a laugh from my belly interrupts my laborious silence. In meditation, says Suzuki-roshi, we realize our original true nature. I didn't expect mine to be simian—though reading Darwin, I suppose, should have tipped me off. I'm glad the little guy is smiling, and smiling impishly, unself-consciously, smiling in his soul.

The joy of these moments is the joy of a child, the joy of aimless play that takes a delightful turn. When that joy is upon me I need nothing more, but of course I always want something more. I want to know, whence comes such happiness? From me, of course. I become happy, and so my world of solitude seems a happy place. But I wouldn't have had this particular moment of happiness if I hadn't heard the grouse. It came with his drumming. Couldn't it be said that he afforded me my happiness?

Not that he intended to, necessarily, and not that the happiness had even been his. He may have had none at all. Later on in the spring, if his hopeful performances fail to succeed in drumming up a mate, I'm likely to interpret them as frustrated obsession: *Maybe THIS-This-THIS-THIS-time*, time after time after time. So—if this happiness didn't originate in me, and not in him, then where? Is it a kind of pervading ether that the grouse stirs which then stirs me, fast as the speed of sound? That would mean that I too could be affording happiness in ways I'm not aware of. Splitting wood last fall, in this same spot, may have conveyed happiness-waves to the grouse feasting on madrone berries directly over my head, evidently not at all anxious about my loud noises. (On the other hand, happy or not, I've done nothing here to cause anxiety in grouse.)

Like any good scientist, though, I'd like a more elegant theory. I'd like to propose the simplest possibility of all—that the grouse *is* happiness, and the trees and light rain around him are happiness too, and I am happiness, because happiness is the original true nature of all being. The word itself affords me some confidence in this theory. Happiness does not mean joy. The word is related to "happen," which comes from the Middle English "hap"—chance, fortune, that which occurs. Haps are what happen, and so happiness amounts to a shortened form of the very happeningness of the world. The nature of happiness, in other words, is the happiness of Nature.

Immediately I object—along with you, reader—that cancer, AIDS, hurricanes, volcanic explosions, and a host of other natural happenings afford little joy to their victims or to anyone else. How can such happenings be considered happy events? Because nobody said that happiness is about human beings, as individuals or a species, or about any other elite of living things. Most of us humans are lucky enough to experience it now and again or most of the time, when we are satisfied, or at least reconciled, with the haps of our lives. Such reconciliation is difficult for terminal cancer or AIDS patients to achieve, but there are many who do achieve it. Those people may not bring an eager joy to the door of death, but they do bring an authentic happiness, and with that happiness they are victims no longer. Their happiness is their triumph.

I acknowledge, as I must, that I probably wouldn't be holding this little colloquy on happiness if I had terminal cancer, and I might not be holding it if I were not a privileged citizen of the richest country on Earth. I can afford such far-blown thoughts because my culture affords me the happiness of a comfortable material existence—so comfortable that I can voluntarily give some of it up for a time and be happy about it. Most don't enjoy that luxury.

But I'm very sure, on the other hand, that there is only a loose correlation at best between material comfort and degree of happiness. On my first trip to Mexico, in Baja California and then the Sierra Madre and deserts of Chihuahua, I saw villages of run-down shacks without plumbing or power, kids begging in muddy streets, poor countrymen trying to hardscrabble a living from barren ground. There was ample evidence of poverty, but there was ample evidence of happiness, too. The streets sounded with shouts and laughs and lively talk, sounds I don't hear so much in U.S. streets. Happiness flashed in eyes and music, in the bright colors of dilapidated homes and businesses. Everywhere, in children and adults, there was a charge, a verve.

And a perseverance. Near Lagos de Moreno, the day before Ash Wednesday, I passed scores and scores of pilgrims strung out for miles along the highway, having walked who knows how far and with who knows how far to go—old men shuffling with canes, boys with radios, women with babies or with bundles on their heads. Here and there in the long procession a family had paused to cook a simple meal over a fire in the shade of a blanket on poles. All were dressed neatly, some of the men in suits. Their faces showed fatigue, some of them, but not impatience or frustration. Some were smiling. They ignored my little truck as I slowly passed. They weren't looking for a ride. They were doing what they considered it necessary to do, which was what they wanted to do. "They look happy," I wrote in my notebook twenty years ago.

When I crossed from Mexicali to El Centro on my way home, it was good to have shoulders on the highway and toilet paper in the bathrooms and water I could freely drink. After six weeks in Mexico, though, I felt uneasy among the immaculate plastic signs and shiny storefronts, the abounding K-Marts and Safeways crammed with customers intent on their shopping. Everything worked efficiently, but it all seemed desolate and sterile. Sleek cars glided along smooth, well-signaled streets, and the drivers looked the way I felt—robotic, as if our souls had been surgically removed for smoother functioning. Nobody looked happy. As I drove north toward home I wasn't ready to renounce my pickup and my contact lenses and other gifts of progress, but I was aware as I hadn't been before that the home I was heading for—a crumbling little cottage on a ranch in the sticks of eastern Oregon that I was renting for fifty dollars a month and sharing with packrats—was a pretty substantial dwelling on this planet, and that if I was wise I would remember never to confuse happiness with the accumulation of money or the owning of things.

March 12

Though I'm drawn to the practice of Zen, I'm reminded reading Thomas Merton that I'm drawn to the *language* of Christianity. How can I not respond to those vast, resonant nouns—*name, word, love, spirit, father, son, hope, God, faith, light, darkness, peace?* To speak or write those words, even casually, is to stir depths I do not know. I'm also drawn to the activeness of Merton's Catholicism. Zen meditation is an active state—in the *zendo* you get rapped with a stick if you confuse meditation with sleep—but not a seeking. You sit not to attain something but to realize the true nature that is already yours. Meditation for Merton— he calls it "inner silence"—"depends on a continual seeking, a continual crying in the night, a repeated bending over the abyss."

Maybe I'm attracted because there's drama in his way, a flavor of narrative, though I can't quite visualize bending over an abyss and don't know why I would do it. I did cry in the night once. When my mother was dying, on a respirator in intensive care, I was strung out with anguish and one night prayed for relief. I didn't know to whom or what I was praying. Later that night, while I slept, help came. I saw my mother as she had been the day before she fell and broke her hip, only now she seemed made of light—her cheerful face, her silvery hair, her lavender skirt and orange blouse, all was radiant. With the vision came the understanding that my mother couldn't live in her body anymore, yet she would live. When I woke into my thinking mind I didn't know *how* she would live, how she could, but the vision was the vision, and it helped.

Since then I've felt inclined to pray once in a while. If you're going to do it at all, it seems a bit cheap to do it only in emergencies. But without an emergency pressing me, I've balked at the problem of whom or what to address. You should know, right? The idea of a God who can hear prayer, who knows individuals and responds to them personally, has always given me trouble. My intellect balks. In fact, it seems to me that such an idea condemns the believer to neurosis or outright insanity, for how can it be squared with the facts of human and nonhuman violence and misery, the horrific deaths and torments that occur every day? How does a caring God countenance the murder of children, the murder of presidents and heroes, and how does a caring person countenance such a God?

And yet, I cry in the night and a helpful vision appears. And yet, in 1997, I'm driving the Pennsylvania Turnpike in a thunderstorm, in heavy traffic, when the van directly in front of me hits a pothole, slams the guardrail, and goes sideways, one door flying open, one of the seat cushions and other objects emptying onto the hardtop, all this in half a second at sixty miles an hour in a driving rain—but I react in strangely slowed-down time, swerving and weaving to miss the seat and an ice chest and the van itself without skidding my rental car sideways, without hitting one of the other cars, as we all—including the people in the van—make it through without harm. I'm a good driver, but I felt guided. I felt the attention of a friendly power.

Luck, God, the power of the unconscious mind—purpose, if any, is hard to discern and surely complicated, but I do pay attention to experience, and experience tells me that to pray may not be an unreasonable thing to do. And so, after meditating and sometimes before a meal, I bow my head and try it. Neither "Lord" nor "Father" nor "God" sound right in my voice, so I address myself to "Spirit whose name I do not know." Ungainly, but for now the best I can do. I give thanks—for the meal, for the day, for the silence, for the river, for the wake-up call directed to my little finger and not to my ankle or leg or skull.

At first I didn't ask for anything. To ask seemed childish, as if I were sitting on Santa's knee. Then I realized—realizations, I remind you, come slow around here—that I didn't have to ask anything for *myself*. I realized I've got a wife at home whose safety and happiness I very much desire. I've got a brother and a niece and two young-adult stepsons, one of them to be married this summer. *Oh yeah* . . . I have in-laws in their eighties, one of them taking treatment for prostate cancer. I have a friend with lupus and a friend with Lou Gehrig's disease, I have two young friends expecting—they've had it by now—their first baby, another couple separated and maybe divorcing. I have a three-year-old friend named Schuyler, whose drawing of a bear hangs on the wall to my side as I write. I've got a lot to pray for.

I have not experienced, in prayer or meditation, the attentive presence of the divine as Thomas Merton describes it: "We confront Him
in prayer knowing Him by Whom we are known, aware of Him Who is
aware of us, loving Him by Whom we know ourselves to be loved." Or,
in the pithier way Meister Eckhart put it, "The eye through which I see
God is the same eye through which God sees me." I haven't known
that, but I have felt close to knowing it, and I consider both men reliable witnesses. I believe in its possibility.

The Christian language I don't believe in is that which insists on the
separation of spirit and matter, the language that kicks God upstairs, out
of sight, and leaves behind a fallen world. Christianity has been vilified
more than it deserves as the source of the western world's environmental woes. Descartes' and Francis Bacon's scientific materialism, which
reduced the universe to dead matter and living things to mere automata,
is far more to blame. Christianity preserves at least the intuition of
sacred origin and sacred purpose in nature, if not sacredness itself. As
evidenced by the views of Wendell Berry, Fr. Thomas Berry (no rela-
tion), and the Evangelical Environmental Network, to cite three very
distinct Christian viewpoints, the Bible rightly understood commands
respectful care for the natural world. How, as Wendell Berry asks, can
love for the Creator be demonstrated by abuse of His creation? Yet there
remains that dichotomy: creator and creation, spirit and flesh, light and
darkness, that which redeems and that which needs redemption. This
dualism is in Thomas Merton:

> My hope is in what the eye has never seen. Therefore, let me
> not trust in visible rewards. My hope is in what the heart of man
> cannot feel. Therefore let me not trust in the feelings of my
> heart. My hope is in what the hand of man has never touched.
> Do not let me trust what I can grasp between my fingers. Death
> will loosen my grasp and my vain hope will be gone.

I too believe in what I have never seen or touched, but it is precisely through what I do see and do touch that my belief arises. In the
manifold things of Nature I sense the unseen presence they embody

and betoken. I perceive this presence through my senses, intuition, imagination, and absolutely through the feelings of my heart. Why would I cultivate distrust of any of those? My heart and senses and psyche are flawed and mortal, but I don't believe they are out to trick me. They aren't laying for me with shotguns. I trust their promptings that there is more, much more, that they can only hint at. The feelings of my heart turn me toward the Spirit whose name I do not know. Whether it knows me I can't say, but at times I sense knowing all around me in this brimming silence. I sense it in the council of trees surrounding my meadow at dusk, in the swirl and slide of the green river. It's in the rank havens where bears even now are stirring toward wakefulness (and one, perhaps, is just getting to sleep), in the flight of the owl and osprey, in the black-tailed deer and in the cougar that takes the deer down. It's the Spirit of beginnings and of endings, of necessity and of chance, of the one way and the many. Its name, though I do not know it, glitters in fire across the sky tonight, is spoken clearly by the whispering river, is as close as the ground I stand on and the breath that clouds and vanishes before me. Death will loosen my grasp and darken my sight. All things are transient, from sow bugs to the stars. And only in their transience and our own, here, now, can we sometimes touch the eternal and taste its joy.

March 13

In the spring of 1970 I finally got my wish to go to jail. In April, after lounging around D.C. for the winter sleeping off my mononucleosis, hanging out with friends, working graveyard for a few weeks at an all-night hamburger house, I hitchhiked to Oregon. I had nothing impelling me but the fuzzy notion that I belonged to the Pacific Coast if I belonged anywhere. I did what I knew. I bought John Sterne's Triumph Bonneville motorcycle—he had upgraded to a Harley Sportster—and hired on setting chokers for Weyerhaeuser again. There was always a contingent of Reed dropouts working in the woods. I lived with them in a suburban house in Vancouver, Washington, across the river from Portland.

One Saturday night that late spring my logging friend Tim Custer and I found it necessary to drink shots and beers at an array of Portland bars, and at closing time were relieving ourselves in an alleyway—quite discreetly, we thought—when we were busted by a couple of plain-clothes cops who had followed us out of the last bar. Custer, more fiery of temperament than I, made the mistake of resisting and took several body blows and a knee to the groin for his trouble. Booked and finger-printed, we spent what was left of the night in the drunk tank of Mult-nomah County Jail. I must have managed to reach John Sterne on the phone, because he put in a valiant Sunday morning buzzing around Portland on his Sportster dunning friends and acquaintances for bail money. He sprung us that afternoon. A few weeks later I stood in a courtroom arguing not that conscience was my guide and highest law, not that the United States government was using the military draft to wage an unjust, unnecessary, and immoral war, but that pissing in an alleyway at 2 A.M. should not be a crime. The judge demurred, lectur-ing at length that in some societies public urination indeed was not a crime, but in the one where he had jurisdiction it indeed was disorderly conduct, and bang went the gavel.

Weyerhaeuser shut down its woods for a couple of weeks that sum-mer when fire risk got too high. I rode my cycle down U.S. 101 to Santa

Cruz to visit my friend Ken Hyams, the one who had bluffed his way into a 4-F deferment on psychological grounds, and when he got jobs for both of us with a wilderness camp in the High Sierra for underprivileged kids, I kissed my logging career good-bye for the second time. Ken and I spent a month amid the sunny meadows and lakes of the Ritter Range, with our underprivileged charges and without, hiking and climbing and fishing. We made an exhilarating ascent of the face of Clyde Minaret, roped together on rock just difficult and airy enough to be fun. Sundown was nearing when we briefly straddled the summit—the sharpest ridge I've ever seen—looking out at a topography of other jagged peaks and ridges flanked with snowfields so precipitous they seemed to overhang. We finished our descent by moonlight, lowering ourselves gingerly down a steep couloir and then feeling our way along a rock traverse to the reassurance of meadow grass underfoot, and the lake where we had camped.

In early fall I bought a new rope and rack of climbing hardware and rode my cycle to Yosemite Valley, where I pitched a tarp in Camp 4, the climbers' camp, and hung around in the mornings looking for a partner. If I hooked up with another novice I had him belay from the ground as I tried my first technical leads, pounding in pitons for protection, jamming my hands and feet into cracks, tenuously smearing my boot-soles to flakes and nubbins of bright granite in a kind of labored, shaky-kneed dance. Once in a while I got lucky and teamed up with an older guy who knew what he was doing. I would study him as he led a pitch, then struggle through the moves that he had made look easy as I cleaned the hardware behind him. I think I realized early on that I didn't have a great gift as a climber and would always struggle, but that was okay. I loved it—the intensity, the whispering of fear that turned now and then to a roar, the exposure, the all-consuming focus of a hard move committed to, and the happy exhaustion at the end of a climb that left me, momentarily, needing nothing more from myself or from anyone or anything else in the world.

I didn't see a connection at the time, but it seems clear enough now that rock climbing gave me something akin to what drugs had been giving me, especially methamphetamine—a sense of heightened awareness and a glow of self-sufficiency, a lively fullness of being. I've read accounts of brain research that link attraction to euphoriant drugs with attraction to high-risk sports such as auto racing or mountain climbing. Both may win the same payoff—a boost in brain chemicals that promote a sense of pleasurable well-being, chemicals that in most people tend to be present at higher levels. I don't know, but as I gave myself to climbing in 1970 I quit using hard drugs. I didn't decide to quit, I just did. My meltdowns on meth had scared me, but I don't honestly know if those alone would have stopped me from using. I found a better way to get high, and it may have saved my life, or at least my health.

I can't imagine a more suitable therapy than rock climbing for kids in trouble with drugs, because it does something that can't be accomplished by any amount of preaching that drug use is unhealthy, that they should just say no and satisfy themselves with the normalities of school, family, friends, and work. Climbing offers them a taste, by means of their own daring effort, of the more vibrant sense of self they've been seeking through drugs, and it even subversively inculcates a healthy Calvinist ethic. Sweet exhaustion, blistered feet, raw fingers, and sore stiffness in more muscles than the climber knew he had make it incontestably clear to him that he has been involved in *work,* and that the work was hard and good. As for human relationships, climbing partners don't inevitably become close friends, but to be tied together on a rope is a mighty bond. You literally entrust your life and well-being to the person who belays you, and you accept the responsibility of that same trust when you belay him. Not a bad exercise.

And, though kids these days tend to get started on artificial indoor walls, climbing sooner or later ropes you into the outdoors. I can't prove that alienation from nature has anything to do with the boredom and disaffection so common among our young, but I do know that they are growing up in a world increasingly enclosed by human constructions, human machines, and human concerns—a world vastly different from even so recent a time as Thoreau's in terms of day-to-day involvement with nonhuman nature. Some are trapped in the human vortex by poverty, some by overprotective parents and their own timidity, many by the sheer overpowering momentum of technological progress.

Climbing—backpacking, kayaking, and other pursuits can of course do the same—turns you outward, not just to observe the wild but to engage it with body, mind, and spirit. You remember how to use those agile feet and prehensile hands that our ancestors spent long ages developing. Glimmers of primal alertness return, a sensitivity to natural influences that stultifies in buildings and cars and the electronic cocoon that thickens daily around us. You get good and scared, good and tired, good and happy in sun and wind and rain. You might get good and hurt, too, but at least it will be a hurt you can feel.

The concept of ecopsychology was widely ridiculed as New Age pap when it arose during the 1990s, but its central insight is downright old-fashioned. It dares to suggest what ancient Greeks or medieval peasants or traditional Native Americans would have found so obvious they would have laughed to hear it asserted, yet the avatars of modern psychology have missed it almost entirely—that along with our relations with humans and human things, the quality of our relations with the natural world no doubt has a significant influence on our psychic and physical health. We are, after all, children of that world. How could estrangement from it not cause us some degree of misery and malfunction? Robinson Jeffers, one of our greatest poets, was a better psychologist than Sigmund Freud when he wrote, "The whole human race spends too much emotion on itself. The happiest and freest man is the scientist investigating nature or the artist admiring it, the person who is interested in things that are not human."

❧

In the 1960s my friends and I derided the dark warnings from Authorities on High that marijuana was a gateway drug, the beginning for all who smoked it of an inexorable slide into hard drugs, addiction, and probable death. Then John Sterne and I seemed to make ourselves poster boys for the very prediction we scoffed at, but it never really fit. The gateway drug for both of us was alcohol, the gateway drug and drug of choice for most Americans. But is there even such a thing as a gateway drug? I remember as a kid in Bannockburn watching my brother and his friends play a game on the grassy hill—ah, that slippery slope—below our house. One at a time, while the others watched, each boy would lean forward, hands on knees, and deliberately hyperventilate until he collapsed and rolled down the hill. They probably weren't blacking out, just breathing themselves giddy and letting go. They were getting high. Kids do that.

And so, one way or another, do most adults. A majority of us use a drug or drugs—caffeine, nicotine, alcohol, marijuana, prescription uppers or downers or mood re-arrangers—for pleasurable, palliative, or consciousness-altering effects. This has been more or less true throughout history. Humans have made wine for as long as we've known grapes. The domestication and cultivation of grain crops ten thousand years ago was aimed at the production of beer as well as of bread. Cannabis has been smoked for millennia for purposes sacred and secular. Early America's taste for the apple, Michael Pollan points out in *The Botany of Desire*, was more about hard cider and applejack than it was about pie or keeping the doctor away.

The antidrug mania of the last two decades, and of other periods in American history—it's a cyclical phenomenon—is rooted in an unwillingness to acknowledge that self-intoxication is as human as speaking, and that in and of itself, self-intoxication is not a bad thing. If we could accept that, we might be able to move on from our absurd societal posture of righteously condemning certain drugs while freely consuming, with appropriate winks and nods—or without even the awareness that winking and nodding is called for—many others. We might begin to focus more on the notion of responsible use, less on the failed policies of prohibition. Any eighth-grader in America can obtain marijuana more easily than he can obtain beer. To score the beer he at least has to steal it or persuade someone of age to buy it for him. The pot he can buy any day at school. We'd gain a better grip on marijuana consumption among our young if we decriminalized possession and regulated sales as we do with alcohol, taxing it heavily and applying the revenues to education and treatment programs for problem users.

We also need to recognize that it makes no sense to speak of a *drug* problem or a *drug* policy—the category is too broad, particular drugs too diverse. Marijuana is one of the most benign intoxicants, legal or illegal, now available to Americans, but the unlucky among those who use it or sell it suffer severe punishments. One federal prisoner in six is a marijuana offender, some of them serving longer terms than murderers do. State penalties can be even harsher: in fifteen states it's possible to get life in prison for a nonviolent marijuana offense. Our societal response to this gentle weed is unjust, vastly disproportionate, and silly. It is driven less by fact than by the ongoing cultural backlash, that began in the Reagan administration, against the real and imagined excesses of the 1960s counterculture.

Psychedelic drugs—LSD, mescaline, psilocybin, and others—pose a more complicated problem, because they are far more powerful than pot and can be intensely disorienting and frightening to unprepared users. They probably shouldn't be sold at the corner drugstore, to adults or to kids. Ideally they should be available only under the guidance of experienced elders as elements of spiritual rite and practice, as peyote is used by the Native American Church, as various psychedelics have been used in many cultures for as long as there have been human cultures. It is a strange quirk, or providence, that creation should provide plant substances that expand human consciousness in such a way that it sees more deeply *into* creation. As Aldous Huxley discovered for himself on mescaline, psychedelic drugs do authentically open the doors of perception. Many of us in the sixties were taking them with that intent—bumblingly, without sufficient preparation or guidance or discipline, but in our own way genuinely seeking. A few of us went insane and a few of us died. Most of us managed to incorporate the experience into our evolving lives, and our lives evolved in new ways—mostly better ways, I would argue—because of it.

I don't know how society should deal with these drugs. I do know that they will always be available, that there will always be a small fraction of the population drawn to them—around 5 percent—and that those who are drawn to them do not belong in jail. Hundreds of thousands in my generation who took psychedelics in the sixties and seventies are thriving today in all walks of life. We are professors, politicians, doctors, artists, and CEOs, and we are mail carriers, ranchers, carpenters, hair dressers, and small businesspeople. It would improve our credibility with our children and grandchildren, as well as open the way for a more thoughtful discourse about these drugs, if we were more willing to speak openly about what they have meant to us.

Methamphetamine, on the other hand, is a corrosive psychic and physical poison, but even this scourge could better be handled through some degree of decriminalization. Users caught in possession should be diverted into mandatory treatment, not prison. Long-term treatment for hard drugs has proven as successful as long-term treatment for other chronic diseases—the one-year relapse rate for both categories hovers around 50 percent—and at least recognizes that drug dependence is in fact a disease, not a moral failing or social deviance that should be punished with a prison term. Treatment is cheaper, too. A year of it costs between two and eight thousand dollars, while keeping an addict in prison—where at present he is unlikely to receive drug treatment—costs more than twenty-six thousand dollars a year.

The manufacture and sale of meth should remain illegal, and penalties perhaps should be increased. It will still be made and sold, though, because its chemical constituents can be obtained from a variety of legal sources, it can be fabricated by any entrepreneurial soul with a chemistry set, and it can be marketed at a vast profit. The supply side is almost as wide open for other hard drugs. Whatever incentives or disincentives the United States government applies to foreign countries, opium poppies and coca leaves will be grown in quantity somewhere in the world; they fuel a black market economy worth many billions of dollars to its bosses, and poor farmers very often have no other crop worth selling. Heroin, cocaine, and other drugs will continue to pour through our borders, with federal interdiction serving merely to raise prices now and then by causing modest market scarcity, and to send some of the less-lucky traffickers—almost never the bosses—to jail.

The War on Certain Drugs makes about as much sense as a fat man declaring a War on Doughnuts in order to control his weight. The drug economy runs on demand. Demand can't be eliminated, but it can be reduced through treatment. Treatment can make a difference only if it's widely available. At present, only a handful of users who need it can get it. Two-thirds of the total of two million Americans now behind bars are there for drug offenses. More than six out of ten of them, released without treatment, will return to prison for similar crimes— even though research has shown that treatment in prison can reduce that 60 percent to 25 percent, and that every dollar spent on it saves seven dollars in medical and other societal costs. For those hard cases unable or unwilling to kick their habits, the most cost-effective as well as the most humane approach is to maintain them, as I believe the British do, on limited doses of their favorite poisons. Self-destruction should be the solemn right of every American, and society would benefit from plummeting theft and burglary rates.

The War on Certain Drugs is costing American citizens on the order of eighteen billion dollars a year, and it exacts nonmonetary costs as well. Property rights and the presumption of innocence are trampled every day by forfeiture laws, which empower police to seize homes, cars, cash, and other belongings when they make a drug bust, no conviction necessary; as a consequence, narcotics units have become self-financing, forfeiture-hungry fiefdoms. Involuntary drug testing in schools and workplaces violates Fourth Amendment protections against unreasonable search and seizure. Alarmist drug-education programs encourage kids to rat on their peers and parents, neighbors on neighbors, and friends on friends, for "crimes" as trivial as growing a pot plant or smoking a joint. Promising research on LSD's psychotherapeutic possibilities was stunted when the drug was criminalized in 1966. President Clinton overruled the unanimous opinion of his AIDS advisers that needle-exchange programs for drug addicts, because they were likely to prevent tens of thousands of new HIV infections, deserved federal funding—Clinton, ever the careful triangulator, feared being seen as soft on drugs. And for the same reason, no political or business leader will voice even the *possibility* of growing cannabis for paper fiber, despite the fact that it yields several times more fiber per acre than do the forests we are clear-cutting for that purpose.

PBS is the only television network to have run a serious feature questioning the War on Certain Drugs. A print columnist now and then gets up the gumption to touch the subject warily. Fewer than half a dozen politicians that know of, none of them with national name recognition, have been brave enough to take a stand in favor of decriminalization. We need more, and as inspiration I offer my own example. I'm not a particularly courageous man, but look what I have lost by making public my drug history and current views on the subject. My longtime aspiration to run for the presidency of the United States is now permanently dashed, and even my lesser ambitions—to serve on the Supreme Court, as chief of the Forest Service, or as Ambassador to Nepal—have come to nothing as well. These are bitter pills to swallow, but at least, with occasional medicinal help, I can sleep at night.

March 14

I've got a bird problem.

A flicker woke me soon after dawn jackhammering the southwest corner of the cabin, and he and his ilk have been drilling trees and yammering without respite all morning. Steller's jays flap about in perpetual aggrievement, directing harsh screeches at the many beings, objects, and phantoms they find unacceptable. Even the usually stoic and decorous robins indulge in cheap exchanges of hostile cheeping over various no doubt weighty issues. It's as though my solitude's been invaded by the vehement political campaigning—pre- and post-election—I was lucky enough to leave behind last November. Must be something in the air. Insects have been welcomed back into the warming world, to drift, whine, and buzz mindlessly about. The droning sweat gnats that plague the summer months have arisen, and it's only March. Wasps are bumbling around with uncharacteristic vigor. Squirrels are chanting their monomaniacal gibberish. Even the Global Warming Frog is at it again, lending his unmusical utterance to the general tumult, and off in the woods that poor solitary loser of a grouse is drumming and drumming and drumming.

Who can concentrate? This is no country for a writer. A sound, a motion, something is forever pecking my beleaguered awareness. I'd like nature better if it wasn't so damned *unruly*. "Let's settle down here!" I want to command from the pulpit of my deck, perhaps with a warning blast from the shotgun, but who would listen? It's spring! The greensward is greener than green, the original idea of green. Daffodils, one-inch daisies, and the first wave of wildflowers are upon us, and soon will follow the plum and cherry and apple blossoms, the golden iris, and the lethally gorgeous perfume of the wild azalea, which lays in wait to knock you over with a single unsuspecting breath—ah, the shimmering gauds and baubles of the season, which may not be the cruelest but surely is the crassest.

It's time to go home. I knew it last night as I stood on the deck, high on nothing but a glass of wine, howling hard as I could into the canyon.

I'll stay through the rest of March, head home on April Fool's Day. I've driven up to the pass and found the snowpack—entirely untracked—at only a foot and a half and subsiding fast. I'll have sixteen days to tidy up the cabin and grounds, and myself, at my leisure. After this mild winter, I know the Brothers will be eager to install the new writer-resident, a young fiction writer from Indiana named Steve Edwards, and to perform the springtime ministrations. Edwards, for his part, has been eager to move in from the moment the Brothers selected him to join the faith. It's time for this winter deadbeat to clear out.

I was howling last night because I'd been fishing in the late afternoon and spotted a rafting party camped upriver from Meadow Creek. They, fortunately, did not spot me. My sharpened animal alertness protected me. I had excellent cover in boulders and scrub oak from which to survey the blithe intruders with my binoculars. Five of them, three men and two women, with two space-age tents and various other bright accoutrements—more of the garish bloomings of spring—conversing cheerily, bounding among the boulders, one of them knocking about with pots and pans as he prepared supper. They were noisy, they had parked themselves precisely at a hole I'd been looking forward to fishing, and, most unforgivably of all, they were young. Absurdly young. Why is it that as I get older the rest of humanity gets younger?

I considered approaching their camp to practice conversation, but what would we have talked about? Whatever dismal news of the world awaits me, I didn't want to learn it from a pack of twenty-somethings on holiday, and neither did I want to answer their questions about my presence in the Rogue backcountry without boat or backpack. Worse yet— my real fear—what if they *had* no questions? What if they merely stirred about semi-politely waiting for me to remove myself and the pall of my company from their happy, youthful, high-tech microcosmos? What if—dear God—I *bored* them?

This is no country for aging men. "Beware the Ides of March," I muttered, not quite loudly enough to be heard, and then rose from my spy nest and withdrew—fell back, trudged uptrail like invaded peoples throughout history, to my secret safehold. At midnight, having eaten and imbibed my modest Dionysian spirit, I went to the deck and cut loose with my exultantly loudest-possible series of wolf/coyote/blood-hound howls and followed with several minutes of my best banshee wailings, trying to sound like a mating cougar or a fifty-pound frog screaming for love. I sent peals and peals of pure, primal, animal ecstasy down to my canyon-mates by the river, of the highest quality and free of charge.

They wanted a wilderness experience, didn't they?

Henry Thoreau liked spring a lot better than I do. He was stirred by the stirrings and promises of the season. He was a man of morning, of renewal, of setting out into the perennial possibilities of his home ground. And so, inevitably, *Walden* ends with the season of beginnings—the chapter "Spring" and a brief conclusion—and in these chapters Thoreau attains some of the book's rhetorical peaks. He observes in a trance of rapt imagination the forms assumed by thawing sand and clay in the raw railroad cut he passes on his way to the village, finding there the boundlessly echoing archetypes of creation—heavy lobes verging into leaves, feathers, and wings of "the airy and fluttering butterfly," as well as veins, rivers, bowels, fingers, and toes. This bank of "sand foliage" convinces Henry David that "Earth is still in her swaddling clothes, and stretches forth baby fingers on every side," and leads him to a conclusion that any Native American would have endorsed, and that within a few decades of our present time everyone alive will take for granted: "There is nothing inorganic."

That railroad bank, an inadvertent collaboration of human artifice and natural process, absorbs Thoreau like no other scene or object in the book, save possibly Walden Pond itself, but it is also in "Spring" that he renders one of the great American credos on the worth of the purely wild:

> We need the tonic of wildness,—to wade sometimes in marshes where the bittern and the meadow-hen lurk, and hear the booming of the snipe; to smell the whispering sedge where only some wilder and more solitary fowl builds her nest, and the mink

crawls with its belly close to the ground. At the same time that we are earnest to explore and learn all things, we require that all things be mysterious and unexplorable, that land and sea be infinitely wild, unsurveyed and unfathomed by us because unfathomable. We can never have enough of Nature. We must be refreshed by the sight of inexhaustible vigor, vast and Titanic features, the sea-coast with its wrecks, the wilderness with its living and its decaying trees, the thunder cloud, and the rain which lasts three weeks and produces freshets. We need to see our own limits transgressed, and some life pasturing freely where we never wander.

In spring, it seems, there is nothing in Nature incapable of evoking Thoreau's enthusiasm. He finds affirmation even in the foul smell of a dead horse by the path to his cabin—to limit the insult to his nose he circles out of his way, but is repaid "by the assurance it gave me of the strong appetite and inviolable health of Nature." Such rhapsodies can sound a bit strained—one melancholic to another, I sometimes sense the man trying to cheerlead himself out of a depression—but in the end, *Walden* wins me over by dint of his resolute passion to attend to Nature in her every aspect with every faculty of his being. He may overexert himself searching out a silver lining to a dark cloud of dead-horse stench, but he does tell you about the horse, as elsewhere he tells of ants rending one another to pieces and of a woodchuck he was briefly tempted to seize and devour raw. There are nature writers whose effusions betray no evidence they have ever bushwhacked a nasty thicket or been harassed by a mob of mosquitoes. Thoreau is not one of them. In his *Journal* especially, where no consideration of audience troubles him, he faithfully renders his occasional irks and disgusts, as when an obscenely phallic mushroom he has gathered deliquesces into a putrid puddle, causing the nature lover to inquire, "Pray, what was Nature thinking when she made this? She almost puts herself on a level with those who draw in privies."

Maybe it's because Thoreau's sympathetic imagination for the things of Nature is so immense and intense that I'm caught up short in *Walden* by his lack of generosity toward human beings. "Through our own recovered innocence," he writes of spring, "we discern the innocence of our neighbors," but the innocence of neighbors is never long on Henry David's mind. In "Economy," the long first chapter, he turns his scorn so frequently on the mass of men he judges as mired in quiet desperation that before I'm thirty pages into the book I want to shout, "Says you! What do *they* think of their lives?" He seems almost oblivious, too, to the privilege that enables his two-year experiment in semi-solitary self-sufficiency. I imagine that most of his putatively desperate contemporaries, if willing to live like him in the manner of a solitary graduate student, would have been well capable of getting by as simply and cheaply as he did (assuming they had a prosperous friend like Emerson on whose land they could squat). They made other choices—marriage, children, and the working of a farm or trade so as to have something to leave those children. Thoreau proposed marriage once; turned down, he wrote one sentence in his *Journal*—"There is no remedy for love but to love more"—and forged ahead with his bachelorhood of letters, pouring his love into language and great Nature herself.

American literature is the richer for it, but Thoreau's snappish side could have used a little softening. Yes, he was writing a manifesto. He wished to rouse his fellow men to a higher calling, but how likely are you to wake a man by telling him how low and primitive he is? When you sit with a poor Irishman and his wife and children, accepting their hospitality during a sudden rainstorm, and tell them at self-satisfied length how wholesomely and inexpensively you live in your small cabin, and suggest that if they too would only live simply, and eschew coffee, tea, meat, and butter, "they might all go a-huckleberrying in the summer for their amusement"—all the while inwardly mocking the Irishman for his deafness to your clearly superior views—is it your aim to wake, or is it to abuse? In such bristly, too-easy judgments, Henry David gives off the distinct odor of some of the less thoughtful attitudes emoted by such as me as we came of age in the 1960s.

But he himself was, of course, a young man—twenty-eight when he went to Walden Pond, in his early thirties as he wrote the book—still learning his craft and forming his soul. In *Walden*, as in his first book, *A*

Week on the Concord and Merrimack Rivers, the prodigious journal keeper was finding his way as a writer of books, and what he found in those two volumes, whatever their flaws, was gift enough. His amplitude of method in *Walden*, combining personal narrative with scientific observation, moral philosophy, spiritual meditation, and ruminations about politics and economy, laid groundwork for all American essayists and nature writers to follow. His lean and vigorous sentences set a stylistic standard that I and countless others have tried to emulate. And the burden of his book, which was nothing less than to suggest organic relations between an individual human life, the life of human society, and the life of the natural universe itself, is even more timely now than it was at its first publication. As our culture lapses ever deeper into its obsession with things and comforts and its sterile orthodoxy of scientific materialism, as it pricks us daily with new wants and pseudo-needs, promising limitless technological progress and delivering limitless distraction and the killing soul-sickness of boredom, we need more than ever to wedge our feet down through the slush and emptiness we have made of our existence and rediscover a sane standing. We have much to learn from the great man whose greatest skill, he wrote, was to want but little.

"There was need of America," Thoreau entered in his *Journal* in 1851, referring to the enervated tameness of English literature, even as he was answering that need by writing the hugely spirited book that would make his name upon publication in 1854. Along with Whitman's *Leaves of Grass*, issued only a year later, *Walden* at its best is the most energetic and most definitively American summons to spiritual wakening that I know. It is a book for youth, as E. B. White observed, and youth can thrive at any age, because "morning is when I am awake and there is a dawn in me." And if Thoreau valorized the prerogatives of youth with too much attitude, I happily accept that too as part and parcel of his greatness. His advice to advance confidently in the direction of one's dreams remains the best possible counsel to offer the young—the only counsel, finally, that matters. If your dreams have not yet come into focus, I would only add, thinking of my own youth, then advance confidently without them. And if you have no confidence?

Advance, my friend, advance.

March 17

My parents came west to visit in the spring of 1971, while I was living in Berkeley and working a white-collar job for a railroad association. They came, traveling separately, to see their first grandchild, my niece Heather, born to my brother and his wife, Rena, the previous fall. Jim had finished his Air Force service and was taking classes at U.C.-Berkeley. He had let his hair grow to his shoulders and was sporting a full beard, the Elvis look-alike now resembling certain representations of Jesus. The four-year hitch in the Air Force had been a stretch of tedium spiked with anxiety—dull work in the military bureaucracy, reassignment to Vietnam always possible. In early 1968, during the Tet offensive, he and his friends had expected new orders daily.

The visit must have gone pleasantly overall, but I don't remember much of the pleasantry. My father and I went to an Oakland A's game—we saw Vida Blue pitch one of the twenty-four wins he would amass that year, his first full season, when he won the Cy Young Award—and the whole family attended a Giants game a couple of days later. In the parking lot afterward my mother and father lost control of the *détente* they had managed to hold together to that point in the visit. One of my friends had invited us for dinner. My mother wanted to go, my father wanted to go to a restaurant instead, and over that weighty issue they wrangled amid the clogged and noisy exit traffic at Candlestick Park. My mother, who surely hadn't had the least interest in going to the game in the first place, spoke sharply in her carefully modulated voice. My father half-shouted back, his expression pouty, his poor sensitive ego wounded yet again.

I don't remember what we did that evening, but the next day, alone for an hour with my mother, I unloaded on her. I was closer to and easier with her than I was with my father. At sixty-three, she was retired, living on Social Security, and beginning a remarkable two decades of vagabonding and spiritual seeking that would take her into solitude in British Columbia, to the Findhorn New Age community in Scotland, and eventually to the ashram of an Indian holy man near Bangalore.

She enjoyed hanging out with young people, even smoked a little dope. Unlike many in her age cohort, my mother didn't react against the sixties counterculture. She pretty much joined it.

And so, she being the available one, I ripped her up and down for dragging their miserable marriage—she and my father were living far apart but still not divorced—clear to the West Coast to dump on me and Jim all over again. It was no coincidence, I told her, that he and I had moved as far west as we could, short of swimming to Hawaii. I gave her both barrels, the one she maybe deserved and the one I was incapable of giving my father.

"I didn't know you felt so strongly," my mother replied, sharply defensive, and maybe she didn't. I had clamped a lid on my feelings throughout my youth, keeping them even from myself. We all had. Being self-enclosed, self-sufficient units had been our means of getting by, the Daniel Way. The only free exchange of emotion came between my mother and father during their fights.

My father would live five more years, and I never did tell him, not even in a letter, how little I appreciated having grown up in a house of drunkenness and anger. I hadn't the courage for it, and I hadn't the stomach. I couldn't bear to hurt him. No one could—not even my mother, who had hurt him again and again, withdrawing betweentimes into resentful remorse. All of us treated Franz Daniel, that titan of a man, like a cake forever in danger of falling.

He was not that circumspect with me. In his motel room one morning I was telling him about my railroad job, a sweet deal I had found through an agency. I drove around the East Bay to the offices of various shippers, inspecting their records to be sure that the rail carriers had charged them the appropriate—that is, the highest possible—rate on their shipments. In a forenoon I could easily accomplish enough work to represent as a full day in my paper reports. Submitting to company standards, I wore slacks with shirt and tie, had shaved off my beard, and had bought a VW bug so as not to be seen during working hours on a motorcycle. It wasn't the most interesting or challenging work in the world, but I thought my father would be pleased that appearance-wise, at least, I was straightening out of my hippie phase.

If he was, he gave no sign. He made one of his little grunts and said, "So you plan to be a railroad dick all your life?"

It was a stiff jab, and it landed. I wasn't a railroad detective—I was more of a traveling clerk, and in fact a member of the Brotherhood of Railway Clerks, an AFL-CIO union—but the implication of my father's deliberate mistake was unmistakable. Railroad dicks were enforcers for management. They harassed hoboes, spied on workers, and roughed up union picketers during strikes. In the view of the labor movement they ranked with Pinkerton rent-a-cops as among the most odious of management life forms.

I responded with my usual sullen silence. My father's indictment stung for a long time, long after he and my mother had gone their separate ways from San Francisco. It stung especially hard because my future had been thrown wide open again earlier that spring, when my draft board sent notice that I had been reclassified from "draft delinquent" to 1-A. I was baffled by this until I called Vince O'Connor and learned the good news. The reclassification meant that the U.S. Attorney for Northern California had declined to prosecute me and had returned my file to the draft board, which now was treating me like any young man freshly eligible for the draft, as if the past three years hadn't happened. I wouldn't be indicted and tried for refusing induction in 1968, and I wouldn't be drafted again, either. Inductees were now selected from the pool of 1-A's by lottery, and my number, which I remember as 364, was so high a perch they couldn't touch me. I was free as a bird.

I don't know why I wasn't prosecuted. Two years ago I filed a Freedom of Information Act request, but I was twenty years too late. The FBI could or would tell me only that I had once been "a person of interest to the bureau," but that my file had been "routinely destroyed in 1978." This was disappointing in that it revealed little, but in a certain way it was reassuring. Given what we now understand about FBI abuses of power under J. Edgar Hoover, it's at least a little comforting to know that the bureau's interest, once gained, could ever be shed. As for the U.S. Attorney's office, I could get nothing from them. I'd like to think that I got off the hook on the recommendation of the FBI man who came to the Waller Street flat that summer morning, he being that impressed with our earnest arguments for civil disobedience, but it would have been the U.S. Attorney's call, not his. Most likely I lucked out strictly on the basis of numbers. Draft resistance peaked nationally in 1968, and no locality had more cases to process than the San Francisco Bay Area. We clogged the machinery of justice to a crawl, and I was one of the fortunate ones the machinery spat back out. There were many others.

This was excellent news, of course, but I felt more guilty than elated. Why had I gotten off, while others were going to jail? Worse than guilt, though, was the sudden loss of the only ordering principle in my life. The prospect of indictment, trial, and imprisonment had been hovering in front of me for three years, scary but also a bulwark—my way of proving myself, my rite of passage to adulthood, waiting for me when the time came. I had committed an act of honorable illegality, and, like Thoreau, I was going to take the consequences like a man. I was going to emerge from the experience wholer, wiser, with a sure sense of who I was. I was going to *earn* the respect from the world I had claimed in 1968 but had not paid for. Now there was nothing and no one to pay. Now I was just a college-dropout railroad dick with no particular skill or talent or passion or virtue or confidence or distinction, and no particular dreams toward which to advance.

Climbing, rock climbing, remained the one thing I could do, the one limited proficiency that gave me a measure of satisfaction and self-respect. I drove to Yosemite Valley every few weeks with a guy I'd met there, a grad student in chemistry at Cal who I got along with and who climbed at about my own middling level. We urged and rivaled each other up some of the shorter difficult climbs at the base of the valley's granite walls, did two of the easiest ascents from valley floor to valley rim—Royal Arches and Washington Column—and eventually barely dragged ourselves up a big wall, a very technical ascent of Sentinel Rock in the withering heat of July. The seventeen-hundred-foot climb took us two days and two nights of struggling at our limits, climbing most of the second day and resting that night without water. It ended with a stumbling descent of the dry couloir behind Sentinel to a cold flowing stream, the happiest sight of my twenty-four years. For weeks after that climb I went about my East Bay life bathed in a warmth of accomplishment, completely forgetting—or not forgetting, but finding completely unimportant—the truth that during almost every move on Sentinel I had been fearful, crushingly tired, in physical pain, and tormented by thirst. I'd been screaming at myself in silence, in fright and anger and genuine bafflement: *Why do I do this to myself? Why do I make myself miserable and afraid?*

Age takes away, and it also gives. I don't climb anymore, but I can answer questions from thirty years ago a little better than I could then. I made myself miserable and afraid, again and again, for the same reason that I occasionally opened up my Triumph to a hundred miles an hour on the Bay Bridge at night, for the same reason that I sometimes risked money I couldn't afford to lose in the Emeryville poker clubs. I was testing my courage. I was trying to find and face up to all the guns in the English arsenals. I was trying to win a stand on some small pinnacle, receiving from myself and others what I had both claimed *and* earned. When I climbed I was trying to succeed at the only work I knew how to do. I was trying to become a man, and I didn't know how.

A full moon tonight, due southeast over Rattlesnake Ridge, and rising toward it, billowing thick out of the cauldron of Horseshoe Bend, the radiant mist, alive as I am, giving itself upward into the light.

March 20

I don't run the economy around here, it runs me. The first humming-bird showed up earlier today. Buzzed to a stop one inch from the sliding glass door and stared, hovering, putting me on notice. I meekly got out the feeder and boiled up a quart of sugar water, and now three of the angry little bastards are dive-bombing one another around the hanging feeder as I watch from the other end of the deck. Still more mania of spring.

At my end of the deck I'm sorting the accumulated recycling of four months, which amounts to an impressive lot of colored glass (wine bot-tles, mostly), clear glass (liquor bottles and pickled okra jars), foot-stomped plastic containers, a few aluminum sardine cans, and bushels of flattened steel cans and can ends. It's very satisfying, in a simple-minded way, to separate the items according to their kinds into black plastic garbage bags. I feel an idiotic desire to take inventory, to count each bottle and can, but I fight it off. These bags will do as is, each in its mute, unassayed bulk, as one measure of my sojourn in solitude.

Other measurements are not so simple. I don't know how to assess my time here. Tomorrow night I'll make my usual 10 P.M. call home, and this time Marilyn will answer, as I asked her to in my message a week ago. It's time to reconnect, to let her know (warn her?) when I'll be showing up, and to learn if there's anything, for better or for worse, I ought to know. Through my months here I've been turning on the phone at our agreed-upon times and she hasn't called, so I'm pretty sure nothing terrible has happened, but I want to hear it in her own voice. At home I have a quick imagination for disaster. If Marilyn is unac-countably late, or even if she's home but the cat isn't and it's after mid-night, my worry can quickly escalate into floor-pacing certainty that the worst has occurred. Here, out of touch for four months, I feel scarcely a twinge of real concern.

But I do want to hear her voice.

And yes, after many blissful weeks of honestly not caring at all, I do want to know whether it's Bush or Gore.

I guess I do have one assessment. I've lived here four months—four and a half by the time I leave—but *been* here less than I expected to be. Henry Thoreau would probably be rolling his eyes, if he had such a habit, and pricking me with well-honed verbal barbs, for all the time I've spent shacked up indoors at the French Provincial Formica table, scratching with my mechanical pencil, impressing the not-quite-soft-enough seat of the Route 66 Distinguished Chair with my rear end, and for all the time I haven't spent beating the trails with the soles of my boots in the health-giving out-of-doors. The Brothers too may well look askance when they hear my report—Brother Frank's prodigious eye-brows raised, his lips pursed, Brother Bradley shaking his shiny head and muttering at the ground.

Well, I apologize to none of them. I have lived as far away as a man can think in order to think, and I have thought. I have lived here to read and I have read. I have lived here above all to write, and I have written, and am writing still. I thought I might find two books here— one about the experience of solitude, the other the story of my coming of age and my father. From the start, though, the two wanted to loop and weave together, and I saw no reason, and see none now, to dis-courage their union. Ask the fact for the form, said Emerson, and I do. I look for the form the story wants to come as, not the form I think it should take. And every sentence I've written here, no matter how far away I might have been while writing it, has been sustained and nour-ished by the fertile silence of this place I love, this blessed canyon, just as surely as every sentence has been nourished by the contents of these steel and glass vessels I'm preparing to haul away.

Can a writer write his way to self-knowledge? Probably not. Yeats said man can embody truth, in the completion of his life, but he can-not know it. Yet one can, I think, write his way to a clearer, broader see-ing of his life, just as a climber sees more when he has reached the top of his climb, whether that be fifty feet or ten thousand feet from his start. I don't know myself any better today than I did four months ago, but I see my life a little better and *feel* it better—I've felt my way back into it, I belong to it a little more surely than I did.

I think I'm ready to make a more specific assessment. I see, having spent this time with my father and my young self, why physical courage was so much on my mind and in my feelings as I grew up, why proving it, or failing to prove it, weighed on me so hard. It weighs to one degree or another on any boy or young man of our culture, but Franz Daniel was a daunting example, and he was my father. Yet I see too, with great happiness, that I never really did have to prove my courage to him. He loved me, worried about me, wanted the best for me. He had his ideas about how I needed to mature, drawing on his own hard-knocks experience, but he didn't need me to be a hero. *I* needed that. I needed to be the star of my story. I never got to be that, but—this is the happiest seeing of all—I've realized I don't need it anymore. It's enough for me now to be in a story at all, as me, as I have been and as I am.

Speaking strictly for myself, refusing induction into the military was not the courageous act some saw it as. It was, to an unformed and very uncertain young man, a course of least resistance that would *pass* as courageous. But still, to do it, and to be willing to go to prison for it, did take a measure of courage. And it took a measure of courage to drop out of college, in the face of my father's and the rest of the family's expectations. It took a measure of courage to climb Sentinel Rock. It took a measure of courage to take up the financially disastrous life of a poet and writer of literary nonfiction. It took a measure of courage to care for my mother at home during her last four years, as she declined with dementia. It took a measure of courage to come here to the Rogue River Canyon, a long way from human company and help.

A measure. Extraordinary courage is something else. I first saw it, I now realize, at a very early age, and not in my father or any grown-up but in one of my second-grade peers. It's been decades since I last thought of this. It would have been 1955. The school day started then with recitations of the Pledge of Allegiance and then the Lord's Prayer, or it might have been the other way around. Though I was essentially without religion, I found the *Our Father who art in heaven* . . . we mouthed each morning inoffensive and even comforting. It gave me a temporary glow of safety from nuclear vaporization and various lesser dooms I imagined. Early in the school year, I became aware that one classmate, a girl from Bannockburn named Susan Landay, wasn't saying the prayer. I recall her sitting, mute, hands in her lap, as the rest of us stood. Some in the class gaped and snickered, some studiously ignored her. I watched her out of the side of my eye, embarrassed for her. I couldn't imagine why she wouldn't stand and recite the prayer with the rest of us.

This may have gone on for a week, or longer, and I'm not sure if Mrs. Augustine, the teacher, spoke to us of the matter and how it had been resolved, or if I deduced that later on my own. But there did come a morning when Susan Landay stood at her desk with the rest of us and added her voice. She didn't say our prayer. She sang her own, her clear soprano rising and falling through our passionless monotone phrasings. I was even more embarrassed for her, and though I'd like to think that I also felt a stirring of respect, I honestly can't say that I did. Respect came later, in memory. But I do remember sensing in her song a tone of conviction very absent from our plodding prayer. I didn't know what she was singing and don't now—it was in Hebrew—but I'm no longer embarrassed for Susan Landay. I thank her for her song.

I don't have that kind of courage. As for the courage I wondered about as a kid and young man, courage in warfare, I'll probably never know. Would I be brave in a firefight? If the first half-hour of Stephen Spielberg's *Saving Private Ryan* is a fair facsimile of pitched battle, I can only guess that I might do as most of those men did. Respond in a frenetic daze to the confused demands of each moment. Shoot or fail to shoot. Get shot or not get shot. Muddle through, if I was lucky, and find myself less courageous than my best hopes, less cowardly than my worst fears. Courage is from the Latin *cor*, heart. Coward is from the Latin *cauda*, tail. I have a heart and I have a tail, which makes me a complete if not exemplary creature, and I have used both. I daresay that each of my ancestors has had and used both, clear back to the prehuman beginnings of my line, and that if any of them hadn't I probably wouldn't be here today in the Rogue River backcountry thinking about courage.

Since I'm making assessments this afternoon, what about the 1960s? Many in my early baby-boomer cohort, when I raise the subject, express a sad wonderment about that decade when we came of age. My brother said it as well as anyone: "Something lived and died then that's never been reclaimed." Is this merely the wistfulness of aging men and women recalling the freedom and devilry of our salad days? I don't think so. No one sings the same tune about coming of age in the fifties or the eighties. Something unique did live in the sixties. Our lives seemed poised on the brink of a new world—or an old world, maybe, a world not of businesses and nations but of humans living in concert with one another as part of the great community of being, living in—yes—peace and love. We glimpsed that world, we imagined it, and in moments as we passed through one another's lives, we lived it.

It could be that this singular spirit was evoked by singular danger. We were the first generation, after all, to live from birth mere minutes away from apocalypse. As children we clasped our hands over our necks beneath our desks at school, as directed, then tried to joke away our fear with an "I see B.M." kind of patter. We grew up with the surreality of backyard bomb shelters touted as rational defenses against obliteration, derisive of those who built them and envious at the same time. The nightly news told us year after year of growing arsenals of multiple thousands of warheads on each side of the Cold War. We walked as if on tiptoes—we did in Washington, D.C., anyway—through that late October week in 1962 when President Kennedy announced that enemy missiles were now in Cuba, ninety miles from the United States, and Soviet freighters were steaming with more toward our naval blockade. I remember staring that week at the Rand McNally world map on my bedroom wall, at all the countries in their soft pastels, my eyes drawn again and again to Antarctica—that would be the place to go, I thought, if only we could get there.

In 1966 and '67, and even later, a better kind of safety seemed near, no more outlandish than the horror of the nuclear age itself. Some of us believed, or half-believed, or maybe just wanted desperately to believe, that our lives were leading us into a world where the missiles might rust in their silos because no one would push the button to fire them, where people might wake from war and the fear of war as if from a bad dream, where all of us might remember who we were and see the world as if for the first time, might walk in green grass beneath a blue sky in a peace we knew was possible because we had glimpsed it and felt it and wished it life. The best of us put their shoulders to the wheel and worked to make the vision true, and many still work today—in non-profits, in intentional communities, in education, in politics, in religion, in thousands of the little ways my father knew the worth of. More of us, though, like me, were far keener on the sentiments of peace and love than we were on work. We did our own thing, as the saying went, and our own thing led us into the seventies and the complications and rewards of adulthood and eventually to the realization that we had pretty much rejoined the very society we had once ridiculed and scorned and romanticized ourselves as having dropped out of.

The sixties have plenty to answer for. Cultural conservatives are right that too many of us abdicated self-control for self-indulgence as a lifestyle. Wallace Stegner was right that too many of us thoughtlessly repudiated cultural tradition and all forms of authority, too many of us considered a rock thrown through a campus window a meaningful protest. Robert Bly is right that the sixties, for all its talk of freedom, produced too many crippled consensus-seekers unwilling to assume the responsibility of leadership. I exhibited some of the poorer behaviors of the decade, and some of the better, and a good deal of plain sixties silliness. When the Beatles brought out "All You Need Is Love," their happy voices brimming over with light and faith, I bought all the 45s I could afford and handed them out to friends and even a few strangers on the street. I meant no irony in this act. I no longer remember what it felt like to believe that five-word sentence, but believe it I did.

Feckless as I and a lot of us were, however, something authentic did move in us. I like it that we believed in love at all, even a love as easy and airy as the Beatles hymned in their song, and that we understood love as essential to human survival. I like it that we opened ourselves with enthusiasm to the strange wind of hopeful energy that stirred the country in that decade. He embarrasses me, that nineteen-year-old handing out shiny 45s, but I won't renounce him. I need him, and the culture needs him, too. There are truths that only the fool can know and speak. He is a wild card; he is wildness itself at work in the human heart and soul. Along with our rationality and sober values and sense of membership in tradition, the fool is latent in us all and will have his say. When the world has turned far enough and that strange wind blows again, maybe then we will at last be ready, whoever *we* are at that time, maybe then we will fill our sails and guide ourselves, with skill, patience, and long work, to the safe harbor of a true community of peace and love.

March 21

In February 1973 I moved back to Oregon with Ann Amundson, the girlfriend I'd been living with for nearly two years. We wanted out of the thickening Bay Area metropolis, and when a job with my railroad bureau came open in Klamath Falls, just north of the California border, we jumped. One of the first things I did in our small rented home was to build, in a detached room out back, a writing platform where I could work standing up. (Hemingway, whom I admired, had at times used such a desk, and I was beginning to suffer back pain from several climbing falls.) I worked laboriously now and then on some short stories and a few ruminations that I hoped might be poems. Nothing came easily. I had to strain for every sentence, as if trying to make a difficult rock climbing move, and frequently scrapped everything I had taken hours to write when I saw it going nowhere.

I had always written well in school, and a couple of teachers in high school had encouraged me to write further, beyond class assignments. I tried now and then, at Reed and after Reed, but the work I produced was stillborn and fragmentary. In the Bay Area I used some of my railroad-financed free time to take classes at a community college in Oakland, untroubled that a Presidential Scholar should have fallen to such a low academic estate. It seemed exactly where I belonged—structured, orderly, not too demanding. I was a month into a composition course when we moved north. The teacher had us write from memory about significant personal experiences, and I recognized the short memoirs I produced for her—about my high school job working with the stone masons, and a road trip with a friend to Quebec and the Gaspé Peninsula in 1964—as the best writing I had done. The teacher saw something in it too, writing on my first piece, "There is the touch of the no-longer-amateur here." I scoffed to myself at her judgment—what did a junior college comp instructor know?—but when we moved to Oregon I built the desk. Looking back now, I'd say it's hard to overestimate the influence of a single sentence of positive recognition on a scattered and groping youth.

Ann, whom I'd met but hadn't been involved with at Reed, was the first woman I had lived with for a sustained length of time. At five-foot-three she was a foot shorter than me, with a pretty, freckled face, an ever so slightly upcurved nose, and stunning straight blonde hair that hung in a shimmering curtain down her back clear to her bottom. We were rarely on calm water for long. I liked living with her but liked my freedom, too—climbing with new Oregon friends, drinking beer with them, holing up in the room out back to put in time at my stand-up desk. Ann wanted more of me, wanted me to want more of her, and didn't want a repeat of her brief marriage to another Reedie that had ended just before she and I got together. To me it seemed I didn't know how to love her any more than I did, which felt like a lot. I understood that it wasn't enough for her but didn't know what to do about it. Ann was the first woman I sometimes cried about in rough times.

In December of 1973 I took vacation and we drove to Missouri to spend Christmas with my father and his sisters. Our little orange Datsun, as we set out, was an incendiary bomb on wheels—it was the year of the first great gas shortage, and I packed the trunk with loaded five-gallon jugs that it turned out we didn't need. My father knew about Ann from my infrequent letters—she had been living with me but had skipped town during his 1971 visit—and seemed delighted to meet her, though when he introduced us to acquaintances he referred to us as "my son John and his wife, Ann," speaking the phrase in a semi-mumbled rush. This from the man who, forty years before, had spent four years in a sexual relationship with my mother before he married her, and who then for a short time shared, or at least withstood, an open marriage with her.

It was, as best I remember, a jolly Christmas. My aunts—the three oldest, Berthe, Frances, and Josephine—doted on us, cooked heroically, and lobbed gentle but searching questions at Ann. They were well ready for me to be married, whether I was or not. They had a few people over to the house to meet us, and my father toured us around Springfield to meet others and see the points of his compass. He had stepped down as chairman of the Unitarian Church but still was active in planning its sessions and still gave "sermons" from time to time. He was on the board of the Springfield Zoo, and was particularly proud of piloting a new project he referred to, with a delighted laugh, as the Franz E. Daniel Memorial Cat House. He was halfway into a three-year term on the city public utilities board, surely the only former Socialist labor agitator ever to serve in that body. Not long before our visit he had moved that the city run water lines into a section of town still served by a private water works, the owner of which was demanding a small fortune to give up his cash cow. My father had boasted to Newman Jeffrey: "I was carried on the TV stations two days in a row calling him a thief and a bastard and the time had come for us to build our own system and leave him with his pipes up his ass."

Clearly my father was in his element—engaged, stirring things up, working for progress, getting the attention he relished and needed. As always, he was very active politically. He had won election from his district to the state committee of the Democratic Party, beating out the governor's personal choice for the job, and was optimistic about the party's prospects in the 1974 elections. I had gotten interested enough to vote in the '72 election and to be thoroughly bummed by McGovern's landslide defeat. My father had worked hard on the campaign locally, writing to Newman Jeffrey, "The McGovern kids had never heard old fashioned bar room stump speaking oratory and they think I invented it." He'd been disappointed by the outcome, of course, but hardly surprised. Now he had long since shrugged it off and was looking ahead, practicing politics where politics lived—on the ground, person to person, in committee meetings and telephone calls, in letters to officeholders and newspaper editors, in speeches to the Rotarians and the University Club and most anywhere else he was invited, in the day-to-day invisible advancement of the work of a just society.

My father was the most politically engaged member of his family, but his sisters too had chosen careers of service—in social work, in public health, in Presbyterian missionary and community work, in teaching at the college level. They seem to have understood from their beginnings that their modest advantages charged them with a responsibility to work for the public good. I don't know how much of this came from the rural but not poverty-stricken culture they grew up in and how much from their parents, but surely George Daniel's values had been shaped by his experience as a successful first-generation American: grateful for his own opportunities, he must have wanted to contribute to the society that had provided them. Grosspapa and Grossmama, for their parts, evidenced no social conscience that I know of, but did have the adaptive malleability that successful immigrants need. There was no Lutheran church in Osceola, so they became Presbyterians. And Grosspapa's politics changed quickly one day when Mr. Tip Cox, a customer he liked and respected, walked into the harness shop, looked Grosspapa in the eye, and said: "Franz Daniel, you're too good a man to be a Republican. You ought to be a Democrat." Grosspapa changed his registration, and the die was cast for generations to come.

My father and I didn't talk much during that Christmas visit. I seem to remember telling him I was trying to write, but I've probably invented that. I doubt I had the confidence to announce to him what I scarcely believed myself. It was Christmas, Ann was with me, conversation was light and social. I remember my father wearing a white cardigan sweater, probably knitted by his sister Josephine, a light blue shirt, and a dark tie. As always I recall him with a cigarette in hand, but now the cigarettes were longer—in a concession to his doctor, he had switched from Chesterfields to mentholated filtered smokes, Salems or Kools. He was probably close to the same weight he'd been for decades, around 220, with an ample belly that his large frame carried well. The skin was a little loose around his throat, but he still looked formidable in a suit. His hair, which he kept slicked back for company and looser when it was just family, still had some darkness in the gray, and something new—a subtle reddish streak on one side in the front, an unaccountable blooming of his old age. "It's the damnedest thing," I remember him saying, and as he said it, a warmth in his blue-gray eyes, I thought he seemed content.

March 23

As I sat this morning, a fly buzzed in the skylight on the slant ceiling a few feet above and behind me. I kept sitting, didn't get up to swat him. Like my thoughts—buzz, quiet, more buzz—it was there, and I could let it be there. It was a sound in stillness. The stillness was there too.

My Muzak's the same. It's still with me sometimes, but it doesn't amount to much. It's oppressive only when I attach to it, when I let it attach to me. I can let it play. There's silence, too.

I've had fine meditations these last three mornings. Somehow, maybe by sheer persistence, I've won through to a deeper stillness and stayed with it a while. The weather's been wonderful—gray showers wandering over, briefly tapping the roof and skylight, then later again. This morning, patches of sun came mixed with little rain squalls in quick succession—exhilarating!—my still shadow forming on the floor before me with every sun.

Seems I'm still settling in here, and in a week I'll be gone. I wonder what six months would be like, a year—if this intimacy, this belonging, would extend itself and take me in still further. But I'm also settling out, my mind and at least half my heart urging me home. I was right. Nothing bad has happened to Marilyn or to family or friends. There was an earthquake in Seattle, the walls waved in Marilyn's parents' condominium, but they came through safely. The baby supposed to be born to our friends Nathan and Dawndae was born indeed, and named Rowan. Bush is president, just as Marilyn told me in the dream. There was high drama to it, she says. She's got clippings for me in a scrapbook. I don't think he'll make much of a president, but maybe he'll grow into the job.

And she, my wife of eighteen years this summer, is fine. So is our elderly cat. I'll go home April first, no fooling.

I don't have a ready knack for relationships. I've been a trial to every one of my long-term lovers; I've had to be taught every step of the way. But what I learned—it's not really learning—what I *became* in loving Cathy enabled me to give what I could to Ann, and what I became in loving Ann enabled what I am with Marilyn. And Marilyn, for her part, is better able than either of the others to love me even in my loner ways. My aloofness, she says, is exactly what attracted her—that, and my mystique as a penniless drop-out rock climbing poet.

It ended hard with Ann. We were together for another two and a half years after that Christmas visit to Missouri, and we weren't. Somewhere along the way we unconsciously loosened ourselves from each other while still in love. Ann, a philosophy major at Reed, started law school in Eugene in the fall of 1974, wanting to do advocacy work for Native Americans. During the school year we saw each other on weekends and holidays. I kept doing what I'd been doing—working, climbing, cross-country skiing, drinking, taking a few writing and literature courses at the local college, Oregon Institute of Technology, and working fitfully at the stand-up cedar desk, pounding away at a few short stories.

If it was climbing that delivered me from hard drugs, maybe also it was climbing that delivered me to writing. When I wrestled to get something right on the page, I kept at it even in frustration with a grittiness I had learned on basalt and granite faces. When I saw for the seventy-third time how lame and amateurish my efforts were and broke off in disgust, I came back in a day or two to have at it again, as I would sometimes return to a climbing move that had thwarted me in the past. The emotional rhythm of writing, the alternation of enthusiasm and dejection with absorbed labor between, echoed the familiar hope and fear of climbing. When I wasn't sure how to advance a story or poem, I reached ahead, feeling for the next move, making it if I could and feeling for the next. I had become a better climber through experience, and that gave me a whisper of hope, as I tapped my yellow pencil on the cedar desk in a rhythm of self-doubt, that I could become a better writer, too. I wouldn't get there fast, as I'd wanted to so badly on the guitar, but if I kept at it I might just get there.

I wrote my father probably one letter for every three of his, but a certain limited easiness entered our correspondence through 1974 and '75. I told him that Ann had helped me realize why I drifted, unable to buckle down to anything in a sustained way—I was afraid to follow through because I might not do as well as others expected me to. I had adopted the high expectations without developing confidence in my abilities, or even knowing what my abilities were. I told my father that I was trying some writing, that I might go back to school in creative writing or journalism. He didn't reply directly to these thoughts, but the tone of his letters seemed to accept that I was evolving in my own direction at my own pace. There were no more cracks of the "railroad dick" variety. And he always sent his love to Ann and me both; she had won a big fan in Franz Daniel.

In Missouri he carried on with his usual busyness and got even busier. He was appointed to a second term on the Springfield Public Utilities Board, became vice-chairman—he could have been chairman, but he didn't think Springfield was ready for a former leftist rabble-rouser in that position—and found himself in a ticklish situation in the summer of 1975, when two city employee unions rejected the city's contract offer and went out on strike. Forty days of federally mediated collective bargaining sessions brought the sides closer to an agreement, but the board lost patience and took up a motion to seek an injunction to force the employees back to work. My father, who in his career had been involved in hundreds of strikes and named in scores of injunctions, was now on the other side of the table. Though the strike was illegal by the letter of the law, he spoke passionately against the injunction: "From my many years of experience, I can say that injunctions have never run railroads. Injunctions have never mined coal. Injunctions have never successfully produced goods and services in any industry. Injunctions never have and will not now provide the essentials for continued operation of this utility. Injunctions sow seeds of distrust, frustration, and anger that have left scars in many cities, and will leave scars in this city." He argued that the two sides weren't far apart and that the negotiations should be allowed more time, but the board voted six to one to seek the injunction.

The court held off, however, instructing the parties to keep talking, and a week later they reached an agreement. After forty-eight days, workers went back on the job. "I'm getting handsful of thank you cards from the workers," my father wrote me, "and they make me feel mighty good."

In January 1976 my Aunt Margaret, one of the two sisters who had settled in Arlington, Virginia, wrote me that she didn't think my father was very well, though "he says so little and certainly doesn't complain." He had spent Christmas with Margaret, sister Georgia, and much of the rest of the family, and he hadn't eaten with his usual appetite. I don't remember being alarmed at all; my father was a strong man, and Daniels live into their eighties and beyond. As the year moved along my own health was much more on my mind. In June, leading the first pitch of what a friend and I hoped would be a first ascent of an eight-hundred-foot granite face at Castle Crags, I took a fall, ripped out four pieces of protection, and hit a small ledge just before the fifth piece held and the rope stopped me. My right ankle took the impact on the ledge and immediately swelled up like a cantaloupe. After an hour drilling the hole for an expansion bolt to anchor me, I managed to rappel off the rock. The ankle was useless, and trying to hop on my good foot with my friend supporting me on my injured side was more exhausting than crawling or sliding, so I crawled and slid the first mile of our descent to my truck, then crawled and poled myself with a big stick for another mile when the terrain leveled out, resting every thirty feet or so. I spent the rest of the summer on crutches and then in a walking cast, off work, putting in the most sustained writing effort I had yet managed—still another way, though not a way I would have chosen, in which climbing delivered me.

If my father felt unwell that spring, there's no sign of it in his letters. In April he wrote Newman Jeffrey with an upbeat assessment of a recent physical. The doctor had urged him, as always, to quit smoking, but he had the "blood pressure of a college boy," and weighed under two hundred pounds for the first time since his thirty-fifth birthday. My father closed the letter with this paragraph: "So, at 72 I'm going strong. And I get one hell of a kick out of life. For me AA meetings—at least three a week—are wonderful. They keep me on my toes and they give me the kind of support I like to get." (He also wrote Jeffrey about finding support in another way: "There's a party getting started down the street, so I think I'll drop over and watch the silly bastards get drunk.") My father resumed chairmanship of the Unitarian Fellowship that spring, was busy with the public utilities board, and was selected as a delegate to the Democratic National Convention, to be held in New York City in July. He expected Hubert Humphrey to win the nomination, but he was increasingly interested in a Southern governor named Jimmy Carter.

In his prime my father would have relished the convention, but he wrote Newman Jeffrey, and later me, that he was too old for the crowds and tumult and rancor. The anti-abortion members of the Missouri delegation turned every morning caucus into a strident fight, and he was already drained by the time the full convention met in mid-afternoon. The highlight of the week for him was the speech by Representative Barbara Jordan of Texas, she of the deep voice and dramatic phrasing. My father told the Springfield *Daily News* that Jordan's speech was "powerful, fundamental, and great. The hall was noisy, and delegates were cramped on the floor. There was disturbance in the aisles. She was the only speaker that held the convention without a sound."

Home from that brouhaha, very optimistic about Jimmy Carter's chances in the fall, my father resumed his activities. But surely by then he knew that something was badly wrong with him. He must have sensed it, at least, for several months, even as he wrote his cheerful letters, denying it and knowing it at the same time and keeping the trouble to himself—the way he was accustomed to bearing adversity, but without the liquor. On Monday, August 16, he came home from a utilities board meeting, telling a colleague "he was feeling awfully bad." He ate no supper that night, and Tuesday he stayed home. On Wednesday he was "very ill," according to his sister Josephine, and she drove him to the hospital.

He called sometime Wednesday afternoon, as I remember. He was in the hospital or about to go there, they didn't know what was wrong, he was very sick. I remember no words except these four: "I'm awful scared, Johnny." Unprecedented words, out of character. I think I understood in that moment that my father would soon be dead, and I couldn't handle it. I froze. I probably stammered. I know I said something automatic, some stupid assurance to him and to me that he would be fine, the docs would get him fixed up and he'd be home in no time. I don't remember what he said back. The conversation ended.

I'm awful scared, Johnny. Once, just once in our lives, my father let down his guard and opened himself, spoke in a way that we both had wanted and hadn't been able to bring ourselves to. I was twenty-eight years old, a should-have-been-grown man, and I choked. I've done some obtuse and destructive things in my life, but there's nothing I regret more than failing my father when it mattered most.

It was about 3 A.M. on Thursday, August 19, when Aunt Berthe called. He had been conscious till close to the end. He had known that he was dying and had answered death with courage and dignity, stripping the oxygen mask from his face.

I was still in such denial that the news shocked me. I hung up the phone and buckled to my knees, sobbing.

March 27

At last, the long desired view.

I had to work like hell to get it. In January I took the Corral Trail to the lower meadows, then up those grassy slopes to the wooded ridge over Meadow Creek, then northeast up the ridge maybe half a mile. I saw some major-league trees, including the biggest Douglas fir I've found around here. A snag still wearing its bark, it must have been seven feet through at the base. The view of the homestead, though, was disappointing—I could see only the mid-meadow area, and the west end of the Brothers' house. I was too close and not high enough to see the whole of the place.

A few weeks later I decided to try Rattlesnake Ridge. I drove out of the homestead to about one mile short of the pass where the road tops out, and skied from there—the untracked snow deep enough to make me nervous about driving further. My mismatched pair of skis—one of mine and one of Marilyn's, hers shorter and lighter—worked fine in the consolidated snow. I liked their representation of our marriage: different yet similar enough, requiring only a bit of care, a bit of thoughtful attention, to keep pace with each other in rhythm.

The four-wheel-drive road on top of Rattlesnake treated me to fine views of the Bunker Creek drainage to the east and my familiar reach of the Rogue to the west, more distant vistas of snowy blue ridges—the clear-cuts standing out in stark geometric white—and a few modest Klamath Mountain peaks. On *top* of the topography for a change, bright openness off both my shoulders, I felt a stirring of the exhilaration of my mountaineering years. I don't care about reaching summits anymore— I'd sooner walk around a mountain than climb it—but to be on high still gives my spirit a jump.

The road ended too soon, though, with Dutch Henry Homestead blocked from view behind Meadow Creek Ridge, the site of my first attempt. The place would have been visible from farther out on Rattlesnake, but that meant an unpleasant-looking thrash through thick manzanita, unskiable, and afternoon was turning to evening in any case.

On the way back to the main road and the truck, I was surprised by a glimpse through trees of a snowy triangular mountain far to the east. Took me several seconds to recognize it as the only peak it could be— Mount McLoughlin, the volcano I saw almost daily from the other side of the Cascades when I was living in Klamath Falls and beginning to write in the 1970s. A long time ago. The mountain seemed to have leapt from that world to this.

And so, today, I did the strenuous but surefire thing. Took the Rogue River trail around Horseshoe Bend and headed up Rattlesnake Ridge from below. It was pretty easy going at first, a steep scramble through scrub oak and tanoak. Then the shoulder I was climbing turned into a narrow ridge of mossy rock outcrops, mostly unstable, studded with small oaks and madrones and big manzanitas festooned with old man's beard. As I got higher I recognized what I was climbing as the shelf I've observed from the cabin that rises transversely across the face of Rattlesnake below a small scree slope. I knew I'd have my view if the trees allowed it, and eventually they did.

Most of the meadow was visible. The most noticeable feature, through binoculars, was the blue pig—the five-hundred-gallon propane tank below and to the right of the cabin. The cabin itself was hard to pick out even with the glasses, its dark wood siding blending into trees and the slope it's built against, but there it was—my home for 129 days now, with its greensward, apple trees, and fenced garden, all framed by the distant daylight version of the council of trees. For some reason it was an immensely satisfying sight.

I didn't expect to be able to pick out the dimensions of the homestead's ninety-four acres, but in a rough way I could. Within the general dark green of the conifer forest, there was a concentration around Dutch Henry meadow of lighter-green mounds—madrones, many madrones. The intensive 1968 logging of the conifers released those Mediterranean beauties—not commercially valuable themselves, thank God— to lift their spreading crowns to the sun. Over years to come, the firs and pines and hemlocks will overtake them and slowly starve them of the light they luxuriate in, but for now, Dutch Henry Homestead hosts something like a ninety-four-acre climax forest of Pacific madrone.

I love to think of the place in that longer perspective, its forest shifting through decades and centuries like a cloak in a breeze, throwing off various tints and textures of green. And not just green. There will be times when the view that so pleased me today will be a desolate scene of black columns and scorched ground. Fire has been a stranger to this part of the canyon for the better part of a century. Dead wood has accumulated on the forest floor, and a proliferation of small trees, dead or dying of sun starvation, stand ready to boost flames from the ground fuel into the crowns of larger, living trees. The heat blazes here in summer, reaching a hundred degrees and more for days at a time. The next fire is likely to be a big one, and the outcome won't be pretty.

Or we won't see it as pretty. Why is our notion of natural beauty so circumscribed, so dominated by the quality of verdancy? The black sticks too are beautiful, like the dead winter weeds Theodore Roethke evoked in a poem as "the beautiful surviving bones," and beautiful too is the burnt-over earth in which seeds and fungi and surviving root systems stir toward wakefulness, ready to send up grasses, wildflowers, and pioneer seedlings of the forest to be. Black char and lush green both belong to the greater beauty of the land in its wholeness, its ceaseless evolution, which appears static to us only because our lives amount to mere shutter snaps of a camera in the course of the land's long time. Fire is the force that drives the land's becoming—fire within the planet, which powers the tectonic plates whose collisions and slow scrapings raise these mountains, and fire here above where Earth meets air in the land's biota, fire even in the mitochondria of our own cells, where a slow chemical combustion generates the energy that sustains our lives. It is the power of Shiva, the Hindu god who dances on one foot with a snake coiled around his neck, his body smeared with ashes—the indispensable ravager, the destroying creator, his beauty so fierce we are forced to turn and shield our faces. He has danced in this canyon and will again, his willful flames writhing and yearning toward the distant stars to which they are kin.

The Brothers know and accept this. It would grieve them to lose the two cabins that they and their parents built, but their faith is not founded in human artifacts, or even in the particular forest and meadow that now clothe the mountainside. They ground their faith in the place itself and in the ever-evolving story of the place, the story that celebrates the place through them and Mother Margery and their order— or their disorder, as Brother Frank prefers. The elder Brother, in his life in the world, is a sculptor and ceramist. He spends his days casting bronze in foundries and curing his clay creations in a wood-fired kiln. He is an intimate of fire. When Shiva dances here at the Rogue, the Brother too will dance, whatever realm he then inhabits, flames of joy in his admiring eyes.

There is no great distance between our earthly lives and the celestial fires of the cosmos. We are made of the stuff of used-up stars, and new beings will materialize from the atoms we are long after our sun has died in violence and returned its matter to the cosmic flux. In the wholeness of time, everything has burned and will burn again. The burning is not heaven, not hell, but Nature. The word means *that which is born*, and this universe gives birth in fire.

Surely it's some inkling of this, some remote recognition, that causes us to stare intently into flames contained in a fireplace or campfire ring. We appreciate the warmth, the cozy aura, but deeper down we are spellbound by a mystery. We have harnessed fire in a multitude of ways since Prometheus stole it from the gods, ways we rely upon and take for granted, but something in us remembers, gazing at the hearth, that it is a wildness we watch. We may have tamed it to our purposes, but fire does not answer to us. It still answers to the gods.

It's odd that a climb to a high place should have put fire in my mind, and kept it there, but there it was as I started down from Rattlesnake— belatedly, in early evening. Dusk was on me well before I reached the river trail. I slipped a few times, once hard, giving much pain to my right little finger. Still not whole, it sacrificed itself yet again to break my fall. You'll be off duty in a few days, I pledged. You'll have a summer of sheer indolence. You can hang out with your bigger siblings as they grip the steering wheel, dance lazily alongside as they tap the computer keys.

It was my father and fire I thought about on my trek home. I remembered our two houses that burned while I was a kid, one from faulty wiring, the other, probably, from one of my father's cigarettes that fell into a wastepaper basket. I remembered my brother and me lowering the absurdly small box of our father's ashes into the ground in Osceola, next to the graves of his parents and little George. A butterfly had lit on the box. My brother coaxed it onto his finger, lifted it, and it flew. I wouldn't know until years later that the Greek word *psyche* means both butterfly and soul.

And I remembered something else, something I haven't thought of in years—an evening long ago when my father and I watched a fire together, and spoke a little in a particular way we had. It was at our cabin in Virginia. I may have been twelve or thirteen. I don't know if my father and mother had quarreled, or if he was brooding about other things, or if he'd had any special reason at all to build a small fire behind the cabin under the tall sycamores, but there he was, sitting on a bench and smoking, staring into the flames. I saw the fire and went out to join him.

"Well, hello there, stranger," he said as I entered the firelight. "Sit yourself down."

"Well, hello there," I answered. "It's an awful nice night, isn't it?"

"Awful nice," my father said. This way of speaking, like friendly strangers meeting at an inn, was something we occasionally did, spontaneously, always in the presence of a fire. I don't remember how it started, only that we did it.

"Are you bound a long way, stranger?" my father inquired.

"Yessir, I am. I'm headed out west. I'm gonna go join up with the mountain men."

My father laughed the soft, back-in-the-throat laugh of his delight. "I reckon you're just the man for it," he said. "I'd go with you if I could. If you run into Jim Bridger, will you tell him I think he's a great man?"

"I sure will tell him," I said.

And we talked on, sporadically, more comfortable in our firelight personas than we were in our own skins. We looked at the fire, never at each other. We watched, spoke, watched some more.

After a long silence—the flutter of flames, a few quiet pops from the wood—my father said something I remember him saying only that once.

"You know something, my friend? I'm mighty happy to know you."

"I'm mighty happy to know you," I said.

A few oblique utterances, spoken to a fire through masks. Nothing more than that, but enough, as I hiked up the trail from the river in the dark, pausing often because I was weary and my ankle was hurting, to bring tears I was happy to cry.

Back in November I wondered if maybe I'd never finished growing up. I haven't. I'm a fifty-two-year-old with a gray head, a bad ankle, and a contrary mind, and I am still my father's child, one of the three he had and loved, sitting next to him by the fire. Becoming a man is a much longer road than I imagined. I don't expect to be done with it any time soon.

March 29

In the funeral home my father lay in an open casket, looking all wrong. His cheeks had been rouged to a rosy glow, his hair combed back and to one side in a ridiculous near-bouffant. A piece of wan, insipid string music was playing, for the man who had raged and soared with Beethoven. I couldn't get myself to go near the casket. Jim went, and did what he could to fix the hair. His own hair, like mine, was semi-long, the spirit of the sixties having settled into the fashions of the seventies. We both dressed West Coast casual, no jackets. I wore my best pants, a pair of brown bell-bottomed corduroys.

Afterward, at the memorial service in the chapel, Jim and I were among the speakers. When my turn came and I went to the podium, I was stunned. The pews were filled, the side aisles and rear of the building were packed with standees, and they were spilling out the open doors to the street. It looked as though half the city of Springfield had turned out. Some wore suits or fine dresses, some were dressed less formally, some were in working clothes. The service had been set at 4:30 P.M. so that working people could attend. How many in the crowd, I wondered, were alcoholics?

I had been writing my tribute on the plane and the bus and had typed it in my father's bedroom, on his typewriter, revising it up to the last minute. I told about Franz Daniel the storyteller, the speaker, the grower of tomatoes and Kentucky Wonder pole beans, the artist of the barbecue, the wager of war against squirrels with a taste for birdseed. I marveled at the tenacity of his faith that a just society could be attained and the tirelessness of his labor to achieve it. I said that he had paid a terrible price for his drinking, and that we in the family had also paid a price. I said that he had fought the toughest fight of his life there in Springfield, and that he had won it. I told the audience that they were unfortunate not to have known my father longer, but blessed to have known him at his best. I told about the funeral he had conducted on that windy spring day for the woman who had killed herself, the woman with three kids—how he was always ready to do the right thing, the decent thing, the necessary thing, and to do it with spirit and conviction.

I said that my father most likely had known that the bill for his bodily self-abuse would come due sooner than he liked, and that he had probably accepted that—not happily, perhaps, but with stoicism. I said that he had lived with courage and died with courage, wanting no oxygen apparatus between him and his fate, his lungs and lymphatic system riddled with a cancer that would have sent most men to the hospital weeks or even months sooner. And I said that I was most indebted to my father for teaching me to *appreciate*—to recognize and value what is worthy and beautiful in food and music and literature and baseball and all human work; to respect and never to denigrate the great good of living, the fundamental decency that all people are capable of and deserve to share in. He was gone, I said, just plain gone, but what he loved in the world lived on:

> Tomatoes still grow fat in August in Springfield, and the fish still bite, sometimes; folks still laugh at a well-told story, still are moved by Beethoven, still are enraged, sometimes, by injustice. My father believed in life. He believed in the future. He believed in those three little kids at the windy funeral, and he gave them something they will never lose. He gave such things to me and to many of you. Rejoice that he lived, and lived a hell of a life, a life so full it overflowed into countless others.

I borrowed a rhetorical device from my father in writing that passage. Two years before, he'd sent me a talk he had given to the Unitarians, titled "On Reaching Seventy," in which he imagined his life in terms of the Gateway Arch monument in St. Louis. The ascending left leg of the arch represented his youth, education, and career, the friendships and love he had known, the joys of good battles fought and the pain of defeats, the motion ever upward. Then the almost imperceptible pause at the peak of the arch, and the long descent toward the right-hand base, toward death. My father said he didn't know where he was on that descending curve, but he imagined the left leg of a second, smaller arch rising out of it, an arch that also reached an apex and plunged to earth. He didn't need to tell his audience that the second arch represented the sober renaissance of his years in Springfield. He concluded:

> I know where my roots are now. When I arrive at the right-hand base of my final arch I shall be at exactly the same place from whence I started—among the hills and bluffs of western Missouri. There will be the colors and the decorations of the fields and woods in the different seasons. There will be the architecture of the trees, the sculpture of the rocks, the gleam of the rivers and the springs. The sun will beat down, the storms will crash, the voices of distant dogs will be heard, birds will cry and sing, perhaps even the wail of the night freight from Kansas City. And I shall be amid those whom I loved, and who loved me. And this love shall be part of the highways and the inhabited places, yes, even continuing to ascend arches. And I shall be at peace.

As my plane flew in to Portland it passed close to the north of Mount Hood, a summit where I had stood three times, but in this moment it looked like a figure of intense dream. It looked so real as to seem unreal. Its sharp peak and crumbly rock ridges and streaks of snow seemed to compose a monument to something inexpressible in words or thought, some greatness akin to the beauty of great music. In my grief I felt my spirit surge. I felt wildly large, awash in possibility, open for all that existence could offer.

Ann met my Greyhound in Eugene, where I limped off wearing the straw hat my father had worn to the Democratic convention. We drove to Klamath Falls. I told her about the memorial service and the burial, about seeing Mount Hood. Her summer job in Portland—where I'd stayed a month with her, writing, after breaking my ankle—was over, her third year of law school about to begin. At home, in the little house on Denver Avenue, she told me. I remember none of her words, none of mine. I remember that we were both in tears. She was in love with one of her professors, had been for a while, and would be moving to Eugene for good.

I pleaded with her to stay, to give us more time, but even in her obvious pain she was firm. She had been steeling herself to do this, and the signs had been there for anyone sensitive enough to read them. For anyone sensitive enough to read, actually. Over the last year she had done her own pleading in a couple of long letters from Eugene: "You care for me, but how can it feel so abstract, so elusive? Where are you, John? Please—there's really only this moment, not so much time after all." I had responded with earnest assurances that I could be what she wanted, that once she was done with law school and we were living together again, things would be fine. But her letters had been about being with me, not about being apart from me.

The signs had been there, but all I felt that night was misery. Ann slept on the couch. I drank some Scotch and took two or three Valiums and lay on the bed in a desolate haze. In the morning she drove north, leaving me the image of her reddened wet face in the car window.

March 30

Today I went down to break up with the river, but amicably, no tears. There was not a human soul but mine—just me and the osprey, the way we began back in November. The osprey seemed to take less offense at me this time, but I may have imagined that. I walked and sat and fished a little. The river moss, I noticed, is already losing its opulent green intensity, fading toward the dingy brown of summer.

The river gave me no last fish. Just as well—it would only have made our parting that much harder. But the river always gives me something. A Canada goose, the very picture of repose, came drifting down the easy current of the pool near which I was sitting. I waited for her to lift off as she approached the vee where the pool narrows into a turbulent rapid. I waited, the goose drifted, and then she was in the rapid, turning this way and that with the urgings of the conflicted currents, cresting through small standing waves, never seeming to struggle or to lose even an atom of her buoyant serenity. She rode the rapid through, stopped on a rock on the far side of the next pool down, held still for many minutes, then winged past me upriver, honking as she went.

In my delight I suddenly felt a pang, a yearning to stay—to keep writing, keep fishing, keep eating cabbage and broccoli and mustard greens (the cauliflower heads are only just forming), keep reading, splitting wood, meditating, howling from the deck—and maybe, just maybe, shoot an out-of-season grouse! If the Brothers found it necessary to boot me from the cabin I could bunk in the woodshed, tossing out well-split logs to the writer-resident upon request, a nickel a log for my trouble, or I could dwell in the little hidden hut Brother Frank built a few years ago to store equipment, spray-painted with a ghastly scowling countenance and the words, *Jesus judges!* Henry David thought he was getting down to essentials in his ten-by-fifteen manse? I'd make do with four by eight! I'd be the Prophet of the Shed, harmless to all who knew me, fierce to those who brought an impure heart and improper offerings. A modern Dutch Henry-gone-hippie, confidant of madrone and Douglas fir, utterer of midnight howls, renowned for conversing with solitary frogs . . .

My eager scenario dissolved before me as I found myself watching the goose again—or *a* goose again—drifting down the same pool and once again expertly and effortlessly running the rapid. I laughed out loud, rose from my rock, and began the trek to the cabin. It's her river, not mine. "A little Madness in the Spring," wrote wise Emily Dickinson,

> Is wholesome even for the King,
> But God be with the Clown–
> Who ponders this tremendous scene–
> This whole Experiment of Green–
> As if it were his own!

As I walked the river trail in the early twilight, the higher country taking its last sun, mist was forming in drifts and wafts close above the river. I've seen it many times from the cabin, clouding large or hanging in soft streaks, but never here at its very creation. The river of air over the river of water slowly filled with fine wisping mist, alive and rising.

Not far below Dutch Henry meadow, in the gloaming of the woods, I passed some fifty feet from two does, both swelling in the belly with young, that I've been seeing now and then for a few weeks. They watched me, stock still. Then one raised her left rear hoof and delicately scratched the underside of her chin.

"Come to dinner," I said. "I'll give you broccoli stalks and cabbage."

I know they heard, but as usual they failed to join me at the red-blanket dining table. I did have company, though, which walked in the door just as I did. Three ticks, leisurely strolling my clothing and skin like petroleum engineers savoring the prospect of their next strike. The warming world of spring has welcomed ticks from wherever it is that ticks spend winter. A world that welcomes ticks is not a world I would have designed, which is precisely why the design of worlds is not left to such as me. Being seeks its own wholeness, fills all voids, finds all forms. It found ticks, and they found me.

Late, very late—just now, as I prepare for bed—I find a *fourth* one, half-embedded in the skin of my left shoulder where it meets my neck. I never felt a thing. The fiendish bastards slip you a local anesthetic when they dig in.

I'm not patient enough as I work the tweezers, and I come away with a leg or two and maybe half a body. Ticks have no integrity. They fall apart under pressure. Well, his half-corpse will just be one more piece of the Rogue River Canyon that I'll take home with me.

March 31

Through the rest of the summer and fall of 1976, I stayed home a lot. My ankle wasn't healing very fast or very well, so I couldn't do much outdoors except limp around and play a little tennis. I eventually had surgery, and even after that the ankle didn't come back to its old self. This I took as a plain instruction to quit climbing. I did go back to work in the fall, hobbling around the rail yards. The hoboes in the Burlington Northern yard commiserated with me, offered me wine and beans, told me their stories. I imagined myself as one of them, riding the freights from town to town like Hank Williams's "Ramblin' Man," who lives that way because he believes it's the life God meant for him. There's always something just over the hill he yearns to see. That wasn't true for the hoboes, though. Most of them had been pretty much run over by life, and they yearned mainly for the next disability or Social Security check and the next jug of wine. The reality of their lives was hard on my fantasy.

Still, I had *motion* in me. I wrote Ann occasional letters of hope; she wrote back kind letters of nope. I couldn't think of her, of us, without pain, but at the same time I knew she was right. We were over, and we had been for some time. We'd had something real between us; now we were each moving on. My father, too—I grieved for him and me both, grieved that I would never hear him call me "Johnny" again, grieved that I had loved him and wanted to embrace him and was scarcely able even to talk to him, even when offered a chance at the end. But it wasn't pure leaden sadness I felt. There was light and movement in my mourning, like wind and sun breaks on a clouded early spring day. In my grieving I felt streaks of soaring joy.

And that disturbed me. Was I happy my father had died? Had I harbored so much resentment that I *wanted* him to die? I didn't think so, but my feelings confused me, left me suspicious of myself. Then, in October I think, a strange and wonderful thing happened. It came during sleep. *He* came, not in his familiar person but his essential being, his true voice. I didn't see him; I heard him. He told me he gardened flowers now, and I saw them—flowers of light in radiant colors. He told me he was happy. He knew that I loved him and grieved for him, and he knew that I felt joy. It was all right, he said. He had known that joy. It was the joy of being alive in one's own life, of going forth into the world leading and following no one. It was the soul's own joy. I felt a surge of love and gratitude, said "Thank you, Franz," and it was over.

I had dreamed of my father before, and I have dreamed of him many times since, more frequently once I realized I wanted to write about him. Some of these have been more intense than my usual dreams, but they have felt and delivered themselves like dreams nonetheless. The 1976 experience was not that. It was a presence, a voice and a vision, and it had the unmistakable quality of a communication. I was present as intensely as my father was. We were I and thou.

My confused emotions didn't suddenly settle in the days and weeks that followed this visit. My grieving didn't cease. But now in my pain it was some comfort to remember my father's voice and those flowers of light, to feel them glowing within me like the embers of a campfire. And joy still came to me, out of nowhere, sometimes with my tears.

It was fall, my favorite season, the time of year I feel most lonely and most alive, the time it feels richest to be alive. I stayed home a lot, applied myself to stories I'd been working on for two years, and started new ones. Two of them—both, not amazingly, about climbing, and losing or not getting a woman—would eventually become my first publications. I started keeping a notebook, jotting down thoughts, images, descriptions, sentences I liked the sound of, quotations I wanted to keep. I bought the biggest dictionary I could find and a used Royal manual typewriter. I read, and when I liked a part of something I read, I tried to study how it worked. Sometimes I copied the sentences in my own hand, hoping in that way to sense how the passage had occurred to the author. I still got drunk with my friends, wasted hours playing pinball, frittered my time in other ways, but I did stay home a lot and somehow that fall I became a writer. It wasn't a decision or resolution so much as a semiconscious realization, like understanding in 1968 that I was going to refuse induction into the army—that feeling of bare feet settling into sand as receding runoff flows over them.

In Al Strehli's song "Sally," an older man counsels a young woman who's being told by those around her to leave the young man she loves. The older man advises her to stick with him, even though "he's young and still unproven, and to himself unspoken." At twenty-eight I had been trying to prove myself for years, and failing, but in the trying and the failing, I see now, something else had been slowly succeeding. As I tried to measure up in the eyes of my father and teachers and bosses, and finally in the eyes of anyone who would look, I was taking my own measure. In a haphazard way I was becoming capable of reflection, of listening to my own being and questioning and making demands. I was becoming spoken to myself, negotiating the terms of my own approval. It would be several years before I answered "I'm a writer" when someone asked what I did, twelve years before I published a book, but I can see now that it was in the fall of 1976 that I gave my consent to the life I am living today. Whatever I ended up proving or failing to prove to the world, I would write.

A life of writing is an evolution, never—like the living land—completed or capable of completion. It has the feel of the life of the ramblin' man in Hank Williams's song, advancing, confidently or not, toward what you don't yet see and very much need to see. I worked hard at those early stories and made them good in certain limited ways, but even as I struggled with them, I knew, dimly at least, that the most authentic thing I had written was nonfictional: the remembrance of my father I had read aloud at his memorial service. I rarely looked at it, but it was there, guiding my way like a faint star, as I soon turned from fiction to poetry, and eventually from poetry to personal narrative—to the work not of inventing lives but of imagining life as I knew it and know it, the work of searching my own experience for the worthy, the majestic, the true.

My father saw only my letters. He died before I could justify his hopes for me, his belief in me. Maybe it had to be that way. Maybe I couldn't have come into my own with his large presence still in the world, even two thousand miles away, but I would write the story differently if I could. I would write my way into my sense of vocation while my father still lived, so that I could go to him and say, "Franz, this is my work." And I would speak those words as I write this book now—not to prove myself to him, not to measure up in his eyes, not even to please him, though I know it would, but simply, honestly, to say thanks.

April 1

The truck is packed with all it can hold, which is about half of what it needs to hold. I'll have to make a second trip in a week or two. I've set the remainder of my things out of the way in the entry porch, next to the considerable remains of the Warhol Wall, which I hereby dedicate to the nutritional needs of writers to come. Surely someone will want that sixty-four-ounce jar of sauerkraut very soon. The cabin is clean as a top, ready for young Mr. Edwards. The French Provincial Formica table is clear for him, and the Route 66 Distinguished Chair is vacant.

The grounds too are in order, apple trees pruned, garden tidy, tools put away, woodshed stuffed. The place looks good. The deciduous members of the council of trees are hazed with new green. Fittingly, for my last day, my favorite weather is here. Mist is on the move, with occasional scatters of quiet rain. And joy of joys, the first golden iris are up—*Iris innominata*, those wild yellow beauties found only here in the lower Rogue River country.

The iris always remind me of Mother Margery, and especially of the ten spring days I spent with her here four years ago, recording her recollections of more than fifty years' experience of this piece of the Rogue Canyon. A short woman of doughty spirit and supreme enthusiasm, with a genius for woodstove cookery and a taste for Bombay Sapphire martinis, Mother Margery remembered the times that she and her beloved Doctor spent here with all the energy and relish with which she had lived them, beginning with the cabin at Horseshoe Bend where the two of them founded their Oregon faith. Well up in her eighties now, Mother Margery comes to the homestead once a year in the company of the Brothers, in her birth month of October, to offer the place her blessing and receive its blessing of her.

Reader, have I written of the Oregon faith too mysteriously? It is nothing esoteric or mystical, nothing more than the spirits of three human beings I honor and wish to shroud in some secrecy, and the intermingling of their lives with many other spirited lives along this reach of a great river. It is the faith of Red Keller and Bill Graiff pursuing their solitude, the faith of steelhead forging upriver and madrone roots deepening their hold in the ground, the faith of dawn light in a misted canyon and the last rich sunshine, green and golden, flooding the steep pitch of Rattlesnake Ridge. The Oregon faith is as boisterous as a drunken miner, as quiet as a cougar's step, as complicated as the Rogue River's currents, and as pure and simple as the first golden iris of spring, which of course is nothing simple at all. The faith, you understand now, is much older than Mother Margery, much older than Oregon, older than the river itself, and the faith is as new as each new writer to whom Mother Margery and her sons entrust the care of this place. The faith of the place is the writer's own faith as she opens her notebook and takes up her pen, and as she writes, the faith lives on in ways and directions no one can know.

I will visit this homestead again—many times, I hope. I have schemed since I first came here to make myself indispensable to the Brothers' advocacy program for impoverished scribblers, and whether or not I am, they generously indulge me. And so I feel no need to make a ceremony of my departure. I'm not here anyway. I'm fully in the grip of the world I'm returning to, like a hiker hustling to break camp and hit the trail home.

Before I slide into the truck and bounce up the drive, though, I do want to say good-bye to my father. I summoned him here and he came, all of him I'm going to know, and I will not leave him rouged and fluffy-haired in his open casket, or packed as a few pounds of ashes in a black metal box.

I have thought long about where and when I want to say good-bye, and I have decided on New Orleans, the French Quarter, in the fall of 1942. My father is thirty-eight, my mother thirty-four. They have moved to this city they love from New York, my father on assignment to organize laundry workers for the Amalgamated Clothing Workers of America. In New York my mother miscarried, but now she has recovered from her deep depression that lasted months, and they are trying again. They are hopeful. Within six months my mother will be pregnant with their first child.

On this particular evening, which is warm but not summer-hot, they have stopped in for drinks at the Court of Three Sisters, an open-air bar that is one of their favorites. They order sazeracs, and it may be that in the liberal New Orleans of 1942 real absinthe adds its delightfully narcotic effect to the general glow of the bourbon. They relax as they have relaxed before at a table with a red-checked tablecloth, my mother in a loose summer dress, something bright, my father in slacks and a light suit jacket. They speak, and there is laughter in their speech. They are in love—with each other, with New Orleans, and with the work they do, the work my father does and my mother did until two years before, when they resolved to have children. The nation is at war in Europe and the Pacific. My mother and father are not in that war, but they have been fighting in America for many years, fighting battles they believe in.

Two rounds, three rounds of drinks, and my father, when they have fallen silent for a while, does something he never does. He looks long at my mother, straight into her eyes, his broad Germanic face flushed and happy. He says, "What would you like right now, most in the world?"

My mother looks at her hands on the red-checked tablecloth, looks again at the man she has loved since the day she met him. In this moment she wants nothing more. She smiles, and says: "I'd love to have this tablecloth."

And so my father stands, lifts their near-empty glasses with one hand and pulls the tablecloth to him, sets down the glasses and wraps the cloth around him beneath his jacket like a sash. He drops what they owe for the drinks on the bare tabletop. He drains the last ounce from his glass, puts on his hat, and they walk out of the Court of Three Sisters onto the New Orleans sidewalk, my father on the curb side, a little bulkier around his middle than before, a cigarette up-jutting from his mouth, his right arm across my mother's shoulders, his hand lightly holding her upper arm.

They are going to a restaurant supper, maybe, or home to their second-floor apartment on Toulouse Street, or maybe to a party and the company of friends who fight on their side in their battles. In truth, beyond such immediate prospects, my mother and father don't know where they are going with their tablecloth, but I do. Like my two brothers, the one who still lives and the one who once lived, I will eat meals at many tables covered with that cloth. I will see my father hammer it with a fist, rattling the glasses and salt shaker, and I will see him, hung over, eat his graveyard stew from a bowl on that cloth. I will see him laugh, and my mother laugh, and the two of them scowl at each other across that cloth. After I leave home I will see it occasionally when staying in my mother's apartment, and then, as she begins the vagabonding of her old age, I won't see or think of it again until 1977, a year after my father's death, when my mother, sixty-nine and still in love with the face across the table in the Court of Three Sisters, tells me, with a laugh and a catch in her voice, the story of how it came to them, and tells me that in a trunk somewhere in the East she still keeps a few scraps of that worn, red-checked cloth.

And so, I say good-bye to them. I have followed them closely for several years now, each of them alone and the two together. I have looked after their lives, eager for all scraps I could find, and now I am ready to let them go. As their figures recede in the warm New Orleans twilight, mixing with other walkers, I imagine that my father with his arm around my mother looks once behind him. I see him but he does not see me, and as his face turns forward again it's as though a great fish, having been fought into the shallows of a river, suddenly feels its freedom and turns away into the dim green depths.

The truck and I bounce up the drive the quarter-mile to the upper house, the Brothers' house, where they will arrive in a few days. Leaving the engine running, I go inside and write a brief note:

Dear Brothers:
Thanks for letting me use the hermitage. It was a very
spiritual experience. I'm sorry the writer's house was

destroyed. Turns out those Bigfoots like to *dance*.

I'm in Mexico now.

You'll never find me.

And now on up the drive, the truck plunging and rising and lurching sideways as it negotiates the water dips, the dug-out troughs that keep the road drained during winter rains. And despite myself, though I know I'll come again, though I know that Marilyn and I may spend a winter here after she retires, I know, too, that things have a way of happening once. What we assume we'll return to, what we think we'll enjoy again and again, turns out not to be there. Or we turn out not to be there. I know for certain that I will never be here again at the end of these particular hundred-and-thirty-four days, and so I go slow. I look around. I feel every jolting bounce and lurch.

And before I'm even to the first gate, I brake to a stop. Ten feet in front of the truck, a large ruffed grouse stands directly in the middle of the road, facing left, one walleye taking in my noisy arrival.

The grouse doesn't move.

The truck doesn't move.

"Don't rub it in," I say.

The grouse takes one slow step and holds, a poised brown elegance.

I honk the horn.

The grouse holds.

"Don't push your luck," I mutter.

The grouse turns its head slightly toward me, and after a while turns it back.

I sigh and pull on the parking brake. I lean back, take the notebook from the seat beside me, open it and begin to write this final scene. When the grouse is ready, when the bird and I get our story straight, I'll travel on up out of the Rogue River Canyon and head for home.

Here Again

Nature is what we know—
Yet have no art to say—
—EMILY DICKINSON

Contradictions have always
existed in the soul of man . . .
We are not meant to resolve all contradictions
but to live with them . . .
—THOMAS MERTON, *Thoughts in Solitude*

November 3, 2001

This little piece of the Rogue River Canyon, to my imperfect eye, looks just as it did a year ago. The meadow grasses tall and sere, Bill Graiff's walnut trees bearing golden leaves, mist on the move in the vault of space above the treed ridges of the canyon. At the river today I found the boulders green with their moss pelts and the osprey right where I had left him. He seemed satisfied when I told him that I wouldn't stay the winter. I watched him bomb the river and rise with a steelhead arching in his talons. Later I caught two fish myself, rapped their heads on a boulder, watched their green-violet aura fade as they quivered to stillness in my hands.

I'm here for a few days to freshen the place in memory. And I'm here, I suppose, to test the experience of my winter alone against the reality of September 11. In my stunned horror that day, and in the sorrow and anger of the days that followed, it seemed cheap, insubstantial, to be writing about time spent in remote landscapes of nature and memory, blithely unaware of happenings in the all-too-real human world. I wondered if the pleasures and tribulations of a sojourn in solitude could matter in the face of such scarcely imaginable violence visited on the American people, with what implications we can't know. I've hardly looked at the manuscript since that dismal day eight weeks ago.

Last spring, I see, I wrote that I hoped George W. Bush would prove capable of growing into the job. Now he has to grow—any president would have to—almost instantly, in ways he couldn't have foreseen, and a lot is riding on whether he can do it. We've invaded Afghanistan, on the trail of Osama bin Laden and al-Qaeda. Given that the Taliban weren't about to hand them over, I think we're justified in that. We were attacked on a military scale, some three or four thousand American civilians killed. We have the right to seek justice. With that right, though, comes the responsibility to focus our retribution on those who have it coming. Already our bombs have taken the lives of Afghans every bit as innocent as those Americans on the jetliners or in the twin towers and the Pentagon on September 11, and they are sure to take more. Smart bombs are directed by fallible humans, and too often do the same dumb work that bombs have always done. Every innocent killed by American air strikes compromises the possibility of the justice we seek. The exaction of justice is the most exacting discipline of all. We'll see if our government has it.

And we'll see, when the numbness and sense of irreality have worn off, just what we Americans will make of this catastrophe. A grievous injury can harden and embitter the injured; a grievous injury can open the soul and spirit and cause them to grow. Vulnerability can be fertile. Already the attacks have pulled us together as a nation in a way I haven't seen in my lifetime. But already, too, the intensely moving displays of the American flag above the rubble of the World Trade Center, and draped on the gashed Pentagon, have devolved into exhibitions of a cheaper kind. Where I live, the image of the flag appears on grocery bags, in almost every advertisement in the newspaper, on umbrellas and refrigerator magnets and a thousand other trivial objects, even on a line of disposable diapers sold at Wal-Mart. Cloth flags hang sodden and sorry-looking on roadside fences, and flap themselves to shreds on the antennas of cars and pickups. Old Glory is everywhere, and there's an aggressiveness as well as a cheapness in some of these displays—something of the tone of an American audience at the Olympics chanting *U – S – A! U – S – A!*, something even of the truculent challenge issued by a householder a few miles from my home who flies a flag on a short pole bearing an easy-to-read metal sign: *BURN THIS FLAG AND I'LL BURN YOUR ASS.*

I don't like the attitude, but of course we reach for the flag. Of course we fold and gather it around us. We're angry, we're fearful, we're hurt in a new way and don't know the severity of the wound. *Everything has changed,* we keep saying and writing, but none of us know how. And none of us, yet, can say how we *should* change.

The world was fast, noisy, and bright when I returned to it, but not in any deeply disturbing way. I blended easily with the flow of traffic once

I reached the populated roads, enjoying the anonymity of motor travel. My hand did not reach for the radio. My first stop—the Myrtle Creek dump, to get rid of recycling and unburnable trash—went fine. I snuck furtive glances at my fellow human beings. No conversation required. In Roseburg I stopped at a Fred Meyer store to get some cash and buy a provision or two, having no grouse or turkey to bring home, nothing at all garnered on my errand in the wilderness except for the makings of this book. As I walked through the parking lot, it seemed that every man and woman I saw looked grim, unhappy, maybe quietly desperate. I hoped I didn't look the same.

The ATM inside the store gave not the usual impersonal instructions but breezily friendly prompts, as if the two of us were buddies: HI! SHALL WE TALK IN ENGLISH OR IN SPANISH? Then: COULD I HAVE YOUR PIN, PLEASE? I punched it in. Then: WOULD YOU PLEASE RE-ENTER YOUR PIN? I again punched it in. I'M SORRY, said the machine, WE'RE NOT COMMUNICATING VERY WELL. COULD I HELP YOU WITH SOMETHING ELSE?

"The only help you're good for is giving money," I muttered. A little heated in the face, I hit the cancel button and started over. When the machine came back with the same stupid analysis, that we weren't communicating very well, I said, "We're sure as hell not! What's your problem?" Evidently I made these remarks in an unquiet voice, which I realized when I glanced over my shoulder and saw several shoppers staring at me. I canceled again and walked out. Halfway to the truck it came to me that I'd been entering a number that belonged to a different card, but I didn't go back. I went to another ATM, a drive-up, where I could do my damn business without the hordes of civilization gawking at me.

Later I stopped at a restaurant, ate a bad salad, and somehow contrived to lose my driver's license. Maybe it slipped from my wallet as I fumbled out some cash to pay the bill. Clearly it's dangerous for an American consumer to get rusty. We need to practice our skills every day. I didn't know the license was missing until it arrived in the mail, thanks to the good people of the restaurant, a few days later.

Things went better at home. Our very plain house looked sumptuous within, altogether too nice for the likes of me, but I managed to adapt. Marilyn and I had a drink, danced a little, and ate a chicken she had roasted. After supper we looked through the scrapbook of clippings she had kept for me, but I found it hard to engage—even the drama of a United States president selected by the Supreme Court didn't interest me much. News is news only when it's new, it seems. Or news is news only when you're among others for whom it's new, when it's swirling in the air through media and conversations, through the mingled awarenesses of many.

The most disconcerting news from Marilyn concerned the phone calls I'd made faithfully every Wednesday night. I had usually talked along for five, sometimes seven or eight minutes on those calls, strewing out my week's cache of Rogue River happenings—oblivious, I now learned, to the screech of the answering machine cutting off promptly at the three-minute mark. (Marilyn had replaced our old machine, but couldn't find a new one that allowed more than three minutes.) On a radio phone you hold down a button to speak, and you must release the button to hear anything back. Because I'd been talking to a machine with nothing to say, I had never released the button. And so each Wednesday night I had gaily rattled on long past the point when the machine quit recording, audible only to myself, the mobile operator, and any radio telephone users in southwest Oregon with their monitors on. Cringe. Seems the operator could have alerted me to this embarrassment, but maybe her professional code didn't allow it. Or maybe she just didn't want to spoil the fun.

To our cat I was no news at all. She accepted a scratch between the ears and resumed her normal neurotic indifference, as if I had never been gone and was worth no more than the little I had ever been worth. That's what I love about cats.

Over the next few days, Marilyn decided that on balance she was glad I'd come back, and I decided that I too was glad. I was unsettled, though, as we both had known I would be. For the first week or two I wanted to see no one but her. I mowed and cleaned the roof and did some other work around the place, and began to type into the computer the 274 penciled pages of this book that I'd brought with me. I didn't answer the telephone; the ring startled me, made my heart race.

Eventually I began to correspond by e-mail, grateful for the silence of that medium, its allowance for waiting and thinking before replying to a message. Marilyn had dropped our satellite TV service soon after I left, and we didn't start it up again. The quiet suits us. My truck is quiet, too. I couldn't find and still haven't found the radio's face, the one I removed when I left home a year ago to keep me out of temptation's way. Did I bury it in the yard? I have no idea.

Within a month, maybe—alarmingly fast—I had pretty much rejoined the main channel of my life, carried along by the flow of events—the domestic chores, a writers conference in Alaska, preparations for my stepson's wedding, the baseball season and the San Francisco Giants, the progress of a small book I had begun before going into solitude. I was happy enough to be back in the shifting winds, mostly pleasant, of human life among human beings, but I wasn't all the way back. I tried to meditate, but I was distracted, nagged by an absence I couldn't define. Something was wrong. Working outside, I would sometimes stop what I was doing and listen for a moment, thinking I had heard something. Then one evening, as Marilyn and I sat out back, the last Swainson's thrushes going quiet in the growing dusk, it came to me. I'd been missing my steady, soft-spoken winter companion, the whispered hush of an unseen river stirring the air like a far-off wind. I smiled when I heard it, and leaned back easier in my chair.

☙❧

I've eaten my fish and fried potatoes, and now, on the deck, I'm listening in the dark to that same, strangely stirring sound, water's voices blended at distance into a continuous shifting chant that flows around and through me. As always its language seems familiar, seems a tongue that I once knew. It tells me, as best I can hear, that Earth is very old and just being born, and it sounds with a kind of confidence, perhaps even courage—a life going on outside of mine, outside of all our lives and somehow inside us at the same time, a life that makes no claim or promise beyond the truth of its own being.

The sounding river cares no more for me, no more for us and our present pain, than it cared for the miners who once shared meals and stories and occasionally murdered one another by its banks, and it cared no more for them than it cared for the Indians the miners and cavalry hunted and killed and drove from the land. And the Indians' long habitation here, their fire smoke rising to a glittering heaven, was no different to the river than the time before, the time of no time, when other lives knew the green and gliding waters.

Sleek otters slipped alongshore. Ouzels dipped into and out of the current. Fish arrived from far at sea, spawned, left their bodies, and small fish swam to sea in the spring. Bears lumbered over sand and stones, deer stepped carefully down to drink, a cougar watched from a crag. The river roared with killing floods, ran thick with torrents of volcanic ash, dwindled in drought to a rank trickle, and freshened again.

Our lives have flowed from exploding stars, from tides of time and gravity beyond our ken. Nothing in Nature can tell us our story, can explain why today some die while others live on, or why we die at all, or why we live. Never asking or choosing, creating itself out of snow and rain, the river gathers all that it touches and finds its way. In surging falls and deep green pools, in chutes and riffles and silent swirls, it bears us on through winding passages of grace and fury, until once, in a stab of sun on streaming water, the entire aching beauty of being comes clear. And the river—the good, green, terrible river—flows on.

FRANZ E. DANIEL
1904–1976

Acknowledgments

Writing a book, especially a book of nonfiction, is an exercise by which a writer reminds himself how hopelessly indebted he is to others.

Cousin Margaret Daniel Fleer, keeper of Daniel family lore and history, was a reliable fountain of information. Anything I've gotten wrong is my responsibility entirely. Cousins Dan Little and David Little shared useful recollections. My brother, Jim Daniel, cheerfully aided my memory with his. Scenes from our youth and what I've tried to know and show of our father would have been far skimpier without his help.

Among those family members now gone, I am deeply grateful to the memory of Margaret Daniel, my aunt and last to die of my father's generation, who again and again put her good memory to use in the service of my research. I am also grateful to the memory of Berthe Daniel, firstborn of that generation, who encouraged my hopes as a writer and told me of the Daniel past long before I imagined this book. All of the sisters—Margaret, Georgia, Frances, Josephine, Berthe, and Agathe— taught me what I know of graciousness by their example.

I honor the memory of my mother, Zilla Hawes Daniel, who also encouraged me, and who spoke frankly and readily about my father and their life together. At the end of her life she could not easily remember his name, but the man himself she never forgot.

Of my father's associates in the labor movement, David Burgess was very helpful, in his person and in his memoir, *Fighting for Social Justice*. Alan Kistler, Dolores Dickman, and Ada Katz provided important recollections. Others I interviewed or who helped in other ways have since died: Philip Van Gelder, Miriam Van Gelder, Victor Reuther, Mildred Jeffrey, Newman Jeffrey, and Alice Cook. I count myself lucky to have known them. They and others with whom my father and mother worked did a lot of good in twentieth-century America. Some of that cohort we now like to call the Greatest Generation did their most valuable fighting here at home.

Missourians who helped me reconstruct my father's later life include Jim Broadstreet and Fred Kieferndorf of Springfield, and Larry

Lewis, longtime friend of the Daniel family, in Osceola. Labor historian Neal Moore turned up right across Weller Street from my father's
former home and gave generously of his time, memory, and writings.
He in turn led me to the Ozarks Labor Union Archives at Southwest
Missouri State University, where archivist Anne M. Baker was most
obliging.

My debt to the Archives of Labor and Urban Affairs of the Walter
P. Reuther Library, at Wayne State University in Detroit, is long and
ongoing. The Franz E. Daniel Collection there, and other collections as
well, provided this son with an unlikely opportunity to research his own
father, personally as well as professionally. The staff patiently tolerated
an untrained historian. I'm especially grateful to William LeFevre for
hunting down a few choice memos among Walter Reuther's papers.

I also did fruitful research, mainly on the California farm labor
organizing drive, in the George Meany Memorial Archives of the
George Meany Center for Labor Studies in Silver Spring, Maryland.
Lee Sayrs was supremely friendly and helpful.

My circle of Reed College friends, class of 1970—Ken Hyams, Victor Friedman, John Sterne, Jim Jackson, Dan Patel, Michael Davitt,
and Cathy Hendricks—most willingly bolstered my recollections with
theirs. I'm particularly grateful to Ken and Cathy for sharing correspondence that evidently I wrote. Dan was a reliable source of medical
information, as was my good friend Jim Steck.

My knowledgeable informants in the life sciences were Gordie
Reeves, fish ecologist with the Pacific Northwest Research Station of
the U.S. Forest Service; Frank Moore, of Oregon State University's
Department of Zoology; and Bruce Bowerman, of the Institute of Mol-
ecular Biology at the University of Oregon. If any point of scientific
fact came out wrong in the book, it's not the fault of those three.

For information on the human history of the Rogue River Canyon,
I wouldn't have gotten far without Kay Atwood's *Illahe*. I am grateful to
Kay, and to Oregon State University Press for bringing the book back
into print. Dave Reed, formerly of the Medford office of the Bureau of
Land Management and longtime friend and guardian of Dutch Henry
Homestead, cheerfully provided historical documents, bureau reports,

and anything else I asked for. What he didn't know, which wasn't much, he knew how to find. Jeff Barnard, of the Associated Press in Grants Pass, got me outfitted with the right fishing gear and techniques, carried my last message to the world, and wrote perceptively about my experiment in solitude.

I'm grateful to PEN Northwest, the regional chapter of PEN American Center, for the fellowship that first brought me to Dutch Henry Homestead and introduced me to its owners in 1994. Dutch Henry has twice now been a lucky place to write. I thank Margery, Frank, and Bradley for affording me the chance to overwinter there, and for the great pleasure of their friendship. If any breach of state or federal regulations occurred during my sojourn at Dutch Henry Homestead, it occurred without the knowledge, consent, or approval of the property owners.

Some of the writing on my father and his labor career dates back to my stint as a research and writing fellow at Oregon State University's Center for the Humanities in 1997–98. I am grateful to the memory of Peter Copek, founder and original director of the center, and also to Wendy Madar, who carries on the center's good work. I thank Tracy Daugherty for his generous advocacy of my application.

A most welcome creative writing fellowship from the National Endowment for the Arts helped to keep the pot simmering in 1998 and '99.

I finished this book in the course of two years as Viebranz Visiting Professor of Creative Writing at St. Lawrence University in Canton, New York. I am grateful to the St. Lawrence community and particularly to the English faculty, who made me feel like one of the Saints.

Jack Shoemaker gave advice that helped me find the wholeness of my story, as did Lisa Ross. Jim Hepworth, Wendell Berry, Ehud Havazelet, Brother Bradley, and Marilyn Daniel read and commented usefully on the text or portions of it. John Laursen was a quick and helpful consultant. Julie Wrinn was a thorough copyeditor-plus, and Nancy Hall was a sharp-eyed proofreader. Jack Shoemaker edited with his customary acuity, and he, Trish Hoard, Heather McLeod, and the rest of the crew at Shoemaker & Hoard turned out a handsome book and saw it into the world. I thank them all, for their work on *Rogue River Journal* and for the happy integrity of their publishing venture.

And lastly I thank the woman to whom this book is dedicated, Marilyn Matheson Daniel, for putting up with and even supporting and loving a guy who does such things as are depicted in these pages.

Written Sources

Edward Abbey. *Desert Solitaire: A Season in the Wilderness*. New York: Touchstone, 1990.

Florence Arman, with Glen Wooldridge. *The Rogue: A River to Run*. Grants Pass, Ore.: Wildwood Press, 1982.

Kay Atwood. *Illahe: The Story of Settlement in the Rogue River Canyon*. Corvallis: Oregon State University Press, 2002.

Kay Atwood, Dennis J. Gray. *People and the River: A History of the Human Occupation of the Middle Course of the Rogue River of Southwestern Oregon. Volume I*. Medford, Ore.: USDI Bureau of Land Management, 1995.

Stephen Dow Beckham. *Requiem for a People: The Rogue Indians and the Frontiersmen*. Corvallis: Oregon State University Press, 1996.

Jackson Benson. *Wallace Stegner: His Life and Work*. New York: Viking, 1996.

Robert Bly. *The Sibling Society*. New York: Vintage Books, 1997.

David Brody. *Workers in Industrial America: Essays on the Twentieth-Century Struggle*. 2nd ed. New York: Oxford University Press, 1993.

Elizabeth E. Budy and John W. Jones. *Lands North of the Wild Rogue: An Historical Overview of People and Events North of the Wild Rogue River*. Medford, Ore.: Bureau of Land Management, 2001.

David S. Burgess. *Fighting for Social Justice: The Life Story of David Burgess*. Detroit: Wayne State University Press, 2000.

"Channeling." Unedited pamphlet reprint of a Selective Service System memorandum issued July 1965. San Francisco: Peace & Liberation Commune Press, n.d.

W. S. Di Piero. "Puppy Love." *The San Diego Reader* (Feb. 11, 1999).

John Gregory Dunne. *Delano*. Revised ed. New York: Farrar, Straus & Giroux, 1971.

John Elder and Robert Finch, eds. *Nature Writing: The Tradition in English*. New York: W. W. Norton, 2002.

Michael Ferber and Staughton Lynd. *The Resistance*. Boston: Beacon Press, 1970.

Todd Gitlin. *The Sixties: Years of Hope, Days of Rage*. New York: Bantam Books, 1987.

Jennifer Hall. "William Fabian Graiff." Unpublished manuscript, 1996.

Robert T. Handy. *A History of Union Theological Seminary in New York*. New York: Columbia University Press, 1987.

Hendrick Hertzberg. "Labor's China Syndrome." *The New Yorker* (June 5, 2000).

Aldous Huxley. *The Doors of Perception: And Heaven and Hell*. New York: Harper & Row, 1963.

Robert A. Johnson. *He: Understanding Masculine Psychology.* Revised ed. New York: Harper & Row, 1989.

Sidney Lens. *Radicalism in America.* New York: Thomas Y. Crowell, 1969.

Lucy Randolf Mason. *To Win These Rights.* New York: Harper & Row, 1952.

Thomas Merton. *Raids on the Unspeakable.* New York: New Directions, 1964.

Thomas Merton. *Thoughts in Solitude.* New York: Farrar, Straus, & Giroux, 1998.

Neal Moore. "Franz Daniel—Reaching for an Understanding." Unpublished manuscript, 1976. Ozarks Labor Union Archives, Southwest Missouri State University.

Neal Moore. Interview with Zilla Daniel. Unpublished transcript, 1981. Ozarks Labor Union Archives, Southwest Missouri State University.

Neal Moore. Interview with Gordon Ross. Unpublished transcript, 1981. Ozarks Labor Union Archives, Southwest Missouri State University.

R. Emmett Murray. *The Lexicon of Labor.* New York: The New Press, 1998.

Thich Nhat Hanh. *The Miracle of Mindfulness: A Manual on Meditation.* Revised ed. Boston: Beacon Press, 1987.

Victor G. Reuther. *The Brothers Reuther and the Story of the UAW.* Boston: Houghton Mifflin, 1976.

Robert D. Richardson Jr. *Henry Thoreau: A Life of the Mind.* Berkeley: University of California Press, 1986.

Robert D. Richardson Jr. *Emerson: The Mind on Fire.* Berkeley: University of California Press, 1995.

Theodore Roszak, Mary E. Gomes, and Allen D. Kramer, eds. *Ecopsychology: Restoring the Earth, Healing the Mind.* San Francisco: Sierra Club Books, 1995.

Laurence Stapleton, ed. *H. D. Thoreau: A Writer's Journal.* New York: Dover Publications, 1960.

Anthony Storr. *Solitude: A Return to the Self.* New York: The Free Press, 1988.

Shunryu Suzuki. *Zen Mind, Beginner's Mind.* Tokyo: John Weatherhill, Inc., 1970.

Henry David Thoreau. *Journal.* New York: Dover Publications, 1962.

Henry David Thoreau. *Walden and Civil Disobedience.* New York: W. W. Norton, 1966.

David Rains Wallace. *The Klamath Knot.* San Francisco: Sierra Club Books, 1984.

T. H. Watkins. *The Hungry Years: A Narrative History of the Great Depression in America.* NewYork: Henry Holt & Co., 1999.

Robert H. Zieger. *American Workers, American Unions.* 2nd edition. Baltimore: Johns Hopkins University Press, 1994.

Rogue River Journal